ARTIFICIAL
HAPPINESS

ALSO BY RONALD W. DWORKIN

The Rise of the Imperial Self

ARTIFICIAL HAPPINESS

The Dark Side of the New Happy Class

RONALD W. DWORKIN

CARROLL & GRAF PUBLISHERS
NEW YORK

ARTIFICIAL HAPPINESS:
The Dark Side of the New Happy Class

Published by
Carroll & Graf Publishers
An Imprint of Avalon Publishing Group, Inc.
245 West 17th Street • 11th Floor
New York, NY 10011-5300

AVALON
publishing group incorporated

Library of Congress Cataloging-in-Publication Data is available.

ISBN-10: 0-78671-714-9
ISBN-13: 978-0-78671-714-9

9 8 7 6 5 4 3 2 1

Designed by India Amos, Neuwirth & Associates, Inc.
Printed in the United States of America

For Sandy, Grace, Alyse, and Grandpa Carl

CONTENTS

ONE

TOO MUCH HAPPINESS

FIVE YEARS AGO, a woman asked me to put her son on Prozac. Rather than follow a professional path after college, her son joined the Navy, which she thought was "nuts," since all the young men she knew became doctors or lawyers. Only unhappy people joined the Navy, she said, so couldn't I give him a little Prozac to raise his spirits and redirect his career? When I hedged, telling her that I was an anesthesiologist and not a psychiatrist, she protested that plenty of nonpsychiatrists prescribe psychotropic drugs these days. I still refused. In the end, her son's career made her so miserable *she* ended up on Prozac. "You're being silly," I told her. "My unhappiness is a disease!" she shot back, which is how her doctor had described it. Something about neurotransmitters, she recalled. Fortunately, her son tried a submarine but discovered he was claustrophobic, then tried a surface ship but invariably became seasick, and so left the Navy for law school. When this happened, she no longer needed medication.

Despite her strange behavior, this woman knew something about American medicine: plenty of nonpsychiatrists prescribe psychotropic drugs for unhappiness, along with other modalities like alternative medicine and exercise, and these practices represent one of the most important revolutions in medicine during the last thirty years. It began with a sincere effort on the part of doctors to help people with everyday psychological trouble; it has evolved into something troublesome, even scandalous. *Artificial Happiness* tells the story of this revolution, explains how Artificial Happiness harms its beneficiaries, and suggests the implications for society when millions of people fight unhappiness with external cures.

Doctors have taken on the responsibility of curing unhappiness—not depression, but everyday unhappiness—through artificial means. The medical practice revolution began in primary care during the late 1960s, when the medical profession faced a serious threat. Patients were rebelling against a century-old trend toward scientific medicine, accusing doctors of ignoring their everyday psychological troubles. Primary care doctors faced most of the criticism, since people saw everyday psychological trouble as a primary care concern. These doctors responded with a revolutionary new ideology, one that brought a qualitative change to patient care and also challenged entrenched interests within the medical profession. Like all ideologies, the new ideology articulated a new worldview, one that aspired to benefit society as a whole and not just a particular interest group, and that rested more on faith than on proven knowledge. This new ideology, which envisioned unhappiness as a disease, led to an enormous increase in psychotropic drug prescriptions, meaning drugs with mood-modifying effects, including antidepressants, antianxiety drugs, stimulants, and narcotics.

The new ideology had a ripple effect in medicine. Rebelling against the overuse of psychotropic drugs, two groups of primary care doctors launched their own ideologies to combat unhappiness. One was built around alternative medicine; the other around obsessive exercise. The sudden and dramatic increase in the use of psychotropic drugs, alternative medicine, and obsessive exercise—each a source of Artificial Happiness—defines the medical practice revolution.

What exactly is Artificial Happiness? John Green, a man I met during the writing of this book, is a good example of someone who feels it.

A thirty-five-year-old lawyer, John fights constantly with his wife over money. He won't divorce her because he fears losing custody of their young son. In the past, he tried Valium to relax, but the drug made him drowsy. Once, an associate phoned on a case. John's wife fielded the call, made excuses, and then screamed, "You can't talk to him! He's already taken his pill!" John finally found relief through Prozac, which lets him live happily inside his loveless marriage. He expects to be on Prozac for years, until his son grows up (and he can leave his wife), or maybe even longer, since by the time his son is grown John will have built up a nest egg that his wife would grab in any divorce.

Although John Green's life is miserable, his mind is happy. His life and mind are out of synch: he enjoys Artificial Happiness. His response to Prozac is typical. For the unhappy patient, life continues by virtue of its own momentum, the cause of unhappiness remains, nonetheless the patient feels better after a couple weeks on psychotropic medication. In John's words, "My wife is still a bitch. I can't stand her. But now I don't care so much. I still feel good no matter what happens." A lack of congruence exists between John's bad marriage and his good feeling. Even John is amazed at how good he feels at home.

Alan Clark also enjoys Artificial Happiness. An ordinary, unremarkable man in his midforties, Alan lost his job loading boxes in a warehouse and couldn't find a new one. His girlfriend resented that he hung around the house while she worked full-time, making him feel ashamed. At night, he would awaken in fear, call himself a failure, then lie in the darkness, worrying, unable to fall asleep. His doctor prescribed Prozac, which dramatically improved his outlook. His girlfriend's insults barely touched him now and he worried less about being unemployed. Sure, he wanted a job, he said, but Prozac put him at ease. So maybe he looked a little less earnestly for that job.

Prozac changed Alan Clark the way it changed John Green. Alan says, "I don't know why. I just felt really good about myself." The good feeling never left him. Alan calls this feeling "happiness," but most people experience happiness in reaction to life. In Alan's case, his good feeling was an unassailable sensation he brought to life—a sensation he experienced for no discernible reason, which mildly confused him since deep down he usually felt good only when life went his way. Yet nothing in Alan's life had changed but a pill.

Artificial Happiness's distinctive feature is its power to resist life. When people enjoy Artificial Happiness they manage to avoid feeling miserable when life is miserable. Measure their misery by degrees during a painful life experience and it never reaches the boiling point. No matter how bad things get, a person with Artificial Happiness goes on feeling well; you can't arouse in him the feeling of total hopelessness.

Enough Artificially Happy people exist now in the United States to make for a new class of Artificially Happy Americans, or Happy Americans for short. These people live full and busy lives, except that what they get from life doesn't penetrate them very deeply. Religion may make them moral, work may satisfy their ambition, but medicine is the real guarantor of their happiness, not life. Rather than mine happiness from their daily activities, some of these Happy Americans get it from the medicine cabinet through antidepressants like Prozac and Zoloft. Happiness comes to them unawares, like sleep, and stays with them until some preappointed time determined by the drug's half-life. How they live and how they feel have little to do with one another.

Bill Mansfield, a thirty-eight-year-old entertainment executive, reveals the dark side of Artificial Happiness. With his New York apartment furnished in swinging bachelor décor, including barbells on the floor and a dresser topped with loose change and some condoms, Bill has a history of recreational drug use. He says with a chuckle how every gentleman bachelor should have four drugs in his medicine cabinet: Ecstasy, cocaine, Viagra, and Ambien. Ecstasy, he reports, makes him extroverted, thereby enticing women to his side at the nightclub, while cocaine works as an aphrodisiac for the women he lures back to his apartment. Although his erectile function is normal, he takes Viagra in part to counteract the mild depressant effects of Ecstasy but also so he can "go all night." According to Bill, the standard for acceptable lovemaking is higher in New York City than in other places, including for a man's stamina during intercourse. One problem with Viagra, he notes, is that the drug helps him maintain, but not actually achieve, an erection. On the contrary, to become aroused, "you still have to like the woman," which he views as an inconvenience. Finally, Ambien helps him sleep at night, counteracting the stimulant effects of the other drugs; it also calms his fears, including whether he'll have enough money to go to clubs, pick up women, pay for their drinks, pay for their dinners, pay for their cocaine, pay for his Ecstasy, pay for his Viagra, and pay for his Ambien so that he can enjoy the good life.

About a year ago, Bill's mood turned glum, which confused him. He was prospering in his condition. He was young, healthy, and working in a job of his choice; he enjoyed plenty of women from all different countries; but for some reason he was unhappy. He grew snappish and irritable and sensitive to arguments between himself and his family; he started to resent life and felt that he had a right to do so. At the same time, he began to lose pleasure in his endless pursuit of women. Everything about his life seemed to bore him. Aware of his new psychology, even a little afraid of it and unsure of its origins, he went to his primary care doctor looking for help.

A more thoughtful doctor might have probed the deep structure of Bill's life and declared: "You're unhappy because you waste your time and money on women who are little more than hookers, who sleep with you because you buy them things, who don't really like you, and whom you don't really like in return; in addition, you succumb to some ridiculous inner pressure to be a sexual superman." Instead, the doctor gave Bill a prescription for Wellbutrin after explaining in a twenty-minute interview how life's stresses can provoke an "imbalance in neurotransmitters," thereby causing a chronic feeling of gloom. The doctor knew Bill was sexually active, which is why he prescribed him Wellbutrin, a drug with fewer sexual side effects than other antidepressants, yet he totally ignored the nature of Bill's sexual and romantic life, as if it were a mere triviality. Wellbutrin stuffed Bill full of Artificial Happiness but by doing so silenced the noise cutting through Bill's consciousness and leading him toward a new outlook on life. To this day, Bill takes Wellbutrin, feels content, and lives as he always has. Artificial Happiness stifles any self-awareness of his pathological life.

The dark side of Artificial Happiness also comes to light in the story of Alice Hudson, whose mind is equally frozen. A sensitive, insecure, middle-aged woman, Alice spent her twenties in what she calls her "I'm sorry" phase. Desperate to be liked, she constantly feared saying the wrong thing in conversation. Even after uttering a simple hello she would catch herself and say, "Oops, I'm sorry. Did I say it wrong?" Still, despite her solicitousness toward others, she found making friends difficult. She was the kind of person whose awkwardness produced in people the desire to tease her. Rather than answer their jeers, she would smile and behave as if the people laughing at her were really her friends; at lunch, she interpreted it as an act of fellowship to be able to buy her coworkers sandwiches at her expense.

One day when she was in her midthirties, Alice was sitting in church when her minister called for people to come forward and give their testimony. Surprised at the impulse that seized her, Alice volunteered. Digging her fingernails into the podium, she talked about her relationship with God; the speech cost her so much effort that at the end she was covered in perspiration. But the rest of the congregation applauded, with one man in the audience so smitten by her that he asked her out for a date. Eventually the two married and had a child. Many times since then she has shuddered while thinking about this experience, yet to this day she considers it her high point as a Christian.

Within a few years, Alice's quirky personality lost its allure for her husband. At best, he began treating her with contemptuous civility. More typically, rather than say hello when she came home from work he took no more notice of her than if a simple fly had flown into the room. Sometimes he mocked her for her insecurities. Sensitive by nature, Alice was defenseless against his reproaches, and his insults moved her deeply and painfully. Occasionally her husband lashed out, wadding pieces of paper up like a fist and throwing them at her. Alice's self-esteem plummeted to the point where she felt completely crushed. When she talked to her minister about her situation and confessed a secret urge to divorce, he reminded her of her obligation to her young child and noted that keeping a marriage intact for the sake of a child was no bad thing. Eventually, she found her way to her primary care doctor, who wrote her a prescription for Zoloft. The drug boosted her spirits and to this day she lives with Artificial Happiness inside a loveless marriage, just as John Green does. Alice's minister knows she's taking medication and condones it, viewing the drug as a means to an end: preserving the family unit.

Artificial Happiness locks Alice in an abusive relationship and robs her of the incentive to change her life. Even marriage counseling she dismisses as unnecessary; since Zoloft surrounds her with an impenetrable fortress of Artificial Happiness, she no longer sees any need to go through the exhausting process of trying to change her husband's behavior. Even more disconcerting is how her minister overlooks her solution because it serves the cause of family values.

Artificial Happiness alarms me. People with Artificial Happiness don't feel the unhappiness they need to feel to move forward with their lives. Sometimes people need a critical mass of unhappiness to push them out of a bad life situation, thereby giving them another chance at happiness; Artificially Happy people lose this impulse to change. With their unhappiness suddenly erased by medicine, they ask themselves: "Why bother? Things aren't so bad." With life artificially clean and comfortable, they stay in their old ruts, stagnate in a pool of sham happiness, and sacrifice any chance for the real thing.

The pernicious effect of Artificial Happiness takes a slightly different form in the case of Linda Jones, a woman who was still able to act while under the influence of a psychotropic drug, but without fully understanding, or even seeing, all the factors and consequences involved. Forty-two years old, Linda endured a troubled marriage for years. Although not abusive, her husband grew into the kind of man who insists on doing things his way. At the very least, he began taking her for granted. After Linda left work early to prepare dinner one evening, he loaded up his plate then went over to the couch and watched TV. Linda usually gave in whenever a conflict loomed, her urge to kowtow rooted in fear. She didn't fear abuse, but she did fear precipitating a hellish conflict that might lead to divorce, single parenthood, and the loss of her material security. Yet there were moments when she did fight back, which shocked her husband and caused him to raise his voice, although the two would eventually make up.

Dissatisfied with life, Linda saw a psychotherapist, who told her that she was suffering from low self-esteem. The psychotherapist recommended that she see her primary care doctor for treatment, possibly medication. When she did, her primary care doctor informed her that stress causes a "chemical imbalance in our brains," which leads to more generalized unhappiness. The first treatment of choice, he said, was exercise, which raises the level of endorphins in the brain. Linda tried the method for a few weeks but failed to improve. She returned and received a prescription for what her primary care doctor called the second treatment of choice: antidepressant medication (in Linda's case, Paxil).

Paxil dramatically improved Linda's spirits, yet it also changed the dynamic in her relationship with her husband. Before, when Linda and her husband fought she defended herself the only way she knew how. After cursing him and delivering a few low blows, she felt ashamed at the pain she had caused him, which evoked tender feelings in her, even pity, showing her husband that it wasn't hatred for him that made her mean but a more general anguish she was feeling, vague and without boundaries. Her sympathy touched him; for a brief moment, he glimpsed the misery he was causing her. Inevitably the whole experience pushed the two closer together. All this changed when Linda took medication. Fortified with Paxil, she no longer felt the sting of her husband's behavior. On the contrary, whenever conflict loomed she just sat in her chair unmoved. Her husband couldn't help but notice this seemingly odd composure, which made him even angrier. The cycle of attack, guilt, and reunion ended; now it was just attack and ignore.

After several months on medication, Linda felt confident enough to sue for divorce as she no longer feared the consequences. When asked if she would have been confident enough without Paxil to get a divorce, she said no. Six months later, with a separation agreement in hand and Artificial Happiness filling her mind, she wanted to start dating but noticed an inability to achieve orgasm, which she attributed to Paxil. She complained to her primary care doctor, who was surprised by her eagerness to meet men. Although he admitted that Paxil had sexual side-effects, he counseled her: "Linda, just stay on the drug until after the divorce." Linda isn't sure if her doctor wanted to mute her sex drive and keep her from dating, thereby preventing her from violating the terms of her custody agreement or instead hoped to keep her from losing the very happiness that had inspired her to sue for divorce in the first place and if lost might cause her to backpedal. Whatever her doctor's motivation, Linda stayed on Paxil. When asked how long she expects to be on the drug, she says, "Until life gets less stressful." When asked when that would be, she replies, "I don't know, but I'll consult with my doctor first."

Paxil guided Linda and decided for her an important question of life. Tiny alterations in her thinking took place, prompting a decision quite out of character for her. At the exact moment when Linda needed the greatest clearness of mind to properly make a decision, Paxil swayed the outcome. Although the judicious use of antidepressants can, theoretically, create a more balanced perspective from which to act, in Linda's case the drug stifled her natural caution, thereby unbalancing her decision. Before taking Paxil, Linda dilated her imagination into the future and saw herself divorced, happy, and free; but she also saw herself without a job skill and two children to support, which made her pause. Once on Paxil, she no longer felt this tension; Linda weighed the pros of getting a divorce, but no longer the cons. She lost a trait she had formerly possessed: an instinct to consider all the different variables in a problem before making a decision. If in the future she does find a better life for herself, she will owe it to good luck more than any careful planning on her part.

Also troubling is how Linda's doctor used medication to insure that her divorce went smoothly. Unlike Linda, her doctor was sensitive to the consequences of her actions—having thought several steps ahead—so he took on the responsibility of strategizing for her. Yet, was it his place to conceal the natural Linda, to manipulate her with medication until she arrived at a point in life he thought best for her?

In both my professional and personal life I meet unhappy people like Bill Mansfield and Alice Hudson—people who might change their situation with the slightest effort. But even that effort is prevented by medicine. Artificial Happiness "cures" them of the desire to change. I also meet people like Linda Jones—people who change their situation but do so because medicine conceals from them the consequences of their actions. Artificial Happiness pushes them off-center as they plot their course of action. I feel sorry for these people and I want to free them from the well-intentioned deceit today's doctors impose on them.

Artificial Happiness establishes a new and dangerous position on the continuum of how people find relief when life goes sour. On one side of the continuum are hobbies like stamp collecting and golf. Many people engage in these hobbies to pass the time. Others do so because they sense a conflict between how they actually live and how they *want* to live (or how they think they should be living), which makes them unhappy. These people plunge into hobbies to distract themselves and not just to pass the time, but since most hobbies are harmless and even serve a reputable purpose (like helping people socialize), society overlooks their behavior. Besides, people who use hobbies to escape unhappiness generally find that life breaks through; society knows that the "cure" offered by a hobby is incomplete and that even golfers and stamp collectors must eventually face up to the truth.

When a hobby fails, some of these people move to the other side of the continuum and stupefy themselves with alcohol or illicit drugs. Unable to divert their attention with an activity, they darken their minds directly. True, most people use alcohol for the same harmless reason they play golf or collect stamps: to socialize and pass the time. But society is more wary of alcohol because of the physical danger it poses to users and because alcohol has the potential to block out life completely and make people reckless and troublesome. Unlike the prevalent thinking regarding hobbies, society judges people harshly for stupefying themselves to escape life and not just to feel cheery.

Artificial Happiness creates a new and dangerous middle ground between hobbies and alcohol. Antidepressant medication has the same power as alcohol to alter a person's frame of mind—to poison the mind and deaden it to life's influence—yet, unlike alcohol, it has the support of a powerful institution: the medical profession. Similarly, alternative medicine and obsessive exercise are as safe as most hobbies and, like most hobbies, even have positive benefits; but they are more effective at shutting out life and causing people to lose touch. Again, because they enjoy the support of the medical profession society looks the other way.

Happy Americans have a strange value system: they worry more about justifying their state of stupefaction than whether their minds are working properly. They don't want to be grouped with drunks and drug addicts; they don't want to feel ashamed. They excuse themselves, knowing that Artificial Happiness carries the imprimatur of professional medicine; they dismiss as antiscientific any accusation that they somehow lead immoral lives. Thus, we have the peculiar situation today of people stupefying themselves and calmly discussing it. Yet respect for science also blinds these people to the dangerous consequences of Artificial Happiness. Happy Americans are not immoral so much as victims.

Life rarely harmonizes with how people want to feel in their minds, so some people bend their minds to harmonize with life: they stupefy themselves with intoxicants. But doing so was never considered proper or respectable, let alone scientific, until today, against the backdrop of a medical practice revolution that sanctions such behavior.

DOCTORS TAP INTO THE PUBLIC CONSCIOUSNESS

Primary care doctors instigated the medical practice revolution, yet in some ways responsibility for the event extends beyond them. Although these doctors aspired to reconnect with patients, they also reacted to a change in the public culture that enveloped them and everyone else. In the second half of the twentieth century, new attitudes toward mental illness filled the air. While the doctors themselves may not have been fully aware of these attitudes, their ideologies reflected them and responded to the deep public insecurities behind them. Precisely because their ideologies struck such widely held chords of belief they succeeded in causing a revolution.

In the early 1990s, to the surprise of many, books about Prozac sold incredibly well. *Prozac Nation*, in particular, tapped into people's anxiety about mental illness. Vividly describing her ten-year experience with clinical depression—the crying fits, the gloom, and the suicide attempts—the book's author, Elizabeth Wurtzel, begged readers to see her problem as a disease rather than as the consequence of personal inadequacy or failure. Fearing the stigma associated with mental illness (which might one day afflict them), many readers obliged Ms. Wurtzel, and with such zeal that not just clinical depression but also everyday unhappiness was labeled a disease. Although primary care doctors had their own reasons for turning everyday unhappiness into a disease, people's sympathy for Ms. Wurtzel and their determination to see mental illness in a new light made the doctors' task that much easier.

Dr. Peter Kramer's best-selling book, *Listening to Prozac,* published around the same time as *Prozac Nation,* also justified the medical practice revolution in the public imagination. Dr. Kramer praised Prozac for increasing self-esteem and reducing negative feelings in his patients when nothing else could. Eager to spread the gospel of what antidepressants could do, he coined the phrase "cosmetic psychopharmacology" to describe how Prozac trims away the ugly parts of people's personalities to produce better, happier people, as a laser removes small skin blemishes. Yet the populist character of Dr. Kramer's book overshadows in importance its pro-Prozac message. Doctors are typically didactic, even condescending, when they write medical books for the reading public. Psychiatrists, for example, talk almost in code when discussing mental illness to maintain a certain distance between themselves and the public. Although psychiatrists want to inform the public they also want to prevent popular interference in medical matters. Dr. Kramer put himself on the same level as readers, occasionally expressing his own uncertainties about life and inviting readers to share their point of view. He shrewdly understood that to make everyday unhappiness a disease, doctors needed to turn mental health into a popular cause.

Critics often blame the popularity of psychotropic drugs, alternative medicine, and obsessive exercise on greedy doctors, greedy drug companies, and greedy insurance companies. Americans, like so many sheep, follow their orders and endanger themselves with psychotropic drugs, or at the very least make themselves look ridiculous with alternative medicine and obsessive exercise. Yet this explanation ignores public moods, which are especially powerful in a democracy. The notion that psychotropic drugs, alternative medicine, and obsessive exercise became enormously popular because they served medical or corporate interests strains the imagination. Moreover, each of these modalities challenged medical or corporate interests. For example, many doctors, including many psychiatrists, opposed (and still do) the liberal use of psychotropic drugs. The entire medical establishment opposed alternative medicine. Many doctors thought exercise medicine was specious. The fact that these modalities became popular in spite of powerful opposition calls into question the interest-based explanation, which also fails to account for the public's enormous enthusiasm for the new approach to unhappiness. So loud was the public clamor for action that at times during the medical practice revolution it was hard to tell whether doctors led the people or the other way around. The explanation lies instead in what sociologist Franz Schurmann called "a realm of ideology." The medical practice revolution sprang not from medical or corporate interests, but from ideology, a system of belief that has at its core deep popular roots.

Nor do critics appreciate the most serious consequence of the medical practice revolution: Artificial Happiness. Critics of psychotropic drug overprescription warn of the physical dangers to patients, including an increased risk of seizures, sexual dysfunction, and, most recently, teenage suicide. Critics of alternative medicine and obsessive exercise adopt a lighter tone since the physical dangers involved are less; they laugh at what they consider to be harmless indulgences. Still, critics of alternative medicine occasionally sound the safety bell, or at least argue that alternative medicine should be better regulated. Yet, by and large, psychotropic drugs are quite safe and alternative medicine and obsessive exercise even more so, which is why critics have consistently failed, for example, in their efforts to curb the use of psychotropic drugs and alternative medicine. The danger from the medical practice revolution is Artificial Happiness itself, not any increased patient morbidity or mortality, and it is from this perspective that my investigation proceeds.

Although doctors purposely created Artificial Happiness, they are not part of any vast medical conspiracy. To the extent that they do mismanage patients, they do so unawares. If anything, doctors sincerely believe they help patients by inducing Artificial Happiness. They truly believe their approach works, a belief intensified by the fact that they have the power to make it work. Their misdeed stems not from malicious intent, but from the mistaken assumption that medicine penetrates every life problem imaginable. This assumption underlies all three ideologies driving the medical practice revolution. Because of the nature of what doctors do it has consequences for millions of people.

With so many people resorting to Artificial Happiness, society as a whole is inevitably affected. The most important things in life begin in a person's mind. Since the mind sets limits on behavior, small changes in the mind may have serious social consequences. When a man silences his misery through Artificial Happiness, he also silences his conscience. Actually, he *must* silence his conscience, since a bad conscience often causes his unhappiness. I speak of conscience not just as a moral instrument, but as something within the mind that appraises a person's entire activity—approving or disapproving, depending on the culture in which that person is raised. For example, the son of ambitious parents may suffer a bad conscience if he's a mediocre student, while the son of underachievers may welcome this status, since the latter lives in the manner he expects to live. Bill Mansfield and Alice Hudson were unhappy because they felt a discord between how they lived and how they wished to live. Their consciences told them that they were on the wrong course in life. Artificial Happiness silenced their consciences, causing them to feel this divergence less. As a consequence, they felt better about their lives and did nothing to change them.

A reckless act sometimes follows when a person silences his conscience with alcohol, since that part of his mind that appraises his activity is turned off. A murderer takes a shot of whiskey before finishing the job. A prostitute takes a stiff drink to numb her mind before work. Soldiers get drunk before sacking a city. Society is able to contain such reckless behavior because intoxicated people are relatively few in number. In addition, alcohol wears off quickly; even murderers and prostitutes come back to reason, after which they sometimes feel remorse for their behavior. But imagine an entire class of people who stupefy themselves regularly and constantly, who remain stupefied throughout the day, and who live not on society's fringes but in the mainstream. Suddenly the problem grows more serious—millions of regular people stifling their consciences to live happier lives, thinking, and therefore behaving, in ways they would not otherwise do. Through sheer numbers these people pose a greater threat to the social fabric than murderers, prostitutes, and thieves.

My concern may seem alarmist, considering that the United States has forty years of experience with Artificial Happiness without Happy Americans proving to be especially troublesome or dangerous. Yet for most of those forty years Artificial Happiness has been an adult phenomenon. Only recently have doctors induced Artificial Happiness in younger people in great numbers, especially with antidepressants. Adults under the influence of Artificial Happiness seem to retain enough of a conscience to be respectful and law-abiding. They can reach back into a past when they lived without Artificial Happiness and be guided by the voice of that past. Their consciences are fully developed by the time they try Artificial Happiness, which somehow steels them against the worst effects of the experience. Children by definition do not have this past. Their consciences are not fully formed; if anything, Artificial Happiness interferes with their formation. Albeit painful, unhappiness is vital to the development of a healthy conscience, for unhappiness teaches a child what it means to feel dissatisfied with oneself, to feel ashamed, to acknowledge that one has made a mess of things, and to hear for the first time the inner voice within that points the way to proper living. Happy Children are relieved of this unhappiness at the very moment they need to feel it, assimilate it, and learn from it.

Artificial Happiness's danger to society lies not in a bunch of middle-aged people hiding from life for the first time, but in the formation of a new stratum of Happy Children who grow up to be Happy Adults and, later, Happy Seniors. An entire life cycle based on Artificial Happiness is emerging in which the only inner experience people have ever known is Artificial Happiness. These Happy Americans know happiness independent of life. For this reason, they can't be controlled through conventional threats to their happiness. Life neither moves them nor threatens them. Totally self-contained organisms, they don't need kindness when they're feeling down; therefore, they don't know what kindness is. They need nothing from others and get nothing in return. Although the prospect is mere speculation at this point, a society composed of such people would be a nightmare.

People today fail to see the negative implications of the change in medical practice and only know that medicine touches their personal lives more than before. From my perch as a practicing anesthesiologist in a community hospital, I've witnessed this change: the increased use of antidepressants, stimulants, and narcotics; the rise of alternative medicine; the rise of the fitness movement; the rise of medical-based spiritualism; and the rise of managed care—*all within the last forty years*. These trends cry out for explanation. I believe a single overarching event explains them—the rise of Artificial Happiness—and that this event portends a sea change in how human beings live and function.

TWO

UNHAPPINESS BECOMES AN
ENGINEERING PROBLEM

ONE SUMMER DAY in 1968, my father and grandfather, both internists, sat in our backyard while my father boasted about his recent accomplishment. Already board-certified in medicine, my father had just received his FACP (Fellow of the American College of Physicians) for a paper he had written on a blood disease called polycythemia vera. This achievement not only set him apart from other doctors but also made possible a whole new appellation after his name, which he thought would convey a sense of greater expertise to patients. Dramatic and grandiose, his heart racing as if greased with butter, my father bragged through lunch, while occasionally glancing at my grandfather's face to discover what impression he had made. My grandfather tried not to let his irritation show, for he disliked bragging. He also seemed embarrassed, for he had begun his medical practice before the era of board certification. Nothing but the testament of a few grateful patients could prove his worth. Fidgeting in his seat, he let out a slight sigh, then mumbled a spiritless "Congratulations."

Sadly, the extra credential brought my father little satisfaction, as frustration and distress dominated his professional life over the next few years. Although he provided good care, some of his patients accused him of washing his hands of all responsibility for their well-being. In the grip of resentment, they shouted at him that he ran away from their personal troubles like a coward or that he was too unfeeling to care. My father found all this incomprehensible; here he was, an expert in polycythemia vera, totally unappreciated. He vented his anger three years later in the same backyard, after a friend of mine, twelve years old like me, mistakenly called my father "Mr. Dworkin." My father snapped: "I didn't go to medical school, finish an internship, finish a residency, and get an FACP to be called 'mister.' It's '*Dr.* Dworkin'!" While my friend and I stood motionless with our mouths open, my mother defused the situation from a distance with laughter and then told my father to knock it off.

The story of Artificial Happiness begins with America's doctors, for doctors write the drug prescriptions and hype the modalities that create Artificial Happiness. Sometime in the late 1960s a change occurred in doctors' attitudes. In the past, doctors counseled, comforted, or simply told unhappy patients: "Live as best you can, for we cannot help you." Today, fully convinced that happiness is a disease and something best treated medically, doctors aggressively prescribe psychotropic drugs and other therapies. The fury shown by patients toward doctors like my father in the late 1960s catalyzed this change.

My grandfather was a doctor of the old school. He knew a fair amount of medical science, although in the early twentieth century, when he practiced, there wasn't much medical science to know, and his methods were a bit sloppy. (He sterilized syringes in the same pot his wife had used to cook the previous day's vegetables.) Nonetheless, his patients loved him because he talked to them about their problems, often quoting from German philosophy to illustrate his advice. There were many doctors like him at the turn of the last century: wise generalists or "father confessor" types—professionals weak on science but thoughtful about everyday life, content to put their instruments aside to talk to patients about personal trouble. These doctors gave patients advice that grew out of their general education and life experiences, not out of any science.

Personal doctoring declined during the twentieth century when the medical profession began the long project of turning medicine into a serious science. To separate themselves from other healers, doctors began emphasizing scientific knowledge over wisdom about life. Their evolution took place in four stages. At each stage, doctors surrendered a nonscientific dimension of patient care to other professionals.

In the first stage, during the first quarter of the twentieth century, doctors turned the *social* troubles of patients over to social workers. At first, social workers just made sure patients took their medicine. However, over time, social workers took over the psychosocial dimension of patient care altogether. As doctors specialized, they found themselves with less time to comfort and reassure patients, to hold a patient's hand during a house call, or to worry about a patient's family or job problems. Even Dr. Richard Cabot, one of the founders of the social work movement, admitted that "Patients shoot by us [doctors] like comets, crossing for a moment our field of vision, then passing into oblivion." Social workers filled this void in patient care.

In the second stage, starting around the 1930s, doctors turned the *emotional* troubles of patients over to psychiatrists and psychologists. Even as late as the 1920s, neurologists, internists, and general practitioners saw bad cases of depression in their offices. Starting in the 1930s, the trend toward specialization, combined with the rising popularity of Freudian psychoanalysis, led to a more rigid division of labor. Mental illness became the preserve of neurologists, who managed disease associated with brain pathology ("organic illness"), and psychiatrists, who managed disease that lacked obvious brain pathology ("functional illness"). Both depression and everyday unhappiness were functional illnesses, and so psychiatrists managed both conditions using psychoanalysis. Over time, most nonpsychiatrists saw psychoanalysis as the natural outgrowth of specialization: surgeons specialized in cutting, radiologists specialized in X rays, and psychiatrists specialized in words. As American doctors specialized (by 1972 almost 80 percent had done so), nonpsychiatrists increasingly saw psychoanalysis as the gold standard in treating mental health, although some patients resisted because of the stigma attached to seeing a psychiatrist.

In the third stage, starting in the early 1960s, doctors turned the *ethical* dilemmas surrounding patient care over to bioethicists. Before the 1960s, the phrase *bioethics* didn't really exist: medical ethics was called *professional ethics*. A doctor had a professional obligation to be ethical, based on the Hippocratic Oath that he swore to uphold on graduating from medical school. At first, professional ethics meant moral conduct and proper etiquette, but as doctors specialized, technical competence overrode other considerations. By the early 1960s, after spending decades engrossed with the mechanical aspects of their craft, doctors balked at answering ethical questions raised by their own technology. Confused and uncertain, doctors looked to theologians and philosophers for guidance, while intellectuals enrolled in special centers to study medical ethics full-time.

Shortly afterward, the field of bioethics was born, eventually replacing professional ethics.

In the fourth stage, also occurring in the early 1960s, doctors turned their *spiritual* duties over to support groups in the community. Busy doctors increasingly ignored their patients' morale issues, so support groups took over that responsibility. Henceforth, when patients felt isolated and in despair, they relied on peers in their support group for comfort. During the next three decades over a thousand different support groups sprang up in the United States, freeing doctors to focus more on the medical side of things.

By the late 1960s, having lost the social dimension of the patient to social workers, the emotional dimension to psychology and psychiatry, the moral dimension to bioethicists, and the spiritual dimension to self-help groups, doctors had been reduced to *mere engineers of the body*. Although outstanding technicians, they lacked any connection with their patients' everyday troubles.

This was a crisis. Already, in the early 1960s, writers in magazines like *Forbes* and *Harper's* were mourning the demise of personal doctoring and writing the epitaph on the "golden age of medicine," with one noted health care consultant during the era complaining that "The doctor may be a learned man in his own field. But in general knowledge he is the worst-educated of our professional men." The public decried that doctors had become cold, overpaid technicians. Nostalgia for the old ways evidenced in television shows like *Marcus Welby, MD*. Books like Ivan Illich's *Medical Nemesis*, Rick Carlson's *The End of Medicine*, and Marcia Millman's *The Unkindest Cut* berated doctors for ignoring the human element in medicine, with Carlson, for example, accusing doctors of equating human beings with machines. From 1968 to 1975 the number of Americans holding positive attitudes toward the medical profession dropped suddenly and precipitously from about three-quarters to just over half, with people between the ages of thirty and sixty-five accounting for most of the decline. Even President Nixon piled on, commenting in speeches on the American people's dissatisfaction with their health care. The medical profession was under assault.

Primary care doctors at the nation's medical schools joined the chorus of criticism. Calling specialty medicine heartless and soulless, many of them urged students to pursue careers in primary care, which was the field of medicine thought closest to the people. The bias in favor of primary care lingered for years. When I chose to specialize in anesthesiology, several of these doctors acted as if I had degraded myself. Their contempt for specialty medicine made even my anesthesia professors squirm with self-consciousness. After teaching me a technical skill then watching me apply it to my patient, one instructor contemptuously told me, "OK, monkey, do your trick," implying that I shouldn't be so proud of my accomplishment and that doctoring involved more than just jamming a tube down someone's throat.

Ironically, primary care doctors contributed most to the upsurge in negative feelings toward physicians, since people expected these doctors to be more attentive than specialists to their everyday problems. It was one thing for a specialist to get caught up in new gadgetry; it was quite another for a primary care doctor to do so, since he or she was supposed to be a wise and compassionate generalist. Because of the stigma attached to seeing a psychiatrist, most Americans preferred to take care of their psychological troubles in primary care. When primary care doctors grew absorbed by technical preoccupations and ignored such troubles and suggested to unhappy patients that they see a psychiatrist, patients felt betrayed and lashed out. My father often came home in a sour mood, resenting patients who had accused him that day of ignoring their everyday problems and working only to pay for his new Buick Riviera. His FACP, a symbol of narrow professionalism, seemed only to make things worse.

In response to this crisis, doctors got back into the game of helping people with their everyday troubles, creating a new ideology that both authorized and justified their interventions. Since they were under the greatest threat, primary care doctors took the lead.

BIRTH OF A NEW IDEOLOGY

For doctors, no matter what society they practice in, science is a powerfully compelling reality, one that governs their professional lives with an iron hand. Science lays down so many rules that doctors easily grow bound by routine. But doctors are also human beings and, like all human beings, they feel and dream and sometimes grow afraid. When threatened with a crisis, even they may seek rescue in some vision. This happened to American primary care doctors four decades ago.

By the late 1960s, physician-engineering had failed. To patients, the medical profession no longer seemed interested in satisfying their aspirations for a happy life. Shocked by the depth of anger, primary care doctors tried to reconnect with patients, but the medical profession's evolution had gone too far to be reversed. Primary care doctors couldn't just start advising people on life again, as they had ceded this task to others long ago. They were more like engineers now, so when they reconnected with patients, they did so as engineers of the body. Responding to public pressure, they embraced unhappiness as a problem worthy of their attention, *but they attacked unhappiness as an engineering problem*—something like a sore throat or a cold, something biochemical that drugs could fix. Primary care doctors, aware of the chaos in their relations with patients and fearing a threat to their profession, responded with a novel idea—unhappiness is a disease—that gave rise to a new ideology and a new policy toward psychotropic drugs.

The new ideology was part science and part faith. In the 1950s, scientists observed that psychotropic drugs blocked the reuptake of neurotransmitters (amines) inside the brain. To explain the salutary effects of these drugs on mood, scientists hypothesized an association between neurotransmitters and depression. Dr. Joseph Schildkraut officially presented this biogenic amine theory in 1965 in a landmark article in the *American Journal of Psychiatry*. The theory remained incomplete, since a decrease in brain amines in itself did not cause depression and several drugs with antidepressant effects failed to increase amines. However, in the late 1960s, during the medical profession's crisis, the biogenic amine theory left the realm of science and became ideology. Primary care doctors expanded the association between neurotransmitters and depression to include everyday unhappiness. Although no article in the medical literature substantiated this position, many doctors embraced it nonetheless, especially since psychotropic drugs gave unhappy patients so much relief.

As happens often, the doctors' ideology came to be known by a single catchword, a brief slogan: neurotransmitters. When doctors invoked this word in the context of mental illness, listeners immediately knew what it meant. A neurotransmitter was more than just a molecule inside a nerve; on the contrary, it symbolized a new worldview, one that proclaimed a physical basis for unhappiness. Primary care doctors wanted medicine to make people happy and they also believed that happiness turned on neurotransmitters. Hence, the word "neurotransmitters" expressed in capsule form the new belief that doctors had a right and a duty to medicate unhappiness. This new worldview, along with doctors' private fears for their profession, formed an essential ingredient of the new ideology.

Although put forward to benefit society as a whole, no ideology is completely divorced from the material interests of a particular group, and the doctors' ideology is a case in point. Primary care doctors suffered during the twentieth century as their sphere of responsibility shrank and that of the specialists grew. Treating unhappiness with drugs reversed this trend, turning the care of unhappiness into a high-tech science that primary care doctors could practice on their own without consulting specialists. Primary care doctors could now do something more than take an old man's blood pressure or wipe a child's runny nose. In addition, by liberally dispensing psychotropic drugs primary care doctors gained the loyalty of their patients. By 1970 an estimated one in five American women and one in thirteen American men were on minor tranquilizers like Valium, with primary care doctors writing the majority of these prescriptions. But the overriding interest of all doctors, at least for the last century, has been to shield the medical profession from public scrutiny and to keep control of medical practice in their hands. This is what makes the change in doctors' behavior during the late 1960s so glaring. When primary care doctors deliberately appealed to "the people" for support for their new approach to unhappiness, exposing the medical profession to democratic pressures, the doctors exposed their theory as ideology.

In the late 1960s, with the crisis in the medical profession ongoing, primary care doctors welcomed, and even encouraged, a decade-old popular mental health movement that had its own political lobby and grassroots organizations. This was a radical departure for doctors, who were traditionally hostile to public intervention into medical matters. Consumer and family activists set up organizations across the country, drumming up support for mental health centers, with primary care doctors urging them on.

Although some of the activists had their own interests—such as gaining employment in the expanding mental health sector—their crusade was also ideological. Like primary care doctors, they saw depression as an illness, something wrongly stigmatized. They also saw depression as an illness whose cure required the patient to remain in society during treatment. These activists worked mostly to integrate sick psychiatric patients into families and communities, and primary care doctors sympathized with their efforts, for they wanted to be America's family and community doctors again. Psychiatrists had fractured mental health therapy into hospital drug therapy and office talk therapy. But now primary care doctors would make it whole again, perhaps not for schizophrenia or severe depression, but at least for everyday unhappiness, treating unhappiness in the office with drugs and in the context of the patient's family and community life. The mental health activists and the primary care doctors shared a common vision.

In the form of "family practice" a new primary care field emerged in the late 1960s in tandem with the mental health movement, again tapping into popular support. With the dramatic fall in the number of general practitioners in the United States—from 112,000 in 1930 to 66,000 in 1965—primary care doctors saw the need to create a new generation of generalists to manage problems ranging from physical disease to everyday psychological trouble. Although specialists laughed at the whole family medicine concept, as creating a specialty within general practice seemed like a contradiction in terms, the public strongly supported it. The name alone—"family practice"—appealed to people. Anything to stop doctors from being a collection of insensitive and dispassionate robots, people shouted.

Primary care doctors encouraged this democratic invasion into medicine because they needed allies to launch their medical practice revolution. They understood that to change medicine's approach to unhappiness the public must hold the same opinions about mental illness as they did. They also understood that for people to trust doctors again a friendly moniker like "family practice" was vital. Popular attitudes formed a vital well of sympathy for primary care doctors to draw on when battling other doctors committed to the status quo.

The appeal to public opinion implies the workings of ideology; it also implies weakness. If primary care doctors had been confident in their professional position, it's unlikely that they would have resorted to ideology or appealed to the public. Instead, they would have tended to their interests in private as doctors always have, resisting public interference and regarding the practice of medicine as so complex that only highly trained professionals motivated by the highest concerns should deal with them. They would have pushed the family practice theme less. They would have interpreted the biogenic amine theory less liberally. But the crisis in the medical profession had disturbed the smooth workings of medical practice.

The most interest-oriented, nonideological doctors in the medical practice revolution are the psychiatrists, who, compared to the primary care revolutionaries, play the role of reactionary conservatives. Because unhappiness forms a natural psychiatric concern, one would expect psychiatrists to have aggressively pushed the new policy. Instead, they fought it. The crisis in the medical profession, which had fueled the revolution, had left psychiatry unscathed. Psychiatrists still talked to patients—unlike physicians who dealt with physical ailments—so the wrath of patients fell elsewhere. Moreover, psychiatrists, especially in the university, had increasingly disowned the unhappiness problem, preferring instead to work on complex psychological conditions like schizophrenia or manic depression, typically in closed-off academic environments.

So when primary care doctors responded to the public's concern with a new approach to unhappiness, psychiatrists were horrified. They mounted a counterattack, which reached a high point in the 1980s, on what they regarded as a crash program in psychological treatment. They ridiculed primary care doctors for taking liberties with the biogenic amine theory (which, after all, belonged to them), condemned primary care doctors for overprescribing psychotropic drugs, and decried the democratic invasion of medicine. To this day, more than a few psychiatrists blame primary care doctors as the "source of all this trouble."

In line with conventional medical thinking, psychiatrists leveled very specific charges. The first was that primary care doctors used psychiatric instruments in ways they weren't designed for. The *Diagnostic and Statistical Manual of Mental Disorders* (*DSM*), the definitive textbook in mental health and a product of psychiatric thinking, was a case in point. A patient must satisfy five of nine criteria in the *DSM* for a diagnosis of major depression, but only two of the nine criteria for a diagnosis of minor depression. These two criteria might include a general feeling of sadness and a loss of pleasure in daily activities—moods typically felt in everyday unhappiness as well as in any pathology. Other diseases in the *DSM* potentially merge with everyday unhappiness. For example, "adjustment disorder with depressed mood," which means unhappiness caused by a difficult life stressor, and "Depressive Disorder NOS (Not Otherwise Specified)," which might mean someone who tells his doctor: "Doc, I'm feeling sad and my sleep is restless. I don't know if I'm depressed or getting depressed, but I'm feeling down. My appetite is fine and I've got plenty of energy, but I'm unhappy." Psychiatrists criticized primary care doctors for using the flexibility inherent in these diagnoses to assign unhappy people a disease and treat them, although in private psychiatrists berated themselves for creating a *DSM* with so much potential for abuse.

Using the *International Classification of Diseases* (*ICD*), primary care doctors found a way to circumvent the psychiatrists' criticism. Unlike the *DSM*, the *ICD* represents a collaborative effort from across the different medical fields. The book assigns numerical codes to all the bad things that can happen to people—not just horrible diseases but also everyday inconveniences—which doctors use to bill insurance companies for their services. One chapter in the book lists common negative emotions, including unhappiness, anxiety, and low self-esteem. When coded, these emotions instantly become "conditions" in their own right, at least from a primary care doctor's point of view, and legitimate targets for treatment even before they coalesce into a *DSM* disease. In the minds of primary care doctors, unhappiness (code V62.1) without any other signs or symptoms, let alone a *DSM* diagnosis, suffices to start therapy.

The strongest charge leveled by psychiatrists against primary care doctors was that of psychotropic drug overprescription, which practically defines the medical practice revolution. In the mid-1950s a flurry of prescription activity followed the introduction of the minor tranquilizer, Meprobamate (Miltown), but that activity was short-lived and modest compared to what came a decade later. As a reaction to the crisis in the medical profession, the new doctors' ideology took root almost immediately. The prescription rate for minor tranquilizers like Valium and Librium began rising dramatically in the mid-1960s, mostly in primary care, around the same time the doctors' poll numbers started to plummet. From 1967 to 1975 the number of prescriptions for these drugs filled in U.S. drugstores increased from 60 million to over 100 million. By the late 1960s, these drugs were among the most widely prescribed oral medications in America and would continue to be so for the next decade.

Compared with the psychiatrists, primary care doctors showed a special predilection for treating depression with minor tranquilizers, yet the prescription rate for antidepressants also exploded in the mid-1960s, rising at an even faster rate than for minor tranquilizers, again with primary care doctors responsible for much of the increase. The number of antidepressant prescriptions filled in U.S. drugstores more than doubled from 1967 to 1975, from 15 million to over 30 million.

Psychotropic drug use soared again beginning in the late 1980s, with antidepressants taking the place of minor tranquilizers as the most popular class. Since Prozac's creation in 1988 and the subsequent introduction of other similar drugs, such as Zoloft and Paxil, the use of psychotropic drugs has *tripled* in the United States, from 40 million office visits resulting in a drug prescription to 120 million in 1998, with antidepressants accounting for most of the increase. (Contrast this with the period between 1978 and 1987, when the number of office visits resulting in a psychotropic drug prescription remained relatively stable.) Psychiatrists correctly blamed primary care doctors for the surge, for of the 80 million new antidepressant prescriptions written between 1988 and 1998 nonpsychiatrists wrote 60 million.

Although some of the new antidepressant prescriptions stem from primary care doctors catching more major depression in their offices, others come from medicating everyday unhappiness. Both major depression and minor depression now get treated with drugs at roughly the same rate. In one study, doctors medicated 77 percent of their patients with major depression, yet practically the same proportion (68 percent) of patients suffering from minor depression received the same treatment. Given the high ratio of minor depression to major depression in the primary care population, possibly four to one, the equivalent percentage of patients being medicated for minor depression translates into many more patients. This supports what the psychiatrists had been arguing since the 1980s: primary care doctors were stretching the bounds of conventional medicine and treating unhappiness with drugs.

As interest-oriented physicians, psychiatrists distrusted change and prided themselves on being responsible, which in medicine means being scientific. The way primary care doctors twisted "their" (the psychiatrists') biogenic amine theory and "their" *DSM* infuriated them, and not simply because they sensed a turf grab. Psychiatrists aspired to keep their discipline a sealed entity, impervious to ideology, for they knew the history of psychiatry. They knew that the involvement of undertrained people in mental health had produced only barbaric monstrosities like nineteenth-century psychiatry, in which mental patients were treated with chains, bloodlettings, and near drownings. But what irked psychiatrists most was the democratic nature of the medical practice revolution, in which primary care doctors used psychiatric instruments to treat mental illness, activists told psychiatrists how to practice, and government, in the form of the National Institute of Mental Health (NIMH), gave laypeople the right to review psychiatric research proposals and even to conduct mental health research on their own. Psychiatrists imagined a dangerous conspiracy: government colluding with primary care doctors and the scientifically illiterate masses to establish a second-rate mental health system.

The insulated atmosphere of psychiatry, especially in academic departments and mental hospitals, made it easy for psychiatrists to think this way. Psychiatrists had the luxury of thinking logically and rationally about mental health because they faced none of the public furor directed at primary care doctors, who were targets of constant abuse. Psychiatrists condemned the primary care doctors' response as antiscientific, and while there is much truth to this criticism it overlooks some of the basic fears weighing on primary care doctors' minds since the beginning of the medical practice revolution. The medical profession's legitimacy as the organizer of health care was at stake. Government loomed and many on the left called for a takeover, while conservatives had their own plan to put health care in the hands of businessmen. Doctors needed to do something radical to arrest their decline. Although the new ideology was bad science by any standard, it did help doctors reconnect with patients and safeguard their profession. One might call these primary care revolutionaries visionaries—leaders who compromised some aspects of the system to save the whole thing.

American psychiatrists were themselves not without blemishes. In the 1950s and '60s they had branded people deviant and abnormal and persecuted them. During this period, intellectuals like Erving Goffman and Michel Foucault slammed psychiatrists for calling unconventional behavior a disease, accusing American psychiatrists, for example, of elevating the cultural prejudice against homosexuality to scientific truth and bullying gays to conform and even drugging them. Primary care doctors were innocent of this crime.

By liberally prescribing psychotropic drugs for unhappiness, primary care doctors actually dodged the whole messy business of defining normal. When unhappiness rather than behavior is the disease, the concept of "normal" loses all relevance; doctors focus on how people feel rather than on how they act. In overprescribing psychotropic drugs for unhappiness, primary care doctors practiced questionable science, but at least they avoided prejudice and intolerance.

Primary care doctors articulated a new ideology because they knew the dangers the medical profession faced and because they knew themselves. Not only did they fear the public's anger toward the medical profession but also their own inadequacy. Although primary care doctors rarely admit to practicing medicine like a trade, many of them privately acknowledge a deep void in their education, stemming in part from years of taking only science classes in college but also from a life limited to the suburbs, the closed environment of the university, and the HMO. Except for a few medical school clerkships spent learning how to talk to patients, many primary care doctors lack wide-ranging life experiences to tap into when trying to be personal doctors. This is a major defect in the training of a physician-engineer. Not surprisingly, in one 1999 study of family practitioners over 80 percent of the doctors felt confident prescribing medication for depression, but only 36 percent felt confident treating depression with counseling. The general internists and ob-gyns in the survey posted similar scores. To the relief of many primary care doctors, the engineering approach to unhappiness makes the long deep conversation with the unhappy patient superfluous.

In response to a crisis in their profession, American primary care doctors conceived of a new order in which medicine would be the dominant force in people's search for happiness. They acted to serve the public against established interests and not to fight the public in the service of established interests. Eventually, however, this changed. The primary care doctors' ideology became institutionalized and joined the realm of interests. By the end of the 1990s, primary care doctors would fight change as rabidly as the psychiatrists had in the 1980s. But the initial purpose behind the medical practice revolution was to bring the practice of medicine back into people's everyday lives. In its own way, however unscientifically, even antiscientifically, the medical practice revolution constituted a progressive force in medicine, at least initially.

THE TRIUMPH OF PRIMARY CARE OVER PSYCHIATRY

Public officials and psychiatrists got a big surprise in 1978. That year Dr. Darrel Regier and his team published an important article in the *Archives of General Psychiatry* examining the findings of the President's Commission on Mental Health, established the year before to identify how the nation's mentally ill were being served. (The mentally ill ranged from those with a diagnosable mental health or addictive disorder to those with a less-definable mental health "problem.") The commission's most important finding was that primary care doctors cared for roughly half the nation's mentally ill. Almost half the office visits to a doctor for a mental health problem involved nonpsychiatrists (the other half involved psychiatrists) and of the nonpsychiatrists four-fifths were primary care doctors, including family practitioners, general practitioners, and general internists. A de facto mental health system based in general medicine had emerged from nowhere.

Psychiatrists reacted with concern, since mental health was their turf. Wondering how primary care doctors had come to play such an important role, they proposed several explanations: First, a shortage of private practice psychiatrists existed in the South and North Central regions of the country, as well as in many of the rural areas elsewhere. Second, health insurance restrictions, including minimal Medicare coverage for mental illness, forced patients to seek care in the general medical sector. Third, low reimbursements rates caused many private practice psychiatrists to refuse Medicaid patients. However, over the next few years, psychiatrists gradually realized that primary care doctors were offering a different mental health product altogether, which explained primary care's unexpected popularity.

A second major article, titled "The Hidden Mental Health Network," in a 1985 issue of the *Archives*, identified this product. The authors observed that primary care doctors saw half the nation's mental health patients and *medicated these patients 78 percent of the time*, twice the medication rate for psychiatrists, although psychiatrists saw the sicker patients. Only one-quarter of the mental illness visits to primary care doctors involved therapeutic conversation, compared to 96 percent of visits to psychiatrists. The new mental health product was a psychotropic drug.

Reacting like any entrenched interest group whose turf is under threat, psychiatrists fought back, looking to other doctors for support. None came forward. Surgeons disliked primary care doctors poaching on psychiatry's turf, but many surgeons during this era had tight working relationships with primary care doctors. Typically, several primary care doctors fed a single surgeon, accounting for the bulk of the surgeon's referrals. Rather than upset these relationships and fight over a remote concern like mental health, surgeons stayed cautiously neutral. Other specialists, such as cardiologists and gastroenterologists, responded similarly, behaving as if the problem was none of their business. In private, some specialists were actually heartened that primary care doctors showed a penchant for engineering medicine. Having organized their practices around procedures to bill for, these specialists feared a plan among insurance carriers to reward cognitive work (like talking to patients) at the expense of technical labor. Although dispensing medication for unhappiness was hardly a procedure, at least primary care doctors weren't spending hours talking with unhappy patients, then demanding that the insurance companies soak the specialists to pay for it.

Most American physicians during this period were committed to economic and professional freedom. They believed in the individual practitioner. Some doctors secretly admired what primary care doctors were doing as an example of what honest enterprise could achieve. From their perspective, primary care doctors were simply being good businessmen. In their fight against primary care, the psychiatrists found themselves alone.

The insurance companies were certainly no help. As interest-oriented organizations geared toward profit, insurance companies saw little reason to get involved in a fight between psychiatrists and primary care doctors, and very good reasons not to. In the 1970s and early 1980s, before managed care, insurance people believed doctors should control the practice of medicine, so they avoided meddling in a debate over clinical responsibilities. By the 1990s, with managed care in full swing, insurance people thought differently. But earlier managed care was still only a regional phenomenon. With managed care still on the drawing board and insurance people foreseeing the important role primary care doctors would play in the new system—as gatekeepers to specialist care—the last thing insurance people wanted to do was antagonize primary care doctors by forcing them to practice one way or the other.

A revolution always signifies change. People previously denied access force their way into a system and demand power. Established interests fight back to regain control and preserve the status quo. In the medical practice revolution, the American people, with primary care doctors as their representatives, reached for the reins of control in professional medicine and demanded change. In making this demand, they upset established interests in medicine and pitted one group of doctors against another.

The revolution proceeded slowly. During the mid-1960s and early 1970s, when psychotropic drug prescriptions began their rise, primary care doctors hesitated to medicate patients who walked into their offices complaining of unhappiness. To the extent that unhappiness was a disease requiring a drug, primary care doctors preferred that a real disease accompany the unhappiness to legitimize their prescriptions. Thus, during this period three-quarters of the visits to primary doctors resulting in a psychiatric diagnosis listed some kind of physical symptom as the chief complaint, such as chest pain, fatigue, or dizziness. In half the patients diagnosed with depression in primary care, another condition, such as hypertension, was listed as the primary diagnosis. A public culture that saw unhappiness as a failure of will and that frowned on giving drugs to the "worried well" still prevailed in some quarters and influenced doctors. Primary care doctors took on established medical thinking but were reluctant to remake it.

Psychiatry's counterattack came in the form of an article. Once surveys established that primary care doctors treated the mentally ill apart from psychiatry, psychiatrists tried to show how inept these doctors were. In a 1980 issue of the *Archives*, psychiatrists Arthur Nielsen and Thomas Williams revealed that primary care doctors failed to diagnose depression in 50 percent of cases. The authors basically set primary care doctors up for a fall. They used a psychology questionnaire called the Beck Depression Inventory, which only psychiatrists knew about, as the standard for estimating depression in a given population; they then condemned primary care doctors for failing to diagnose depression at the same rate as that found with the Beck Inventory. The point of the article was to encourage primary care doctors to recognize their inadequacies and collaborate with their elder psychiatrist brothers.

Psychiatrists hoped collaboration would introduce conservatizing forces into primary care. They didn't expect primary care doctors to stop prescribing psychotropic drugs altogether, but they believed greater collaboration was a step in the right direction and that over time primary care would grow civilized under the weight of professional responsibility. Psychiatrists envisioned a mental health system with primary care bound to psychiatry (not one where primary care doctors referred less than 4 percent of their mental health patients to psychiatrists, as was then the case).

At the very least, psychiatrists wanted to sweep aside the cloud of idealist rhetoric coming from the mental health movement, which was united in its hostility toward organized psychiatry. Many of the movement's members were former inpatients still fuming over the abuses and indignities they had suffered in mental hospitals at the hands of psychiatrists. Other members, distrusting psychiatry on principle, spoke of empowerment and self-help. Psychiatrists wanted to divide this movement from its primary care supporters by showing how primary care doctors were failing the mentally ill in their own way.

Unfortunately for the psychiatrists, the Nielson-Williams article had the opposite effect: the article gave primary care doctors the green light to prescribe antidepressants for minor depression (everyday unhappiness). Before the article's publication, primary care doctors felt more comfortable hooking all forms of depression onto the diagnosis of a physical ailment, with the physical ailment itself almost overriding in importance, whether the depression was major or minor. When the Nielson-Williams article accused primary care doctors of failing to diagnose and treat both major *and* minor depression, primary care doctors realized they could aggressively diagnose and treat minor depression as a distinct problem, one that might still be tethered to a physical diagnosis but that would also stand as a reputable diagnosis in its own right. However, the primary care doctors would use *their* paradigm to treat minor depression, not that of the psychiatrists. They would treat minor depression with drugs.

The psychiatrists had tripped on one of their own instruments: the Beck Inventory, which is a series of questions designed to determine whether a person is depressed. When answered by many individuals the Beck Inventory estimates the prevalence of depression in a given population. The problem is that the diagnosis of depression depends on how the test is scored. For example, in one study of patients in a British general practice, 48 percent of patients were "depressed" when a score of 11 was required for the diagnosis, but only 25 percent were depressed when the cutoff was raised to 17. (The higher the score the more severe the depressive symptoms but also the less chance of falsely diagnosing people as depressed.) By taking general questions about everyday mood, scoring them, and then calling everyone above a certain score "depressed," the psychiatrists generated as many depressed people as they wanted.

This bias inherent in psychiatry had serious consequences when Drs. Nielson and Williams joined their theoretical estimate of minor depression's prevalence in the United States— 12.2 percent—to a call for primary care doctors to get more aggressive. They used a Beck score of 13 to 17 to diagnose minor depression in their particular study, but in the real world they recommended an even lower threshold (a Beck score of 10), so that fewer "depressed" patients would go unrecognized. Statistically, a Beck score of 10 would catch enough Americans with unhappiness to produce a 12.2 percent prevalence of minor depression in the general population. In 1980 the prevalence of minor depression in the primary care population was only 2.3 percent; thus, Drs. Nielson and Williams accused primary care doctors of underdiagnosing the condition—except that dangling a quota of depressed people (12.2 percent of the population) before primary care doctors was like hanging red meat before a hungry animal. Resentful of being called inept by the psychiatrists, eager to help unhappy patients, believing unhappiness was a disease, determined to save the medical profession from itself, and now armed with a lower threshold for minor depression, primary care doctors felt within their rights to diagnose minor depression even more aggressively. Although Drs. Nielson and Williams didn't expect the new patients caught by primary care to be systematically medicated, primary care doctors had their own plans.

The medical literature cited Nielson-Williams for the next twenty years, although psychiatry journals like the *Archives* continued to publish other articles during the 1980s showing how primary care doctors underdiagnosed and undertreated depression. These articles shared the same modus operandi: use a depression inventory that only psychiatrists knew about to document the amount of depression in a given population, then show how primary care doctors failed to diagnose this number. The articles' goals were also fairly uniform: effecting better service integration, tying primary care closer to psychiatry, and discouraging the federal government from expanding the mental health sector in primary care.

The dilemma psychiatrists faced during this era was that the one great revolutionary vision in mental health came not from psychiatry but from primary care. Psychiatrists lacked a viable solution to the unhappiness problem. They sympathized with people's concerns, but they preferred that unhappy people take the sensible path of slow, deliberate effort, including multiple sessions of psychotherapy. Primary care doctors, on the other hand, had a real solution to unhappiness—medication—based on their assumption that unhappiness was a neurotransmitter problem. Although the psychiatrists' solution had theoretical merits, the primary care solution had operational consequences. Primary care doctors believed that only their solution could rescue the medical profession's falling poll numbers while meeting people's demand for relief. True, their science wasn't perfect, but from their perspective they were making the best of a bad business. Psychiatrists constantly misinterpreted the motives of these doctors during the early stages of the medical practice revolution, assuming aggressive prescription behavior among primary care doctors was about grabbing market share. The misunderstanding intensified the feeling of resentment on both sides. Psychiatrists saw primary care doctors as occupying a more primitive stage of physician evolution, now with the temerity to become uppity; primary care doctors saw psychiatrists as ethereal academics practicing a rarified form of mental health therapy and blocking what the people wanted.

The two groups fought along this line until 1988, when Prozac was introduced. Suddenly, matters became urgent. Safer and more effective than earlier antidepressants, Prozac became the psychiatrists' most prized possession. The beauty of Prozac was that it gave the clincher to the rapidly emerging doctrine among some psychiatrists that psychopharmacology, rather than psychotherapy, formed psychiatry's future, a doctrine first advanced in the early 1970s when studies showed psychotropic drugs benefited depressed patients more than psychotherapy. The doctrine stalled so long as psychotropic drugs caused serious side effects: people occasionally died from antidepressants. But when one little pill, Prozac, could do what all the other pills did, safely and more effectively, and *more* than what psychotherapy could do, the doctrine seemed vindicated. At the same time, psychiatrists saw that if they lost control of Prozac, it would only be a matter of time before primary care absorbed other psychiatric diseases besides depression. Since Prozac was incredibly safe, any doctor could prescribe it.

Prozac's mere existence created a crisis for doctors; the question of control was urgent. Psychiatrists believed that Prozac, along with mental health in general, should remain in the hands of highly trained mental health professionals. Primary care doctors thought otherwise. Other physicians agreed with primary care doctors, convinced that any doctor should be able to prescribe Prozac and that Prozac was just another drug. Since primary care doctors had already been prescribing psychotropic drugs for twenty years, the debate's outcome was inevitable. In the end, primary care doctors won de facto control over both Prozac and much of mental health through the triumph of their ideology.

Primary care doctors succeeded because their ideology had action consequences and was also believable, at least compared to psychiatry's vision. Primary care outlined a worldview that seemed reasonable—unhappiness is a disease—while psychiatry failed to define unhappiness with any precision and was awash in competing schools of thought and contrasting styles. The public never really understood them; even many doctors gave up trying.

Americans traditionally gravitate toward general ideas because general ideas let a busy person explain many things at once in the shortest amount of time. Compared to the psychiatrists' arcane explanations for unhappiness, the primary care doctors' more straightforward explanation—unhappiness is a disease—was grasped quickly and easily by both the public and other doctors, letting them understand something important without much effort. Slowly but surely Americans came around to primary care's way of thinking on the issue. Because primary care doctors were the only physicians prepared to act on this thinking, they prescribed most of the Prozac for most of the minor depression in America. Both the drug and the disease quickly became identified with them.

Because medical training tends to produce cultural uniformity in students that professional associations later reinforce, psychotropic drug ideology spread rapidly among young doctors. Family practice residency programs expanded their commitment to mental health in the late 1980s. Around the same time, general internal medicine programs added mental health training. Because a third of all American women use ob-gyns for primary care services, ob-gyn residency programs added mental health training in the early 1990s. These programs taught residents the operational consequences of the new ideology: unhappiness is a disease best treated with drugs. Program graduates imbibed the message, which is why doctors trained since the 1980s prescribe antidepressants more quickly than older doctors. Psychotropic drug prescriptions increased dramatically after Prozac's discovery, with primary care doctors finding and then medicating the other depressed Americans whom psychiatrists claimed had been missed. By the end of the 1990s, psychiatrists admitted that the 50 percent failure-to-diagnose figure was no longer accurate, taking away their most important weapon in their war against primary care. Primary care doctors had won a resounding victory.

But it was neither Prozac's discovery nor the triumph of primary care over psychiatry that pushed the antidepressant prescription rate into the stratosphere. In the late 1980s something important happened to primary care doctors. They stopped being idealists; for them, antidepressants became a source of power.

THREE

FROM IDEOLOGY TO
INTERESTS TO SCANDAL

URING THE COLD War, Andre Snezhnevsky, the Soviet
Union's leading psychiatrist, invented "sluggish schizophrenia," a disease that anyone could suffer from without even
knowing it; once diagnosed, the patient had to be locked up and
knocked down with psychotropic drugs lest the disease "progress." Snezhnevsky colluded with authorities to imprison political
dissidents in hospitals on the basis of this phony diagnosis, then
defended his decisions with ideology, not science, for ideology let
the diagnosis of sluggish schizophrenia be anything he wanted
it to be. Ideology leverages more power than science, which
allowed Snezhnevsky and his disciples to blur the distinction
between healthy and sick, and label any troublemaker a sluggish
schizophrenic. In one example, a dissident's mother protested her
son's forced hospitalization for sluggish schizophrenia. When
the psychiatrists agreed to release him, she demanded that her
son be released that morning. A psychiatrist warned her: "You

better be careful not to demand anything or he'll turn out to be healthy in the morning but ill in the evening."

However, a psychotropic drug scandal arose in the Soviet Union not from the bad science in Snezhnevsky's ideology, which was obvious, or from the ideology itself but from that ideology's institutionalization. Sluggish schizophrenia became a weapon in the conflict between the Soviet state and its citizens.

The ideology of American primary care doctors gave rise to a second psychotropic drug scandal for similar reasons: it became a weapon for use in interest-group politics. After beating the psychiatrists and taking over a large share of mental health, primary care doctors started wielding power. Once they did, they went from being agents of change to agents of inertia, eager to defend their turf against other doctors and even against patients. Their ideology ceased to have a liberating effect on society and instead became repressive.

The change was already evident in the mid-1980s when surveys showed primary care doctors pushing psychotropic drugs on hesitant patients. In one 1985 study, two-thirds of family physicians cited lack of patient willingness to be treated for depression as a barrier to care. Patient resistance continued through the 1990s, although it declined somewhat as more people adopted the doctors' ideology after publication of *Prozac Nation* and *Listening to Prozac*. Something odd was going on inside the doctor's office. Instead of helping patients with everyday unhappiness, doctors seemed to be *inflicting* care on patients, pushing psychotropic drugs, and making patients wary.

Another sign of change came in the early 1990s. Interest groups typically obsess about their own concerns at the expense of the big picture. They work to expand their power base, stealing other interest groups' turf to do so. Primary care doctors began operating in this fashion, creating new indications for psychotropic drug therapy—bulimia, obsessive-compulsive disorder, weight loss, premenstrual syndrome, pain, and smoking cessation—and grabbing turf away from other physicians, and not just psychiatrists. Treatment of these conditions with psychotropic drugs represented "off label" use of these drugs (meaning for a purpose not evaluated by the FDA in approving sale of the drug); thus, even government looked askance at the takeovers. The progressive impulse in their ideology had waned; instead, primary care doctors used their ideology to grab property.

The new nature of the crisis facing doctors precipitated the change—managed care, which seemed to be digging in for the long haul. Doctors envisioned a new threat to their profession— except for primary care doctors. On the contrary, primary care doctors gained new powers under managed care, including the power to treat patients who before would have gone to specialists, and the power to control access to specialists. Primary care doctors enjoyed their new situation and occasionally gloated to specialists about how the tables had turned. Yet, to keep their favored position, they had to do two things. First, they had to control as much clinical turf as possible to show how indispensable they were and how most medicine could be practiced in a primary care setting, saving the insurance companies money. Second, managed care demanded efficiency, so primary care doctors had to show how their approach to unhappiness could be systematized and made efficient.

To accomplish these tasks, primary care doctors turned their ideology into a useful bureaucratic tool. If unhappiness is a disease, then other everyday behavioral problems are also argued the primary care doctors. Although the science behind the "unhappiness is a disease" concept was a stretch in its own right, primary care doctors extended their ideology to cover other mental illnesses. They also used their ideology to reorganize primary mental health care.

Gradually, primary care doctors distanced themselves from their patients, not by growing benignly neglectful as in the past, but by growing elitist: scientific expertise, to the extent that psychotropic drug ideology involved any, now mattered more than patient bonding. Primary care doctors were again eager to defend their interests against all challengers, even patients.

The Macarthur Foundation Initiative on Depression and Primary Care, begun in the 1990s, gives a good picture of what depression treatment in primary care is like today. Although the multimillion dollar initiative basically supports the primary care approach to unhappiness, several publications associated with the initiative reveal some disturbing trends.

In one study, a doctor prescribed antidepressants to *convince* his patients they were depressed. He worked on the assumption that the improvement following antidepressant treatment justi-fied the medical intervention in the first place. Another doctor prescribing antidepressants reported:

> Some people, you can't tell when they walk in cause they're gonna mask that [depression], and I think you have to probe a lot, you really have to dig for it.

A third doctor said:

> You have to try it [the medication]. If the patient's not feeling good and there's the possibility [of depression], you have to bark up that tree to see if you make them feel any better.

The doctors' ideology became a basis for hounding unhappy

people into taking a psychotropic drug. Unhappiness became an engineering problem until proven otherwise; the only way to prove otherwise was with hindsight, after a drug trial had failed. Under these circumstances, doctors were given a license to treat all unhappiness with medication.

In another Macarthur-funded study, actors trained to display minor depression visited primary care doctors under cover, complaining of a headache. Each actor played the same character: a twenty-six-year-old data entry clerk, recently divorced, with a ten-pound weight gain and a feeling of sadness. In an office visit lasting on average only sixteen minutes, the doctors considered this symptom, and then, with no other prompts, diagnosed minor depression 50 percent of the time and prescribed medication more than 50 percent of the time. An additional complaint, "I've really had a tough year," triggered doctors to think about depression in another 30 percent of cases. Sixteen minutes is a short visit, given that doctors typically waste the first few minutes of any new patient visit on basic identifying information, such as a history of allergies or previous surgeries. For these doctors to diagnose minor depression and write a prescription after a sixteen-minute interview means they were determined to find unhappiness and medicate it.

Once the doctors in the study sensed unhappiness in their patients, they asked these patients about their home life, work life, and social network—not to counsel them, but to convince *themselves* that their patients were unhappy. The best way to do so was to make sure their patients had a good reason to be unhappy. A good reason ruled out somatic illness as a cause of unhappiness, letting the doctors prescribe a psychotropic drug immediately. A curious contradiction existed: doctors looked for a life problem to explain a patient's unhappiness and then treated that unhappiness with drugs on the assumption that a drug could "cure" the unhappiness even if the life problem was not ameliorated.

The crisis occasioned by the rise of managed care transformed both the doctors' ideology and the doctors. When the medical practice revolution began, primary care doctors were idealists. Touched by patient complaints, they approached unhappiness as a disease in the effort to reconnect with patients and save the medical profession. Their science was off, but their intentions were true; when patients came to their offices complaining of unhappiness, doctors felt for them, even if that meant fudging their diagnoses and tacking on a somatic complaint to legitimize psychotropic drug therapy.

Under managed care, doctors began using their ideology to persuade patients to accept psychotropic drugs. With institutionalization the ideology's purpose had shifted. Doctors no longer saw their ideology as a quasi-science with a larger social purpose; rather, they saw it as a real science that demanded submission from patients. The concept of "unhappiness is a disease" stopped being a bridge to patients and became a justification for doctors to act unilaterally.

In one Macarthur-funded study, a doctor described depression as a "destination" at which one could arrive in different ways depending on a patient's reactions. Using depression questionnaires, he gathered "evidence" to get his patients to admit to being depressed, almost as if he were trying to get wily criminals to confess. In his hands, ideology had degenerated into an instrument of control. Rather than bind him to patients, psychotropic drug ideology divided him from patients; not only had he lost a sense of their problems, he even started to see his patients as adversaries.

Circumstantial evidence confirms the trend. The average patient visit to a primary care doctor lasts thirteen minutes and the average patient has six problems. To apply formal *DSM* diagnostic criteria for depression takes eight minutes. Given that most primary care doctors investigate medical problems before psychological problems, the chances that a primary care doctor would devote more than half of a patient's visit to a mental health problem are almost nil. Thus, the vast majority of unhappy Americans get only a brief look over before being prescribed a psychotropic drug.

Even when patients do suffer from minor depression, drug treatment is often unnecessary. One study shows that between 40 and 75 percent of the improvement in minor depression comes immediately after visiting a doctor, or at least in the first week after the visit—well before the psychotropic drug kicks in. Doctor-patient interaction probably explains the patient improvement, and both common sense and serious research suggest that unhappy people feel better after talking to someone. Yet, despite evidence that empathy and friendship work as well as medication in minor depression, primary care doctors continue to prescribe aggressively for the condition.

In the life of every ideology, a moment comes when that ideology turns into dogma no longer fed by popular forces. Psychotropic drug ideology is no exception. Starting in the late 1980s, rather than help doctors reach out to patients, psychotropic drug ideology gave primary care doctors an advantage in their bureaucratic fights. The fact that so many activists in the mental health movement came to resent their old primary care allies for overprescribing drugs and dictating to patients says much about how this ideology operates today. An ideology that once cultivated public opinion now no longer needs popular support. With the crisis in the medical profession over and the original reason for the ideology gone, psychotropic drug ideology persists, but as a simple doctors' tool.

ADHD: A SECOND TURF WAR

Dr. Charles Bradley performed spinal taps on children in 1937 as part of a neurological workup, which led to some of the children getting headaches due to a loss of spinal fluid. To increase the body's production of replacement fluid, he prescribed a stimulant, Benzedrine. Although the drug did little for the headaches, Dr. Bradley heard from teachers that the children's learning and behavior improved. The children themselves called the medication "math pills" because it raised their test scores.

Dr. Bradley had accidentally stumbled upon the first treatment for the condition now known as attention deficit/hyperactivity disorder (ADHD), a syndrome marked by inattention, with or without hyperactivity, and causing serious social and learning impairment. Today, millions of American children and adults carry this diagnosis and take stimulants like Ritalin. Although some of these patients deserve treatment, others are victims of a turf war between primary care doctors and psychiatrists. In their struggle against psychiatrists, primary care doctors applied their ideology to ADHD, then pushed the operational limits of their ideology simply because they had the power to do so, which caused some patients to be wrongly diagnosed with ADHD and treated for it.

Dr. George Still first defined the ADHD phenomenon in 1902 when he described forty-three children with defiant behavior and limited attention spans. He attributed the phenomenon to a "defect in moral control" rooted in some neurological deficit. From 1902 until well into the 1960s, doctors continued to see these symptoms as the result of a brain injury, which is why doctors performed in-depth neurological exams when evaluating children for the condition. Although clear evidence of brain pathology was lacking, neurologists called Dr. Still's symptom cluster "minimal

brain damage" in the 1930s and 40s and "minimal brain dysfunction" in the 1950s and 60s, with both definitions presuming the
existence of some injury. When Ritalin came onto the market in
1955, neurologists still felt certain that a brain lesion would soon
be found to cause ADHD. However, until it was they hesitated
to prescribe Ritalin in large quantities.

In the 1960s, a debate raged between neurologists, who saw
attention deficit as a neurological problem, and psychiatrists,
who increasingly saw it as a behavioral problem. The neurologists'
continuing inability to produce a brain lesion caused psychiatry
to win by default: the American Psychiatric Association awarded
ADHD its present name in 1980 and inscribed it in the *DSM*
as a set of behavioral symptoms. Biological markers and other
laboratory findings became irrelevant when diagnosing the
condition; a simple behavioral checklist replaced the detailed
neurological exam. Henceforth, doctors screened for ADHD
by asking patients about eighteen different symptoms, with a
positive response to twelve establishing the diagnosis.

By making ADHD a behavioral problem, psychiatrists had
won a victory over the neurologists. But then primary care doctors won a victory over the psychiatrists. Primary care doctors
argued that because Ritalin works in ADHD, ADHD must be
a brain problem—since otherwise Ritalin wouldn't work—the
same line of argument they used to push antidepressants in
unhappiness. What neurologists had failed to establish with
their scanners—a physical basis for ADHD   the primary care
doctors accomplished through inference; a simple drug effect
turned attention deficit into an engineering problem. The Ritalin
effect became a subset of psychotropic drug ideology, causing
attention deficit to join everyday unhappiness among the ranks
of physical diseases.

At first, laypeople welcomed the aggressive posture toward

ADHD, as primary care doctors helped thousands of children underperforming in school whom psychiatrists had ignored. But then psychotropic drug ideology became severed from its popular roots; it justified primary care doctors grabbing control of ADHD and steering patients toward treatment. Ritalin's mass prescription followed, not in psychiatry or neurology, but in primary care, especially in pediatrics and family practice, with the take-off point roughly the same as that for antidepressants. Between 1985 and 1995, stimulant prescriptions written by psychiatrists barely changed, but in primary care they *increased sevenfold*. Approximately 800,000 American children ages five to eighteen (2.8 percent of children in this age group) were taking Ritalin in the late 1980s. By 1995, 1.5 million American children were taking Ritalin; by 1999, an estimated 5 million children took Ritalin. The numbers for adults shock even more. As a condition, adult ADHD didn't even exist before the late 1970s; today, doctors estimate that anywhere from 8 million to 13 million American adults have the condition. Already, a quarter of the affected population receives treatment.

That Ritalin and antidepressant prescription rates exploded around the same time and among the same doctors means that Prozac's discovery alone can't account for the new emphasis on psychotropic drugs. Although Prozac was new, Ritalin had been around for almost thirty years; thus, something other than Prozac's discovery must have prompted the increased prescription rates for antidepressants and stimulants. I argue that both drugs became instruments of power for primary care doctors, justified by their ideology.

Political conservatives see a different ideology causing ADHD; they think doctors overprescribe Ritalin because a secular ideology destroyed the family and created hordes of undisciplined children who need drugs to be controlled. They see increased Ritalin use as a consequence of the culture wars, not of a doctors' ideology. Facts suggest otherwise. During the 1980s a growing number of children took Ritalin for inattention without the hyperactivity that produces discipline problems; in other words, doctors wrote new Ritalin prescriptions for more than just rambunctious children. In addition, adults newly diagnosed with ADHD account for some of the Ritalin increase and these people, by definition, aren't juvenile delinquents. Nor are they adult delinquents. Adults with ADHD often have trouble organizing their homes and remembering to pack their children's lunches; they are not necessarily holding up banks.

Primary care doctors overprescribed stimulants because they sensed the power in their ideology and used it to grab turf at the expense of good science and good patient care. They cited patient improvement with Ritalin to retroactively justify their aggressive diagnosing of ADHD, although Ritalin therapy improves even a normal child's learning and social skills. They rushed children through the evaluation process, sometimes diagnosing ADHD after a mere ten-minute interview. They diagnosed ADHD without the necessary evaluations from both school and home. They bent people's behavior with stimulants because they had the power to do so and because they sincerely believed their approach worked. They grabbed turf with confidence because their ideology told them they could. And they succeeded: primary care doctors now account for 75 percent of the office-based visits for ADHD.

PAIN: A THIRD TURF WAR

Several years ago, I treated a sixty-year-old man for hip fracture pain with narcotics. During the day the man rarely complained of pain, but in the evening his narcotic needs soared. Eventually I discovered the reason: the man's irritating son visited every night around dinnertime. My patient felt stress during these visits, which aggravated his pain and led to a transitory spike in his drug needs.

The case illustrates how all pain has both a psychological and a physical component, each capable of exacerbating pain. The psychological component explains, for example, why a man suffering from a sports injury often tolerates his pain better than a man with pain of unknown cause. The former can explain his pain and put it in perspective—even blame himself—and know it not to be life-threatening, while the latter has no explanation for his pain, feels his pain to be unjust, and imagines all sorts of mortal terrors. Unhappiness exacerbates pain, and pain patients with mysterious illnesses or difficult home lives often need more narcotic. Doctors, including me, feel compelled to give it to them in the short-term, but ultimately the extra narcotic treats the unhappiness as much as the pain.

On the back of this phenomenon, primary care doctors penetrated the area of chronic pain, fighting not psychiatrists or neurologists this time, but anesthesiologists. In the past, doctors rarely treated chronic pain. In the first half of the twentieth century, the medical profession divided pain into clinicopathological pain (pain associated with a tissue lesion) and psychogenic pain (pain without a tissue lesion, or something "in the patient's head"). Because chronic pain often lacks a visible tissue lesion, doctors ignored it and attributed the patient's complaint to neurotic behavior. New research in the 1970s and 1980s showed chronic pain to be a real phenomenon, even in the absence of a tissue lesion, as in, for example, pain caused by dysfunctional activity of the sympathetic nervous system. Doctors' views changed, and rightly so, for doctors had grossly undertreated pain for years. Yet pain also has a psychological component—an unhappiness component—and here the problem began. Primary care doctors invoked their ideology to medicate all the dimensions of the pain experience, including the psychological one, leading to a dramatic increase in narcotic prescriptions.

Narcotic prescriptions took off around the same time as anti-depressant and Ritalin prescriptions. U.S. consumption of morphine stayed flat for decades, until 1985. Before then, doctors used morphine mostly in the hospital, and even then rather sparingly, consistent with the prejudices of the times. The World Health Organization (WHO) in 1985 released its three-step ladder for cancer pain treatment; after this date, morphine consumption steadily increased. Physician-dominated organizations in the United States continued the WHO's work, claiming that doctors grossly undertreated pain (which they did). Annual morphine consumption in the United States increased from roughly 1,000 kilograms to 3,000 kilograms between 1985 and 1990. The availability in 1986 of a new sustained-release morphine preparation called MS Contin made it especially easy for doctors to prescribe narcotics. The physician-led campaign on pain picked up steam in the 1990s, with new guidelines for the treatment of chronic pain published in 1996. Narcotic prescriptions rose dramatically between 1993 and 2001, with sales of morphine, hydrocodone, and oxycodone increasing 300 percent, 360 percent, and 1150 percent, respectively. Primary care doctors wrote the majority of these new prescriptions, especially in the area of noncancer pain.

It strains the imagination to think that primary care doctors coincidentally started prescribing more narcotic (an age-old drug) at the exact moment they began prescribing more Ritalin (a thirty-year-old drug) and more Prozac (a new drug). Something else was going on. True, good reasons account for the increase in narcotic prescriptions, including the medical profession's past neglect of pain that needed to be made up for, plus the fact that elderly patients do better with oral narcotics than they do with aspirinlike drugs. (Narcotics are kinder on the stomach.) Since pain management falls under the purview of anesthesiologists, these doctors were especially guilty of underprescribing, even, at times, of withholding narcotics in the recovery room for fear of inciting addiction, Nevertheless, the treatment of unhappiness in pain accounts for some of the increase in narcotic prescriptions. Primary care doctors grabbed turf away from anesthesiologists, expanding their ideology to cover the unhappiness associated with pain and using a single medication to knock out both problems.

In the privacy of their hospital departments, anesthesiologists often complain about how primary care doctors treat both pain and unhappiness with narcotics. Yet the ideology of primary care doctors has seduced them more than they realize. Anesthesiologists often perform regional blocks for pain, which primary care doctors are not trained to do. These blocks prevent impulse transmission along nerves coming from the afflicted part of the body, thereby leaving the mind unchanged. Thus, inherent in the practice of anesthesia is the ability to separate pain and unhappiness, making anesthesiologists less prone to medicate both experiences with narcotic. Still, anesthesiologists criticize primary care doctors for overprescribing narcotics mostly because they think primary care doctors prescribe the wrong drug. They think unhappiness in chronic pain should be treated with antidepressants, while only pain should be treated with narcotics. Thus, even anesthesiologists accept the primary care notion that unhappiness is a "disease" best medicated. They simply want to use a different drug.

Primary care had won another victory.

THE END OF ACT ONE

The American psychotropic drug scandal, like the Soviet one, arose from a crisis situation. A threat faced primary care doctors, who responded with a plan to combat that threat. With public opinion behind them (and also forcing them), these doctors crafted a new ideology to help unhappy people, while offending doctors committed to the status quo. Gradually, primary care doctors returned to the cold, hard world of interests—protecting their turf, raiding other's turf, and telling patients to shut up and take their pills. They stopped being visionaries, their psychotropic drug prescriptions grew reflexive, and scandal arose.

But the medical practice revolution had yet to run its course. On the contrary, the psychotropic drug scandal signifies only the end of the revolution's first act. A second crisis arose from changes wrought by the first. In this second crisis, a group of primary care doctors, disgusted with the drug approach to unhappiness, rose up in rebellion, put forth a new ideology, and upset physician elites, with the engineering approach to unhappiness now representing the status quo. These rebel doctors, harnessing popular forces as the primary care revolutionaries of old did, took the medical practice revolution into its second phase.

FOUR

THE REVOLT OF THE ENGINEERS

O N JANUARY 22, 1944, Allied soldiers sailed toward the Italian coast, stormed the Anzio plain, then stared dumbfounded into the moonless night when their gunfire went unanswered. It was a trap. Within two days, German divisions counterattacked, pinning the entire invasion force down on a tiny beachhead four miles wide and five miles deep and turning Anzio into a bloody debacle. Caught between the sea and the enemy, the Allies burrowed underground; pilots looking down from above had the illusion of thousands of giant moles at work. Among the invasion force was Major Henry K. Beecher, MD, who made an important medical discovery during the battle, one that foretells the second chapter of the medical practice revolution.

Trained at the Massachusetts General Hospital (MGH) where he practiced anesthesia before the war, Beecher cared for the wounded with morphine at a makeshift field hospital on Anzio's perilous "Hell's Half Acre." Although sandbags surrounded the tents, German artillery—especially "Anzio Annie," the German's giant 290-mm railroad gun—regularly pounded the area, killing people so often that patients sometimes deserted to the front. Soldiers with ghastly shell fragment wounds inundated the operating theater daily.

Beecher was no stranger to trauma or to morphine, having treated burn victims during the famous Boston Cocoanut Grove disaster two years before. When a busboy at the Cocoanut Grove restaurant lost his balance screwing in a lightbulb and holding a lighted match in his other hand, a nearby artificial palm tree caught fire. Flames shot up, fire spread rapidly, patrons panicked and rushed around blind in the smoke; outside, horrified spectators heard the sound of fists beating against bolted doors and watched the stack of burned bodies, wedged in death, grow six feet high in the revolving doors. Ambulances whisked hundreds of victims to the hospital, where most died in the halls. Beecher tended to the few survivors, observing that morphine, although helpful in treating their pain, did little to control their hysteria.

At Anzio, Beecher made another observation about morphine and psychology. Despite suffering horrendous injuries, even worse than in the Cocoanut Grove fire, the victims needed less morphine. Three-quarters of the badly wounded men denied having serious pain and hardly asked for the drug. Beecher was amazed. One nineteen-year-old soldier suffered a meat cleaver-like wound from a mortar shell that cut through eight ribs, a lung, and a kidney, yet he felt only as if he was "lying on his rifle." He needed just a little sedation to make him comfortable.

One day, swamped with casualties, Beecher ran short of morphine, at which point he injected saltwater into the wounded men's buttocks before surgery, telling the men it was morphine.

Incredibly, the men tolerated their operations as if they had received real anesthesia.

To explain these odd phenomena, Beecher reasoned that a wounded man's unique psychology reduces his morphine needs. Injury releases a soldier from duty on the front line—where he faces discomfort, anxiety, and the real danger of death—and gives him a ticket to the relative safety of the hospital. His troubles are over, or at least he thinks they are, and happiness reduces his pain. As for the soldiers injected with saltwater, their happiness at being wounded and safe, combined with their belief that they had received morphine, let them tolerate surgery with subpar anesthesia.

At Anzio, Beecher disproved the longstanding assumption that pain perception involves the simple transmission of impulses along nerves without psychological input. Forty years later, a small group of primary care doctors applied Beecher's discovery to general medicine and advanced the medical practice revolution. They proposed that happiness helps people fight disease no less than it helps wounded soldiers fight pain. Their ideas merged with a scientific theory called *psychoneuroimmunology* (PNI) to produce an ideology that justified making sick people happy, then later justified making everyone happy, since happy people supposedly had less chance of falling ill.

According to the new ideology, unhappiness was not a "disease" so much as a risk factor for illness, although it remained something doctors had to treat, again drawing on Beecher's Anzio experience. Beecher's deception with saltwater is one of the first recorded cases of a doctor knowingly treating a medical condition with a placebo. Placebos are drugs or modalities that are actually ineffective for the condition for which they are prescribed. They just make patients happy, or less unhappy, and work only because patients believe in them. In the late 1980s, primary care doctors drew on Beecher's method and prescribed placebos for some medical problems that supposedly had unhappiness as the common root, and sometimes for unhappiness in its own right in the form of mild depression. However, they used more than saltwater to treat unhappiness, finding in alternative medicine a treasure trove of placebos with which to please patients.

Although physicians had dismissed alternative medicine as quackery for most of the twentieth century, a new crisis in the medical profession compelled some primary care doctors to resurrect it. By the late 1980s, the free fall in the public's respect for doctors that began in the late 1960s had stabilized, but some primary care doctors wondered at what cost. Physician-engineers appeased people's anger by treating unhappiness as a disease, yet their reliance on psychotropic drugs had sunk all hope that doctors might reengage patients in a personal way. It also made medical practice incredibly boring. The daily office routine in primary care now consisted of slotting patients into diagnostic categories and treating them according to cookbook algorithms, even in cases of unhappiness. By applying the right drug to every condition, how were doctors any different from experienced housekeepers who chose the right key for every door? Some doctors practicing in this regimented environment felt robbed of half their humanity. They saw in alternative medicine, with its religious themes and emphasis on cultivating belief, a chance to redeem medicine and restore the personal element in doctoring that had inspired them to go into medicine in the first place.

Just as psychotropic drug ideology resonated with the public, so did alternative medicine ideology. In the late 1980s many Americans searched for a third way, beyond medicine and organized religion, to deal with their everyday troubles. They saw doctors, with little depth of human understanding, prescribe psychotropic drugs for unhappiness and they grew disgusted. Medicine was now more science-oriented than ever. Yet organized religion seemed totally irrelevant and antimodern, a sweet dream to help the weak and the superstitious forget their miseries. If doctors concentrated on rational knowledge at the expense of life's mysteries—limiting their understanding of unhappiness to neurotransmitters—then organized religion concentrated exclusively on the unknown and therefore seemed to know nothing. In this environment, people migrated away from both medicine and organized religion in search of new solutions to unhappiness. Alternative medicine benefited from these migrations and got people's attention.

During most of the twentieth century, few Americans used alternative medicine. Then in the early 1990s alternative medicine consumption skyrocketed. From 1990 to 1997, the amount of money spent by consumers on alternative medicine increased 45 percent. By 2000, consumers spent more money for alternative medicine therapies than they did out-of-pocket in the entire allopathic (mainstream) medical system, their strong commitment to these therapies unmasked by the refusal of most insurance companies to cover them. By 2003, over 80 percent of Americans used some kind of alternative therapy. Although alternative medicine ushered in a new approach to all disease, therapy for everyday unhappiness figured prominently, with a quarter of alternative medicine users in the United States seeking treatment for anxiety or depression. Some primary care doctors began playing dual roles. Like their physician-engineer colleagues, they treated major depression with psychotropic drugs but prescribed alternative medicine therapies such as herbs, meditation, magnets, and aromatherapy for minor depression. By putting their imprimatur on alternative medicine they encouraged unhappy patients to try alternative medicine on their own, without direct physician involvement.

In the late 1960s, doctors' fears for their profession gave rise to a psychotropic drug ideology, which drew on popular support and remade the practice of medicine. This event replayed itself in new form in the late 1980s: doctors' fears for their professional integrity gave rise to an alternative medicine ideology, which many Americans supported and which led to the establishment of a parallel medical system.

High-minded primary care doctors promoted alternative medicine with the noble goal of marrying East and West: alternative medicine's personal, individualized approach to therapy with allopathic medicine's technological sophistication. These doctors were idealists, eager to harmonize their respect for science with their love of humanity. But alternative medicine ideology, like psychotropic drug ideology, contains serious contradictions, and after the initial progressive impulse waned doctors who practiced alternative medicine began to export these contradictions to their patients, driving a wedge between themselves and the very people they wanted to help. Instead of forming a personal bond with patients for humane purposes, they seduced patients into believing in alternative medicine and rationalized doing so by arguing that a happier patient is a healthier patient. They made people happy at the expense of their intelligence. Like psychotropic drug ideology, alternative medicine ideology lost its visionary quality and became a physician tool.

Except for the spinal adjustment technique used in chiropractic, which has been shown to be effective in low back pain, alternative medicine has questionable value. Randomized, controlled, double-blind clinical trials—the basis for determining a therapy's benefit in allopathic (scientific) medicine—have yet to prove the benefit of most alternative medicine. Supporters cite positive treatment associations—for example, ginseng for the common cold or homeopathy for asthma—but whether patients would have improved on their own, without these therapies, or whether patients improved simply because they believed in their therapy (the placebo effect) is unclear. Granted, it is hard to perform double-blind studies in alternative medicine, since the identity of an alternative medicine therapy is hard to conceal during a test. But my concern is not whether alternative medicine induces Artificial Happiness through real biochemical effects or through the power of suggestion. After all, even many alternative medicine doctors don't care; most are satisfied just knowing that their therapies work. My concern is that alternative medicine doctors purposely induce Artificial Happiness, whatever its origin, because they believe happiness fosters good health, which to them justifies intervention in all cases of minor depression. This link between happiness and health, the foundation of alternative medicine ideology, has given rise to a whole new source of Artificial Happiness.

FROM GEORGE WASHINGTON TO PNI

Alternative medicine killed George Washington. After Washington developed a tonsillar abscess, doctors bled him up to three quarts in twelve hours, then dehydrated him with calomel and emetic tartar. True, Washington's doctors didn't know their treatments were worthless placebos, let alone dangerous; on the contrary, they believed their therapies had value. But ignorance doesn't keep treatments from being placebos, and doctors have unknowingly used placebos for thousands of years. Even as late as 1950, 40 percent of general medicine involved the use of placebos, a judgment made only with the benefit of hindsight.

The difference between then and now is that now doctors *knowingly* use placebos. In the past, doctors thought their therapies worked. Even as late as the nineteenth century, doctors rarely gave patients worthless sugar pills to make them happy. Doing so would have been considered deceitful. Today, primary care doctors involved in alternative medicine do just this, and not simply to get irritating patients off their backs; the reality is that they believe happiness aids in the cure of disease.

To understand how this ideology took hold, we need to trace the placebo's history in Western medicine. In 1785, a medical dictionary first defined the placebo, referring to it as a "commonplace method or medicine." By 1820 the placebo had evolved into a "medication given more to please than to benefit the patient," which remained the definition up to 1950. All during this period, *placebo* was a pejorative term. Doctors viewed placebos as unethical—a form of low trickery—and rarely admitted to using them.

Surgeons, for example, insisted that only drugs could be placebos, which absolved them of the charge, since they just cut on people. Psychiatrists offered a similar defense, noting that they just talked to people. Both erred, since a placebo can be a drug or a modality like cutting or talking. For example, a surgeon can make an incision, do nothing, then sew the patient back up, and if the patient's symptoms improve because he thinks he received a real operation, then the surgeon's cutting constitutes a placebo.

Internists prescribed drugs but claimed to prescribe only active drugs, while placebos, they insisted, were inert. The internists also erred, since drugs don't have to be inert to be placebos. Actually, no drug is truly inert: even sugar and water are not inert. Sugar, for example, when prescribed along with insulin to treat cases of high potassium, is very effective; only when it is prescribed for diseases where it has no effect, such as the common cold, is it a placebo. In any event, most doctors well into the middle of the twentieth century distanced themselves from placebos.

In the second quarter of the twentieth century, some primary care doctors began using placebos to get troublesome patients out of their hair. As a child growing up in the 1960s, I saw the tail end of this practice, with my father giving vitamin B_{12} "pep shots" to neurotic middle-aged women. Although vitamin B_{12} lacks any bioactive pep effect, many of these women left his office crying, "*Gevalt!* I feel fantastic!" while my father just smiled and shook his head. Still, even doctors like my father felt pressure not to overuse placebos.

In the 1950s the placebo's status changed along with its definition. Placebos found a legitimate use as controls in the new double-blind drug studies. By 1963, the FDA required such studies to prove both the safety and efficacy of a new drug before its release, earning placebos a permanent role in medical research. Consistent with the placebo's new role, doctors redefined the placebo (wrongly) as any "inactive, or inert, medical substance." Equally important, academic physicians, and especially Dr. Beecher, began investigating the placebo effect in clinical medicine.

After the war, Beecher went back to the MGH with his Anzio experience uppermost in his mind, eager to explore the placebo's role in pain and other subjective symptoms. He wanted to see if doctors could treat symptoms by just imitating therapy, the way he had at Anzio, dispensing fake medicine with only a promise that the medicine was real. Beecher published a landmark article in 1955 titled "The Powerful Placebo," in which he reviewed fifteen clinical studies where doctors had treated patients' symptoms with placebos. He concluded that 35 percent of patients could be adequately treated with placebos alone across a wide range of symptoms, including headache, nausea, wound pain, and seasickness.

Beecher's article put the placebo effect on the scientific map. Still, the old prejudice against placebos prevailed and most physicians remained leery of them. Researchers spent the rest of the decade trying to delineate the particular patient type that responded to placebos, in part to wall off candidates for placebos from the main body of "normal" medical practice.

In the 1960s the "autonomy" movement and two big scandals slowed the growing interest in placebos. The autonomy movement, which pushed new concepts like "full disclosure" and "informed consent," lambasted doctors who withheld knowledge from patients in the spirit of "we know best." Then two scandals rocked the nation. First, without their knowledge, seventy-six women received placebos instead of birth control pills in a clinical study; to everyone's outrage, seven of the women became pregnant. Then, in the early 1970s, journalists exposed the infamous Tuskegee study. Black men with syphilis had been purposely treated with placebos from 1930 to 1972, without their knowledge and long after effective therapy had been discovered. These scandals embarrassed the medical profession and discredited placebo use.

During this tumultuous period, placebo science quietly moved in a new direction in the nation's research labs—toward Artificial Happiness. Scientists asked two questions. First, placebos treat subjective symptoms, but can they treat disease? Second, if placebos work on disease, how is the placebo's influence on the mind translated into real biochemical effects? Stanford University researchers Drs. George Solomon and Rudolph Moos published a paper in 1964 titled "Emotions, Immunity, and Disease," outlining an approach to these questions. They theorized a link between psychology and the body's response to stress, citing examples from their own practice. In one case, for example, a thirty-eight-year-old devoutly religious spinster plunged into depression, then developed severe polymyositis (an inflammation of skeletal muscle) after being impregnated by a man who had promised to marry her, but instead stole away with her life savings. With Solomon and Moos's paper, unhappiness and poor health became linked.

Eleven years later, psychologists Robert Ader and Nicholas Cohen provided the first lab evidence of Solomon and Moos's theory by showing how behavior could condition a rat's immune system. They fed rats a harmless saccharin solution, then followed those drinks with injections of a lethal immunosuppressive agent. The rats learned to associate the harmless saccharin with the immunosuppressive agent, such that, when some of the rats stopped getting the immunosuppressive agent but continued with the saccharin drinks, the rats kept dying at the same rate. By changing rat psychology, the researchers had turned the placebo saccharin into an immunosuppressive agent. They showed that psychology had a direct effect on health.

Ader and Cohen's study gave birth to psychoneuroimmunology (PNI), a term that Ader himself coined. The field revolutionized placebo science. In Beecher's era, around World War II, doctors ameliorated people's subjective symptoms with placebos but never believed placebos could actually cure disease. With the rise of PNI, doctors adopted the attitude that if placebos pleased patients to the point of arousing Artificial Happiness, the happiness itself activated the immune system to fight infections, control tumor growth, and heal wounds. Although psychoneuroimmunology remained just a theory, it seemed intuitively reasonable to physicians, many of whom factored it into their worldview the way other doctors had done a decade before with the biogenic amine theory.

More research boosted the placebo's value. In the 1950s, doctors assumed placebos worked only on neurotic patients. In the 1960s and '70s, studies showed that anyone could respond to placebos. These studies made everyone a potential placebo candidate and showed that placebos worked best when patients liked their doctors. Combined with PNI's claim that happiness cured disease, the new thinking initiated a paradigm shift in medical practice. Doctors stood ready to use placebos in all their patients, to develop better relationships with patients to maximize placebo effectiveness, and to do so in the name of good health.

Doctors tried placebos in different diseases, using both Beecher's method of imitating therapy and PNI's method of evoking happiness, but additional research pushed them toward PNI. Beecher, it seemed, had erred. In his pioneering article, he claimed that fake pills caused 35 percent of patients to respond as if they had received real therapy. Subsequent reviews showed this not to be the case. German researchers Gunver Kienle and Helmut Kiene demonstrated that some of Beecher's patients had improved on their own or had been treated with an active drug besides the placebo. All fifteen studies cited by Beecher in evidence of the placebo effect were flawed. Another article by two Danish physicians, titled "Is the Placebo Powerless?" opened up a second front against Beecher. Reviewing more than a hundred clinical trials, they found placebos had no significant clinical effects except in the treatment of pain—the very condition that Beecher had treated at Anzio to get the placebo ball rolling! The authors agreed with Kienle and Kiene that Beecher's method of imitating therapy was useless.

Doctors realized that to make placebos work they had to focus on making patients happy. Happiness was the key; the placebo itself was just a useful prop. Merely dispensing pills, pretending therapy, as Beecher had done, wasn't enough. The deception had to be more artful. Doctors had to inspire patients, excite patients, and entertain patients. In other words, doctors had to become artists and showmen—and more than just engineers.

A full-fledged placebo movement with happiness as its central focus took shape. Only one thing was missing: enough doctors wanting to cultivate the placebo deception. Implementing placebo science on a mass scale required doctors who wanted to be personal doctors again, who wanted to be more than just engineers, who wanted to motivate patients and make them happy, and who would take the time to do so.

In the 1980s, a new crisis gripped the medical profession, supplying this missing item.

DOCTORING GROWS BORING

"I hate this!" Dr. Michael Saxon screamed in 1985, referring to his medical practice. "It's so mindless!" From cries like these rose alternative medicine, which put placebo science into practice.

Dr. Michael Saxon finished his family practice residency in 1982, started a medical practice, and hated it. He wanted to be a personal doctor but managed care warned him to keep his office visits short, which prevented him from developing meaningful relationships with his patients. Sheer boredom with this practice style caused him to think seriously about leaving medicine, although he earned more than a six-figure income.

Many doctors during this era resented managed care for a variety of reasons. Dr. Saxon resented being a physician-engineer; other doctors resented the loss of their professional autonomy. Either way, rather than fight managed care, these doctors simply resigned themselves to the new situation and sought satisfaction outside of medicine. Some female doctors went part-time to raise their children, especially if their husbands were the primary wage earners in their families. Male doctors started businesses on the side, including, among my own friends, a computer consultancy, a long-distance phone company, a hair transplant business, and a publishing company. Dr. Saxon learned to draw, enjoying creative possibilities denied him in medical practice. At the office he followed rules and procedures; in his studio he felt like the master of a medieval paint shop. In 1990, he started a gallery, expecting to leave medicine altogether, but the business failed and Dr. Saxon found himself back on the medical factory floor, a full-time grunt working on the line.

Dr. Saxon had also experienced a personal crisis. Having grown up secular, majored in science in college, and slept with lots of nurses, Dr. Saxon had geared much of his life toward material things and achievement. Rather than question these goals, he contented himself with thinking that he lived as everyone lives—or wants to live. But he grew bored with his big house and pretty physical therapist wife. His peers called family and work the real business of life, but these activities felt increasingly to Dr. Saxon like the habits of life. Living as others did, or because others prized the way he lived, no longer sufficed. Seeking an outlet for his restlessness, Dr. Saxon had an extramarital affair but it proved unsatisfying. By the time his business venture crumbled, he suffered a real crisis of the spirit.

Around this time, Dr. Saxon chanced upon Buddhism and ancient Chinese philosophy and read several books on the subject, including one in particular, *Shambhala: The sacred path of the warrior*, by Chogyam Trungpa. In these books he found answers to questions about life. He embraced Buddhism and meditated daily. He flew to Nepal and talked philosophy with a Buddhist monk. Inspired by his trip, he took classes in ancient

Chinese medicine, forging the synthesis of the personal and the professional that he had been looking for.

In the mid-1990s, Dr. Saxon integrated acupuncture and herbalism into his medical practice. His office betrays the new emphasis. Two pictures hang on the wall next to his medical school diploma, one of him backpacking in Nepal, the other of him standing next to a Tibetan monk inside a Buddhist temple. Next to a soulless brown counter topped with steel instruments stands a beautiful Asian sculpture. Dr. Saxon practices alternative medicine roughly 50 percent of the time, although he calls alternative medicine a money loser. Because he spends more time with his alternative medicine patients he can't recoup his office costs, even though he's paid in cash. Still, he feels better about himself as a professional.

Other doctors followed Dr. Saxon's path in the late 1980s and early 1990s, supplying the missing piece needed to turn placebo science into a full-fledged movement: doctors who hated being engineers and who embraced alternative medicine as their salvation. The revolt against physician-engineering began in primary care, since primary care doctors more than specialists felt the most disenchantment with the decline of personal doctoring. Although statistics are scarce, spokesmen for alternative medicine's licensing boards, including the American Academy of Medical Acupuncture and the National Certification Commission for Acupuncture and Oriental Medicine, agree on a basic trend: in the late 1980s and early 1990s the vast majority of doctors taking classes in alternative medicine, often out of professional frustration, were primary care doctors. Specialists came later, in the mid-1990s, typically anesthesiologists, in part because of a surplus of anesthesiologists at the time (alternative medicine helped them to diversify) but also because anesthesiologists treat chronic pain, which has a psychological element that placebos work on. Only in the late 1990s did other specialists, including some psychiatrists, take classes in alternative medicine in large numbers. Even then, primary care doctors continued to dominate the field.

Many of the early alternative medicine doctors were hotheads. They ridiculed conventional medicine and imagined themselves competing with allopathic doctors for the future of American health care. Although alternative medicine lacked the infrastructure to care for every American if allopathic medicine suddenly disappeared overnight, these alternative medicine doctors saw the consequences of overturning the established order as a wash, making life inconvenient at first but at least giving something better a chance to emerge. Their ranting had a utopian quality, full of talk about a democratic, decentralized health care system organized along alternative medicine lines and run by and for the people.

These alternative medicine doctors provoked a vigorous counterattack, as their ideology cut deep into the realm of interests and offended the entire medical establishment. Psychiatrists once again defended the old order. Already sensitive to the charge that psychotherapy was a placebo, the last thing psychiatrists wanted to support was alternative medicine. They joined the chorus of contempt and laughed sarcastically at the whole alternative medicine movement. However, the entire medical establishment rejected alternative medicine. Establishment physicians worried that the ignorant masses might be lulled, even mortally so, into substituting useless placebos for real therapy. They called alternative medicine doctors irresponsible, even crypto-anarchists with malevolent intent, for why else would these people be quarreling with fifty years of allopathic medical success?

The two camps simply held different worldviews. Alternative medicine doctors believed that the engineering model of disease was inadequate; more irrational forces were at play in health and disease, and all illness had a spiritual component. These doctors denied using placebos; on the contrary, they said, alternative medicine deals with spiritual forces that allopathic doctors had no knowledge of. Because these forces were different in each patient, personal doctoring was vital; only personal doctoring could identify a patient's unique spiritual balance, which decided treatment. (For example, if ten patients present to an acupuncturist with peptic ulcer disease, each one might be treated differently.) Establishment doctors called the whole thing rubbish and insisted that science and spiritual ideas be kept separate. Because spiritual forces couldn't be measured scientifically they bordered on religion, these doctors charged. They didn't begrudge churchmen their turf; they simply believed that a rigid division between the two fields was the indispensable basis for any kind of rational medical system.

Establishment doctors were convinced that if they stood up to the radicals, the radicals would cave. They adopted a three-pronged strategy: belittle, ignore, and attack. First, in public forums, they called alternative doctors "hucksters," "kooks," and "witch doctors," and alternative medicine "mumbo jumbo" and "nincompoopery." One editor of a medical journal, writing of his visit to an alternative medicine clinic, thought for sure that he smelled marijuana. Doctors at the FDA ensured that even the more reputable examples of alternative medicine, such as acupuncture, remained classified as "experimental." Second, they pretended that alternative medicine didn't exist. Most patients found their way to alternative medicine doctors on their own and not through a referral from an allopathic physician. At medical conventions, the subject of alternative medicine rarely came up except as an object of derision. Third, they attacked, with allopathic doctors filing complaints against alternative medicine doctors, prodding state health departments to revoke the latter's medical licenses.

Simply put, the medical establishment hated alternative medicine. One has to have spent some time with doctors in the late 1980s, in the hospital elevators and cafeterias, to understand how deeply rooted these sentiments were. Establishment doctors pointed to alternative medicine providers, some of whom were foreign-born, practicing medicine in squalor that no self-respecting American physician ever would. To the medical establishment, these people seemed hopeless. Their scientific level was so low as to be virtually nonexistent; they chanted, prayed, and deceived patients in their weird languages. The conditions in which they worked were worse. No member of the medical profession would climb five stories to a dusty attic in Chinatown to practice medicine, or brew potions in an open pot on top of a stove and then clean up the mess. Deep down, establishment doctors' rejection of alternative medicine combined a strong belief in Western science with a tinge of racism. They believed in allopathic medicine's natural superiority just as they believed in the West's natural superiority; further, they thought that by attacking alternative medicine they were keeping patients safe, preserving the medical profession's dignity, and selflessly serving the cause of Anglo-American progress.

Against all odds, alternative medicine doctors triumphed over the medical establishment because their ideology had popular support. Patients liked the fact that alternative medicine doctors spent time with them. After an examination by an alternative medicine doctor, patients said they "felt seen." In addition, many patients unconsciously looking for a new faith but distrustful of organized religion found themselves drawn to alternative medicine.

The first evidence of victory came in the form of hospital-based alternative medicine clinics. Alternative medicine left the obscure environment that had given it an air of shadiness and took up residence on hospital campuses. Ever attuned to public opinion (at least compared to doctors) hospital administrators brought alternative medicine into their facilities not because proven science demanded it but because their marketing surveys revealed intense public interest in the field. These clinics gave the field legitimacy and demonstrated how popular forces could bend the practice of medicine against strong resistance from the medical establishment.

The real breakthrough came in 1991 with the creation of the Office of Alternative Medicine at the National Institutes of Health (NIH), the nation's premiere allopathic medical institution. As sociologist Franz Schurmann notes, popular ideologies typically enter the social fabric through the state. The most extreme form is a revolutionary takeover of the entire government, but even the creation of a small bureaucratic structure that consumes its share of the state budget signals the triumph of a new ideology. Although the office's initial budget was only two million dollars, the creation of an Office of Alternative Medicine inside allopathic medicine's inner sanctum represented a coup. Allopathic physicians protested, calling the new bureau the "Office of Astrology"; the Institute's director even resigned. Doctors complained that the office had more to do with "political correctness" than with good science; they were partly right but they failed to recognize the populist current in what was happening: the office reflected the people's will, voted into being through Congress.

During the 1990s, pressure from below continued the office's expansion. First, the revolt against physician-engineering grew in size; a small cadre of physician idealists swelled into a large army, with primary care doctors leading the way. By 1994, nearly one-quarter of America's family practitioners were using alternative medicine in their own practices. According to a report prepared for the Policy Institute for Integrative Medicine at Jefferson University Hospital, by 2002, as many as 100,000 American doctors—14 percent of all physicians—had received some kind of education, training, licensure, or certification in one or more alternative medicine modalities. The budget for the Office of Alternative Medicine tracked the growing physician interest, growing to forty-five times the original number by the end of the decade.

Second, with the end of the Cold War, Americans grew increasingly determined to find new solutions to unhappiness. During the twentieth century much unhappiness was due to external causes—for example, war, economic depression, fascism, or communism. Neither religion nor medicine seemed like relevant solutions; people simply needed to get politically active. During the 1990s, with the end of the Cold War, the increasing success of the civil rights movement, and the final acceptance of the hybrid capitalist-welfare state as the best social model, the external forces of unhappiness seemed tamed and the need for politics muted. As these causes of suffering diminished, age-old internal ones resurfaced, such as loneliness, boredom, and confusion, which were like elemental forces with no name. Americans who suffered at their hand suddenly felt powerless, because now misfortune had no clear remedy. Political strategies were no longer appropriate, organized religion seemed irrelevant, and allopathic medicine, with its overreliance on psychotropic drugs, seemed soulless. So Americans turned to alternative medicine for relief. Dr. Adriane Fugh-Berman, an herbal medicine expert who worked at the office in the early 1990s, recalls the enormous number of phone calls from laypeople inquiring about alternative medicine during this period—more calls than to the established bureaucracies at the NIH, and much to the latter's envy. Callers inquired about alternative medicine and everyday unhappiness, looking for solutions to a problem that now neither religion nor medicine nor politics could treat.

ALTERNATIVE MEDICINE LOSES ITS VISIONARY QUALITY

"All I know is that it works," Dr. Saxon nervously replied when I pointed out that alternative medicine's value remained unconfirmed and that PNI remained just a theory. "My depressed patients feel happier. My obese patients lose weight. My arthritis patients feel less pain. Alternative medicine works," he insisted.

Although a dedicated physician, Dr. Saxon was caught in a personal contradiction about which he was still of two minds. On the one hand, he admired Western medicine and seemed embarrassed that alternative medicine failed to meet Western standards. On the other hand, he disliked what many Western doctors had become: engineers who treated diseases instead of people, who saw only the mechanical side of disease, and who were wholly ignorant of life's psychospiritual dimensions. Rather than face the contradiction squarely, he buried it. Whether he believed in alternative medicine or simply forced himself to do so no longer mattered, because, to his mind, he got results. He befriended patients and forged close personal relationships with them, which he enjoyed, but less to honor the patients than to cultivate the placebo deception—to make his patients happy and boost the chance of his therapy's success. Alternative medicine stopped being an ideology in which personal doctoring was the primary motivation and instead became a means to an end, a technical instrument for achieving goals, similar to what happened to psychotropic drugs a decade before.

Alternative medicine's transition from ideology to interests began when the medical establishment reached an accommodation with alternative medicine. In the early 1990s, most physicians still looked at alternative medicine with revulsion, but they took a practical approach to the problem, reflecting their own interest orientation, and saw the advantages of domesticating alternative medicine, bringing it into the university, and turning it into allopathic medicine's junior partner. At least that way they could control the phenomenon. As the editor of one medical journal put it, "We want [alternative medicine] investigated under *our* control where *our* doctors can lay down the rules" (journal editor's italics). In 1990, one American medical school offered alternative medicine courses; by 2003, over seventy medical schools did. Alternative medicine doctors teaching the new courses complained that the schools only tolerated their presence and that the courses were just a sop thrown to idealistic students who identified with "the people" more than with the medical establishment. Their suspicions were justified. Although establishment doctors were reconciled to alternative medicine's popularity, their hostile attitude toward alternative medicine warmed only slightly, into semi-indulgent contempt. Controlling alternative medicine didn't mean liking it.

The accommodation with alternative medicine threatened non-MD alternative medicine providers. Nothing was more irritating to the medical establishment than the professional pretensions of these providers, who had the audacity to think they could consult with physicians as equals and to imagine that they had something worth teaching doctors. These non-MDs needed to be put in their place, and the sheer number of allopathic doctors involved in alternative medicine made doing so an easy task.

As of 2003, roughly 4,000 naturopaths (non-MD providers who prescribe herbs), 3,000 homeopaths, and 10,000 acupuncturists practice their art. One hundred thousand medical doctors easily swamp them. Already doctors comprise a third of all acupuncturists in the United States The medical establishment controls, or at least influences, the licensing of these non-MD providers in many states, limiting some competitors and disqualifying others. Dr. Marc Micozzi, a leading expert on alternative medicine, notes that doctors might one day be the gatekeepers to all alternative medicine. To see a naturopath or an acupuncturist, patients will need a referral from a doctor. Already a common practice model is for a doctor to run an alternative medicine clinic, with several non-MD providers practicing alternative medicine under his or her direction.

When the medical establishment extended the olive branch to alternative medicine doctors, these doctors grabbed it, even going so far as to change the name of their field. Alternative medicine became "complementary medicine" as alternative medicine doctors tried to show how they wanted to add to allopathic medicine, not to destroy it. The field's name changed again in the late 1990s, this time to "integrative medicine," implying an even closer relationship with allopathic medicine, with alternative medicine so assimilating itself into conventional medical practice as to make the two styles inseparable. Alternative medicine doctors also emulated allopathic medicine's academic style, resulting in a degree of organization in alternative medicine that never before existed. Like their counterparts in allopathic medicine, alternative medicine doctors set up conferences, wrote test protocols for new therapies, and published textbooks and journals—all designed to make alternative medicine more credible in the eyes of the medical establishment.

Alternative medicine doctors leveraged popular support to

gain legitimacy, but they could push their advantage only so far, given the medical establishment's enormous power. Reaching an accommodation with established medicine was shrewd politics. Some alternative medicine doctors opposed accommodation, regarding it as a vast conspiracy on the part of the medical establishment to soften up alternative medicine for the final kill, which to some degree it was. But these idealists were increasingly few in number, and the medical establishment found enough alternative medicine doctors to work with who feared deviating too far from Western principles and who wanted to "settle down." Besides, most alternative medicine doctors doubled as allopathic doctors and they benefited from the new restrictions placed on non-MD alternative medicine providers. In addition, a close association with allopathic medicine transferred allopathic medicine's respectability to alternative medicine.

Yet the accommodation between allopathic medicine and alternative medicine papered over a fundamental contradiction in alternative medicine ideology. An ideology that hoped to marry Western and Eastern medicine proved increasingly flawed.

Treating unhappiness with alternative medicine exposed the looming contradiction. Alternative medicine doctors pushed herbs like St. John's wort and kava in opposition to conventional antidepressants, then stressed how the herbs worked on neurotransmitters the same way as conventional antidepressants did. On the one hand, alternative medicine doctors condemned the one-size-fits-all approach to unhappiness built on the biogenic amine theory; on the other hand, they cleaved to the theory that gave rise to it. When accused of treating unhappiness with the placebo effect, alternative doctors denied it, insisting that allopathic medicine's instruments were too clumsy to measure what they did. Then, working the other side of the road, they noted that conventional antidepressants also rely to some degree on the placebo effect, a factor that legitimized their prescriptions.

Unable to resolve the contradiction in their ideology, alternative medicine doctors grew evasive, even devious—again, especially when treating unhappiness. In physical disease, it matters whether a placebo works. A placebo may hearten a cancer patient, but the cancer still grows, eventually exposing the placebo as useless. In unhappiness, a placebo's value need never be proven, since unhappiness is completely subjective. If an unhappy patient feels better after taking a placebo, who can argue with him? After all, he is the person who feels and no one else. Alternative medicine doctors finessed this exception into an example of Eastern medicine meeting Western standards for cure.

Unable to explain alternative medicine's mechanism of action except through the placebo effect and craving to be accepted as mainstream by the medical establishment, alternative medicine doctors increasingly fell back on the logic of PNI. Although PNI was just a theory, it offered vital middle ground between real science and the placebo effect, for it linked the placebo effect to measurable effects on the immune system.

The data on PNI were conflicting and hardly a basis for inducing Artificial Happiness in millions of patients. Some studies showed that unhappiness, in the form of stress, weakened the immune system, while other studies showed that unhappiness strengthened it. In one study, depressed patients exhibited a significant decrease in lymphocyte activity. However, other studies showed that the quality of a patient's mood—happiness versus unhappiness—mattered less than the accompanying behavior. Happiness and unhappiness elicited similar immune effects, causing some researchers to speculate that only depressed patients who "give up" suffer immune system suppression.

Although common sense recognizes that severely depressed people sometimes fall ill, linking everyday unhappiness to physical illness through the immune system was a stretch. The studies yielded contradictory results; some of the immune system changes observed might have been artifact. For doctors to say on the basis of the data that unhappiness causes immune system changes—and consequently sickness through those changes—is like watching a person get into a car, then seconds later watching the car move and deducing from this observation that the car moves because someone gets into it.

Ideology—not science—let alternative medicine doctors connect unhappiness to ill health through the immune system just as a generation before, ideology—not science—let doctors connect unhappiness to neurotransmitters. Torn between East and West, these doctors cleaved to PNI to defend their discipline. Unable to prove the existence of spiritual forces to account for alternative medicine's action and eager to make peace with scientific medicine, alternative medicine doctors told establishment physicians that they tweaked the immune system through the placebo effect, thereby treating physical disease, or even just unhappiness itself, in accordance with conventional science.

The new emphasis on PNI rendered alternative medicine's personal connection with patients a mere instrument. Alternative medicine doctors drew closer to patients to facilitate a therapy's action, not because it was the humane thing to do; whether they deceived patients with alternative medicine no longer mattered so long as patients improved. If patients with minor depression felt happier through alternative medicine, then the deception was worth it. Such was the logic of PNI. To the extent that personal doctoring facilitated the deception, it became a useful means to an end.

Some of the 100,000 allopathic doctors who came late to

alternative medicine embraced the new logic, for, unlike the original idealists, these doctors went into alternative medicine more to diversify their practices than to restore a personal connection with patients. They focused on concrete matters—immediate gain or loss for themselves—rather than on fulfilling some operational worldview. This meant making alternative medicine profitable, which required practicing it in cookbook fashion, limiting patient visits to twenty minutes and thus violating the original spirit of alternative medicine. Already comfortable with practicing allopathic medicine this way, this second generation of alternative medicine doctors dished out herbs, acupuncture, and magnets in the same brisk manner that they dispensed psychotropic drugs. Once they subtracted the spiritual baggage from alternative medicine and spoke less to patients, alternative therapy took roughly the same amount of time.

Alternative medicine became a form of spiritual engineering. Even those alternative medicine doctors who spent time with their patients, such as Dr. Saxon, fell in step. They mistook the extra time it took to customize an alternative medicine prescription with the thoughtfulness once associated with being a personal doctor. True, doctors who prepare special potions for individual patients show a personal touch. But what made physicians in the past "personal doctors" was the personal connection they developed with patients outside of the therapeutic relationship. Sometimes that personal connection took the form of stern counsel for a misdirected life; other times it was composed of nothing more than pleasant conversation or a pat on the back. Either way, personal doctoring was not a treatment with a specific goal like happiness. If anything, it suggested a distinguished and urbane professional deigning to illuminate a less well-educated patient about life. By tailoring therapy to the individual patient to please that patient, alternative medicine doctors imagined themselves to be replicating this experience, only now it was *through* the therapeutic relationship, not independent of it, that these doctors exhibited the personal touch. Unhappiness became one more problem to be fixed through engineering.

Patients under the influence of alternative medicine feel Artificial Happiness. Although life is unchanged, they imagine feeling better because they believe the therapy works; they yield to the power of suggestion. In my experience, the more outrageous the therapy, the more likely unhappy patients believe in it—"No one could make up such a lie," they think. This causes some alternative medicine therapies to be truly bizarre. Reason weakens and emotion strengthens. Once hypnotized, patients imagine everything in the world is possible and take whatever their doctors tell them on faith because without science they have nothing but their doctor to help them differentiate between lies and truth. In the end, patients endow alternative medicine with a value inconsistent with reason, and the doctors support this action because it gets "results." Patients fail to see the full horror of this design or to raise their voices in complaint because they just want to feel happier, even if this means only vaguely recognizing the true nature of how their good feeling comes about. Their state of mind can best be compared to amiable senility.

Alternative medicine started out as a way to restore the personal element in doctoring; it ended as a tool for doctors to leverage power over patients. For brief moments, I have exercised such power. Here is an example: anesthesiologists prefer spinal blocks to general anesthesia for Caesarian sections because general anesthesia increases the risk of a certain kind of pneumonia. In one case, a patient of mine had a patchy spinal block that dwindled toward surgery's end, causing her pain. Not wanting to put her to sleep, I asked her if she felt pain, or just pressure. "Feeling deep pressure is common under spinal anesthesia," I reminded her. It was pain, she insisted. "Are you sure?" I asked, wrestling in the back of my mind with the decision to put her to sleep. "I bet you're feeling pressure. And feeling pressure is normal." Looking confused and vulnerable, she winced and said, "Well, maybe it's pressure. I just never knew that pressure could feel so much like pain." By manipulating this woman and supplementing her patchy spinal anesthetic with extra narcotic, I got her through the last ten minutes of her surgery without having to put her to sleep.

This is real power: convincing someone that pain—the most basic human feeling—is not pain but something else. Imagine such power exercised over unhappy patients, not for minutes but for months or years, and one begins to appreciate the scale of the deception in alternative medicine. True, any power can be abused, even with good intentions. But the abuse in alternative medicine is worse because many doctors practicing the art don't even believe in what they're doing. They only believe that they should say that they believe. They believe they should tell patients that the liver corresponds in nature to wood, the lungs to metal, and the spleen to earth; that bile is made up of fire and water; and that drinking the midflow of one's urine is beneficial—all ideas from ancient Chinese and Ayurvedic medicine. But deep down they do not believe these things. The healers of former ages who framed these therapies could believe in them, but many alternative medicine doctors, with their extensive training in scientific medicine, cannot. Afraid to condemn an activity they have committed themselves to, or consoling themselves with the thought that science will eventually come up with a satisfactory explanation for how their therapies work, alternative medicine doctors content themselves with deceiving patients into happiness, convinced by their own pseudoscientific arguments that hypnotizing patients into happiness is a good thing.

Unhappy patients desperately want to close the gap between how they feel and how they wish to feel; vulnerable and confused about life, their sad minds lay open to strange thoughts and images. These patients go to alternative medicine doctors, who bring them to a state of weakened rational activity, filling the emptiness in their lives with romantic notions and grabbing hold of them with useless substances. No matter what the motivation behind this activity, the end is slavery. Alternative medicine doctors have twisted alternative medicine's honorable impulse toward personal doctoring into something monstrous.

Curiously, alternative medicine patients actively participate in their own deception. Patients must believe in alternative medicine for it to work; swallowing it or feeling it on the skin isn't enough. Hence, patients become enthusiastic coconspirators in the trick perpetrated on them. The solution to this problem is not more "patient autonomy." On the contrary, alternative medicine thrives in an environment of personal freedom. It's no surprise that alternative medicine blossomed in the United States after the autonomy movement of the 1960s and not before. Being drilled into stupidity or treated like a rag dummy works fine when receiving psychotropic drugs, but not when taking alternative medicine. To experience the most intense placebo response, patients must be free to believe in their therapy and sufficiently informed to do so. They must be able to listen to the dictates of their own mind before submitting, thereby making faith in their therapy all the more secure. Dr. Beecher showed that ignorance is compatible with the placebo effect, but possessing some knowledge actually intensifies it: enough knowledge to respect science and consent to therapy but not enough to dare question doctors on their prescriptions. Rather than obstacles to a flourishing alternative medicine movement, autonomy and freedom are necessary preconditions.

From the beginning, alternative medicine was about deception. But no matter how great the deception perpetrated on patients, it was outweighed by the noblest elements of alternative medicine ideology. Alternative medicine doctors could point to hundreds of examples of real friendship growing up between doctor and patient, with doctors taking time to listen to patients and treat them with respect, in stark contrast to the behavior of physician-engineers. When the ideological impulse in alternative medicine waned in the late 1990s, the deception began to stand forth without the protective cover of ideology. That it persists despite this nakedness shows how deeply entrenched alternative medicine has become in the realm of interests.

THE SPECIAL CASE OF MIND-BODY MEDICINE

"I won't pray with you," I told my patient. "Nor will I," insisted the surgeon. The patient was a thirty-five-year-old woman scheduled for routine gall bladder surgery. Her primary care doctor accompanied her to the operating theater and asked that we all pray together, believing that mind-to-mind communication before surgery would strengthen her physiology during the operation. He also wanted the woman to listen to whale music under anesthesia.

"Well, we really should pray," her doctor said.

"Yes, we have to pray!" the woman repeated defiantly.

Sensing a standoff, I tossed the patient a bone. "Listen, I'll put the headset on your ears during surgery and you can listen to all the whale music you want, but I'm not going to pray with you."

"Not good enough," she insisted, crossing her arms. "We have to pray. Otherwise, I'm not going in."

Desperate to start the operation so he could get back to his office, the surgeon relented and agreed to pray. I held out. Finally, the surgeon pulled me aside and sternly said, "Damn it, Ron! Just pray, for God's sake. It's not going to hurt you and I need to get this case going."

In the end, I agreed. Before going into the operating room, we all held hands and prayed—the surgeon, the patient, the primary care doctor, and I—the surgeon rolling his eyes and mouthing a silent, "Thank you, thank you," in my direction.

In the late 1980s, some primary care doctors embraced not only alternative medicine but also a parallel field called "mind-body medicine." Many mind-body modalities, such as meditation, prayer, psychotherapy, biofeedback, and hypnosis have existed for decades, even centuries. What makes mind-body medicine a new field is the link it proposes between mental health and physical health, which doctors produced scientific evidence of starting only in the 1970s.

Harvard cardiologist Dr. Herbert Benson pioneered mind-body medicine. In 1977, after years of studying stress reduction in transcendental meditation, Benson showed how meditation increased longevity and improved quality of life. He coined the phrase "the relaxation response" to describe how mental calm boosts physical health. In the 1980s other scientists followed Benson's trail. In 1986 a connection between meditation and chronic pain reduction was shown and in 1992 a connection between meditation and blood pressure reduction.

In the 1980s, the word *stress* became a buzzword—the media spoke of an "epidemic of stress"—with stress becoming a synonym for the unhappiness arising from everyday trouble at home and work. A growing mind-body movement harmonized the different activities of the various practitioners (often psychotherapists) and lowered people's stress levels for health purposes. These practitioners at least induced—if not Artificial Happiness—Artificial Calm, as patients felt relaxed after their treatments, although nothing in their lives had changed.

The idea of eliminating stress before surgery also grew popular, the argument being that positive emotions experienced prior to the induction of anesthesia strengthened the patient during the operation. Dripping pleasant music into the ears of an already unconscious patient supposedly conferred additional protection through some kind of action on the subconscious.

Primary doctors involved themselves in mind-body medicine around the same time they embraced alternative medicine. At first glance, the alliance between alternative medicine and mind-body medicine seems unnatural. The original creators of traditional alternative medicine aspired to manipulate people's "energy fields," not to make people feel less stressed. Ancient Chinese doctors imagined restoring the body's essence, or Qi, while ancient Indian doctors imagined harmonizing the body's spirit with the Wo'ope—the natural law of creation. These healers wanted to achieve a mystical balance of forces, not please patients.

To say, for example, that ancient Chinese doctors bled people to make them happy implies that these doctors didn't really believe in their therapy and that the whole thing was a charade deliberately orchestrated around the placebo effect. But the overwhelming evidence suggests that ancient healers did believe in evil humors, supernatural forces, and energy fields, all of which bloodletting supposedly influenced. Besides, if happiness, not mystical energy fields, had been the key to understanding alternative medicine's mechanism of action, then alternative medicine doctors wouldn't have wasted so much time trying to prove the existence of these fields through modern scientific techniques. They would have admitted that their therapies worked through the placebo effect—and thus would have been done with the matter.

Alternative medicine ideology sanctioned the alliance between traditional alternative medicine and mind-body medicine. When alternative medicine doctors failed to prove the ancient healers' explanation for why alternative medicine worked, they gravitated toward PNI. They argued that even if alternative medicine worked through the placebo effect, the resulting happiness had physiological consequences, which legitimized the whole enterprise and made it scientifically respectable. Since mind-body medicine had always been about making people calmer and happier (as opposed to playing with people's "energy fields"), alternative medicine doctors saw the discipline as a natural extension of their ideology.

Today, any activity that delights people counts as mind-body medicine. Hence, we have "dance therapy," "music therapy," and even "humor therapy." Mind-body medicine, justified by PNI, gives alternative medicine doctors the right to tie any cultural activity into medicine so long as the activity draws a smile.

Alternative medicine doctors leverage great power through mind-body medicine, for it lets them trespass on any cultural activity for medical purposes, then influence that activity from a distance. I recently attended a meditation session at a Buddhist center. Exotic Asian images adorned the walls; people bowed when they entered the room and then squatted on raised red pillows; a metal dragon sat on the teacher's table. The grave and solemn atmosphere recalled ancient times, yet the teacher devoted most of his sermon to recent neuroscience investigations at Harvard Medical School. People in the audience saw nothing contradictory in this; they imagined themselves participating in a purely cultural activity. Mind-body medicine had circulated through this meditation center in an incredibly sneaky way, supplanting Buddhism's ideas about the mind with scientific ones while leaving Buddhism's art and mythology intact, without arousing suspicion.

Although many mind-body activities border on psychotherapy, primary care doctors, not psychiatrists, push them—another testament to the primary care nature of the revolt against physician-engineering. Dr. Hunter "Patch" Adams, an internist, leads the humor therapy movement. Dr. Larry Dossey, an internist, leads the health-through-prayer movement. Dr. Deepak Chopra, an internist who connects religion to science, sells thousands of books on mind-body medicine. Dr. Andrew Weil, an internist, guides the self-healing, stress-reduction movement. And as mentioned above, Dr. Benson, an internist, started the whole thing.

In some ways, mind-body medicine is more intellectually honest than alternative medicine. The original practitioners neither justified their activities through a clever manipulation of scientific data nor built a rationale for practicing fifth-century medicine on the back of a questionable theory like PNI. Unlike alternative medicine doctors, the original mind-body practitioners lacked an ideological system. They were simply empiricists who believed in what they saw and acted accordingly. When a relaxation technique cured insomnia or lowered blood pressure, they used it and accomplished much good—for example, helping people lower their blood pressure without resorting to pills.

Still, mind-body medicine targets unhappiness. When a patient's sole problem is unhappiness, all the negative consequences of Artificial Happiness follow. People detach how they feel from how they live and sometimes avoid making the life changes they need to find real happiness.

ANOTHER END AND ANOTHER BEGINNING

The Communists in pre-1989 Eastern Europe banned alternative medicine, or at least tightly controlled it. These people knew ideology when they saw it. They well understood that alternative medicine involved more than just therapy, that it challenged the stereotypical models of existence perpetuated under communism and created political rivals in the form of alternative medicine doctors who managed, and ultimately controlled, people's minds. Ironically, even Maoist China put severe restrictions on alternative medicine, despite the fact that ancient Chinese medicine forms a core component of the field. The Chinese communists shared the same fears as their Eastern European counterparts. They fixed the problem by turning ancient Chinese medicine into a Western scientific application—like physician-engineering—and importing Western medicine's diagnostic categories, compelling healers to prescribe acupuncture and herbs in cookbook fashion.

In a way, by adapting themselves to allopathic medicine, today's alternative medicine doctors operate within the medical establishment much like their colleagues did under communism: docile, conciliatory, no longer meddling in medical politics, and supplying the practical know-how with which to make alternative medicine a useful reality. Fully domesticated, alternative medicine no longer haunts the medical establishment like a nightmare.

To a large degree alternative medicine doctors "sold out." Still, these doctors fill an important void in medical practice in the area of physical disease, a circumstance that compels me to excuse at least some of their deception. Allopathic doctors gear medicine toward complete and ready answers, reflecting their engineer's mentality, but when confronted with patients suffering from untreatable diseases they often lapse into silence. Sometimes they utter a few blunt, straightforward words about the inevitable outcome—which does little more than knock sick patients on their heads—and with such determination that one wonders what conceit there might be in forcing sick people to know the unvarnished truth about their futures. In contrast, alternative medicine doctors have persuasive dreams and seductive legends at their disposal. They can tell sick people that their unique history as human beings caused their illness, or that once their psycho-spiritual centers are awakened health may return. The ability of alternative medicine doctors to dazzle patients and inspire hope attests to an elemental truth about human existence, that the only way for sick patients to stop believing in something is for them to stop living. When allopathic medicine reaches the limit of what it can do and physician-engineers tell sick patients to live as best they can, patients naturally transfer their affections to alternative medicine. Making room for a dream in a sick patient's mind, which alternative medicine does, is not a bad thing.

My concern with alternative medicine involves the treatment of everyday unhappiness, not physical disease. True, alternative medicine doctors, unlike physician-engineers who treat both unhappiness and major depression with psychotropic drugs, have separate treatment tracks for these conditions. They use alternative medicine for unhappiness and reserve psychotropic drugs for major depression. Still, alternative medicine doctors dramatically enlarge the amount of Artificial Happiness in America, not only because alternative medicine is inherently safe (so unhappy people more readily accept it) but also because alternative medicine doctors convince people to see unhappiness as a threat to health—the logic of PNI. Psychotropic drug ideology never made this connection between health and happiness. This idea incites fear and drives more unhappy people into medicine's arms.

As ideology, alternative medicine survived a decade before degenerating into a physician tool. But alternative medicine was not the only ideology to arise in response to the overprescription of psychotropic drugs. Around the time that one group of primary care doctors conceived the alternative medicine solution to unhappiness, another group of primary care doctors conceived the exercise solution to unhappiness. Drawing on popular support, these exercise doctors crafted an ideology more enduring than the first two ideologies and with more social ramifications. With the public's help, these doctors pushed the medical practice revolution into a third stage.

ENGINEERING FOR THE MASSES

"**T**HERE GOES THE smallest fellow in the class!" jeered two Harvard students in 1850 as George Windship walked across the college green. An underweight, sixteen-year old freshman, Windship suffered taunts daily, with one bully in particular throwing his books down the stairs every time they met. Sick of the abuse, Windship told a friend, "Wait two years, and I promise you I will either make my tormentor apologize or give him such a thrashing as he will remember for the rest of his life." After two years of intense gymnastics, Windship confronted his old enemy, his muscles coiled tight like steel springs, ready to punch. At the last minute, he experienced a change of heart: exercise had not only made him stronger, but also healthier, even happier, which so pleased him that he dropped his fists and thanked his old enemy for inciting the regimen that proved so beneficial.

Several months later, Windship joined a crowd assembled around a weight-lifting machine. Eager to show off his new strength, he proudly lifted 420 pounds. Then he watched, to his surprise, everyday wagon drivers and porters lift far more; this taught him that real strength required resistance training in addition to gymnastics. He enrolled in medical school to study strength development, challenging along the way the conventional wisdom that vigorous exercise was dangerous. In anatomy class doctors taught that lifting heavy weights risked fracture of the thigh bone, but Windship proved them wrong, showing how the thigh bone could safely bear up to 3,000 pounds. He began lifting weights on his own, training on an apparatus built from ropes and barrels and earning a reputation as a local strongman. After graduation, with a medical credential and a performer's nature, he barnstormed the country, touting exercise's health benefits through exhibitions of great feats of strength, lifting 1,250 pounds with his hands and 2,700 pounds with a yoke, although he himself weighed only 148 pounds. He quickly gained fame as the founder of America's first medically approved fitness movement, with other doctors putting his equipment in their private offices, including the first set of graduated dumbbells ever patented and a lifting apparatus that was a forerunner of the Universal Gym.

Two decades later, in 1876, although seemingly in good health, Windship dropped dead of a stroke at the age of forty-two, his health-through-strength movement dying with him. His death at a young age seemed to contradict his claim that strenuous exercise increased longevity. Establishment doctors long suspicious of Windship felt vindicated, while public support for strenuous exercise melted away, resulting in seventy years of physician disinterest in exercise.

Still, Windship casts a long shadow over American medicine, anticipating by a century both the physical fitness movement and the third stage of the medical practice revolution. In the 1960s, a physical fitness movement grew up among specialists who prescribed exercise for heart trouble. This was science. In the 1980s, a second movement grew up among primary care doctors who prescribed exercise for unhappiness, based on "endorphin theory." This was ideology.

A new crisis in the medical profession precipitated the rise of this new doctors' ideology. During the 1980s, restored public confidence in the medical profession showed doctors that a liberal approach to psychotropic drugs could work a miracle for their image, but the miracle depended on patients becoming wards of physicians. Believing that unhappiness was a neurotransmitter problem, primary care doctors aggressively prescribed psychotropic drugs, hooking millions of people on medication. A new concern swept the medical community—the fear of doctors controlling people with pills—sparking a new insurrection in the physician ranks. In the 1980s, while alternative medicine doctors protested the decline of personal doctoring, another subset of physicians, citing patient overdependence on drugs, rallied around exercise therapy. These exercise doctors also saw unhappiness as an engineering problem—a problem of neurotransmitters—but they wanted engineering for the masses, a way for people to enjoy Artificial Happiness without doctors and pills, which exercise therapy promised.

A doctors' ideology is not deliberately invented; it unfolds naturally. But to do so, it needs three essential ingredients: first, pressure on the medical profession, from within or without, causing doctors to panic; second, a new worldview regarding how medicine should be practiced; and third, a scientific theory justifying the change in course. In psychotropic drug ideology, doctors winced when people called them cold and insensitive. They responded with a new worldview—unhappiness is a disease—and a new therapy—psychotropic drugs—backed up by the biogenic amine theory. In alternative medicine ideology, doctors fretted about the decline of personal doctoring. They responded with a new worldview—psychology's influence on the body—and a new therapy—alternative medicine—backed up by psychoneuroimmunology. In exercise ideology, doctors feared patients' overreliance on psychotropic drugs, and they also responded with a new worldview—the illogic of the separation between preventive and curative medicine—and a new therapy—exercise—backed up by endorphin theory, which ties happiness to the body's release of opiates during exercise.

In each case, a cadre of idealistic primary care doctors mixed science with hope to craft a new policy toward unhappiness, one enthusiastically embraced by the public but spurned by the medical establishment. These doctors were revolutionaries, convinced that an entirely new approach to unhappiness was needed, not just a patch here and there. What distinguishes exercise ideology from the other two faiths is that exercise ideology gave everyday people the leading role in creating Artificial Happiness, making it the most democratic ideology of all.

RUNNER'S "HIGH" AND THE SECOND WIND

One running fanatic describes the happiness he feels during exercise:

> Thirty minutes out, and something lifts. Legs and arms become light and rhythmic. My snake brain is making the best of it. The fatigue goes away and feelings of power begin. . . . Then sometime into the second hour comes the spooky time. Colors are bright and beautiful, water sparkles, clouds breathe, and my

body, swimming, detaches from the earth. A loving contentment invades the basement of my mind, and thoughts bubble up without trails. I find the place I need to live if I'm going to live. The running literature says that if you run six miles a day for two months, you are addicted forever. I understand. A cosmic view and peace are located between six and ten miles of running. I've found it so everywhere.

The year 1973 was an important time in the history of Artificial Happiness. That year, three groups of scientists, each group working independently, discovered the opiate receptor, launching a chain of events that culminated in the third stage of the medical practice revolution.

For centuries doctors knew morphine was the ingredient responsible for opium's euphoric effects, but they could only guess at how morphine worked. Discovery of the opiate receptor proved that morphine worked by attaching itself to special receptors inside the animal brain. A new question arose, however: since opiate receptors apparently exist in every vertebrate, from hagfish to humans, do vertebrates have their own source of opiates—endogenous opiates—to match the receptors that exist naturally? Put another way, if an opiate receptor exists naturally then shouldn't a substance exist naturally to bind to it? Otherwise, what was the evolutionary point of the receptor?

In 1975, John Hughes, working with rat and pig brains in Aberdeen, Scotland, solved this new puzzle, successfully purifying naturally occurring opiates. He called the substances "enkephalins," later termed *endorphins* by Eric Simon at NYU Medical Center. Endorphin was a contraction of "endo" (for endogenous) and "orphine" (for morphine). Avram Goldstein, who discovered endogenous opiates in the human pituitary gland in 1976, encouraged the scientific community to drop the terminal "e."

Neuroscientists mused about the purpose of these substances, with some doctors convinced that endorphins were part of the body's pain-suppression system, while others argued that endorphins varied the pitch of emotional states. Yet neuroscientists weren't the only professionals intrigued by endorphins; almost immediately, exercise specialists and psychologists joined the debate.

Since the 1960s, exercise specialists had been trying to explain the "second wind," the improved performance of runners during the second half of a marathon race. Runners described the second wind as a kind of euphoric experience, similar to the high experienced on drugs. In 1979, biologist Candace Pert and colleagues made the first attempt to link exercise-induced euphoria with endorphins. They forced rats to swim in a bucket of ice water for five minutes, then they let the animals recuperate before decapitating them and studying their brains. Compared to the control rats, which merely sat in ice water, the exercised rats showed evidence of increased opiate receptor activity after fifteen minutes of recovery, which returned to normal after forty-five minutes of recovery. Pert attributed the increased opiate receptor activity to an exercise-induced release of endorphins, which attached to the opiate receptors, or possibly tighter binding by preexisting endorphins. They also hypothesized a psychological change in the exercised rats during the period of increased opiate receptor activity, which they called "relief euphoria," although they never actually interviewed the rats on this matter.

Since real narcotics cause euphoria, the idea that endorphins also cause euphoria seemed reasonable. Sports psychologist David Pragman officially formulated the endorphin theory in 1980, arguing that endorphin release during exercise *causes* the runner's second wind. To further cement the link between endorphins and real narcotics, he termed the euphoric experience "runner's high." Although pure conjecture, the theory seemed intuitively reasonable to doctors and became a prejudice among many of them, much like the biogenic amine theory and psychoneuroimmunology.

In the early 1980s two studies seemed to confirm the theory, hardening the prejudice. In one study conducted by Edward Colt of Columbia University, the endorphin increase associated with running correlated with running intensity: a relaxed jog led to an endorphin increase in 45 percent of runners, but a strenuous run led to an endorphin increase in 80 percent of runners. In a second study, runners showed an increase in endorphin levels in the presence of high levels of lactic acid, the waste product of muscular activity that causes the burning sensation during exercise. These facts dovetailed nicely with endorphin theory, which argued that endorphins increase with exercise to counteract lactic acid-induced pain—and promote happiness almost as a side-effect, just as real narcotics do.

As evidence for endorphin theory mounted, newspapers and magazines sang in chorus, popularizing endorphin theory and making the word "endorphin" part of everyday usage. In casual conversation, people referred to endorphins when explaining their good feeling after exercise. Jogging, my friends joked, would "get those endorphins going."

So secure seemed the tie between exercise and endorphins and so innocent the motive for its popularization that endorphin theory simply spread by word of mouth like a new bit of common sense. But from the outset serious scientists doubted endorphin theory. In 1982, only two years after Pragman had coined the term "runner's high," a team of scientists injected runners with naloxone, an opiate antagonist, to counteract the mood changes associated with running. If endorphins were responsible for "runner's high," then naloxone, which competes with endorphin for attachment to the opiate receptor, should reverse the endorphin effect. It didn't, suggesting that something other than endorphins caused runner's high. In another study, scientists compared endorphin levels in ten runners with those in sedentary people. Surprisingly, the runners showed a *decrease* in endorphin levels. A third study also yielded a contradictory result, showing no real correlation between improved mood and endorphin levels in marathon runners. Although the mood of the marathon runners improved, more than half of the runners showed no increase in endorphins at all.

There was another reason to doubt endorphin theory. Endorphins circulate not only in the brain but also in the body's general circulation, where they serve as temperature regulators. The body maintains a rigid barrier between the brain and the general circulation (called the "blood-brain barrier"), such that some drugs injected into the body's bloodstream never penetrate the brain. Since scientists hyping endorphin theory had only measured endorphin levels in the general circulation, which lack a direct correlation with endorphin levels in the brain (where runner's high occurs), it was a leap of faith to link a change in the amount of endorphin in the body's bloodstream with runner's high.

A third problem arose when scientists discovered more than one kind of opiate receptor in human beings and then discovered that not all opiate receptors cause euphoria when bound; in reality, sometimes the opposite feeling results. Since no one knew which receptors endorphins attached to, any link between increased endorphin levels and exercise-induced euphoria was pure speculation.

Oliver Stoll, of the Sports Science Faculty in Leipzig, Germany, summed up the state of endorphin theory in a review article: If endorphin theory is true, then it is only true for highly trained individuals and not for the great mass of everyday gym people. More likely, he concluded, endorphin theory is just a myth.

None of this evidence put a dent in the theory's support among the public or among doctors. Rather than forsake an idea they instinctively liked, people kept their minds on the beaten track. As professionals, doctors should have expressed some skepticism, but, like the public, they found it easier to believe in endorphin theory than question it, since questioning it took time and investigation. If endorphin theory ceased to be *certain* fact, it remained established fact.

Doctors clung to endorphin theory for another reason: it complemented the biogenic amine theory, which loomed large in doctors' minds at the time. In the early 1980s the doctors' ideology built around psychotropic drugs took off, causing tension between primary care and psychiatry. By positing a new connection between mood and brain chemicals, endorphin theory strengthened the argument among primary care doctors that unhappiness had a physical basis, justifying the expanded role for psychotropic drugs.

However, a subgroup of primary care doctors had an altogether different reason for keeping faith with endorphin theory. These doctors saw in endorphin theory a way to fight the growing trend toward psychotropic drugs. Although endorphin theory was questionable, a questionable theory is often the first ingredient in an ideology's creation. Even when a questionable theory ceases to be supported by science it can take on new life as an ideological symbol. This is what happened to endorphin theory. Some primary care doctors used endorphin theory to bolster the biogenic amine theory. Other primary care doctors embraced it for a countervailing purpose, turning it into a symbol of what people could do for themselves without doctors. Endorphin theory contained within it the seeds of a new and opposing ideology—exercise ideology—one that undermined the case for psychotropic drugs.

EXERCISE DOCTORS CHALLENGE THE STATUS QUO

"As long as my patient drinks less alcohol than me, he's doing fine," one doctor wisecracked in the 1970s when explaining why he refused to counsel his patients about lifestyle. Many American doctors thought similarly during the decade, whether about drinking, smoking, or exercise—not because they were lazy or because they lacked knowledge about lifestyle and health but because they held a particular worldview. For over a century, a rigid division between prevention and cure had dominated doctors' thinking. Doctors saw their role as curing disease rather than preventing it. The division had deep roots in Anglo-American philosophy, mirroring the larger division between government and the individual. Government agencies practiced preventive medicine (including sewage treatment and food inspection), protecting the health of the community the way the military protects the security of the nation. Doctors in the private sector treated sick individuals the way merchants serve individual customers with individual needs. As this paradigm solidified over time, preventive medicine grew synonymous with public health, while curative medicine became identified with private practice. For a doctor to counsel a healthy person about lifestyle—in other words, to practice preventive medicine—was tantamount to trespassing the public health functions of government. At the very least, it violated official etiquette. Eager to keep government on its side of the fence and curative medicine in private hands, doctors meticulously adhered to the century-old paradigm and left lifestyle counseling to public information programs. Even as late as 1984 only 15 percent of American doctors advised patients to exercise. Doctors also disliked telling other people how to live. Although the surgeon general's office issued a report in 1979 linking lifestyle to disease prevention, most American physicians thought it more offensive to lecture people on their personal habits than to let them fall ill.

Finally, many doctors sneered at the whole notion of exercise therapy, viewing activities like weight lifting and jumping rope as little more than ways to condition athletes. They saw exercise as a branch of high school physical education, not real medicine—something that gym teachers with whistles taught, not doctors in white coats. At most, they saw exercise science as a harmless plaything for PhDs, in contrast with the more serious therapies that MDs dealt in and that carried some risk.

Even the notion of exercise as harmless was relatively new, which made doctors ignoring exercise that much more understandable. As late as 1950 most physicians feared exercise's impact on the heart. They believed, for example, that the common irregularities of sound and beat in an athlete's heart were pathological rather than variations on normal, and part of a larger syndrome known as "athlete's heart" that shortened lifespan. Athletes even risked heart rupture, doctors warned, although no such case had ever been recorded.

Attitudes changed in 1957, when several cardiologists debunked the notion of athlete's heart and praised exercise as beneficial to heart patients rather than harmful. Unheard since the days of Windship, the new thinking provoked bold newspaper headlines like "Exercise Called for All Heart Patients!" and "Exercise Is Good for Mending Heart!" Several years later, after learning that exercise helped in the rehabilitation of musculoskeletal diseases, orthopedic surgeons championed the activity. Still, exercise remained of little interest to primary care doctors, as evidenced by the infrequency that these doctors counseled patients to exercise.

Although endorphin theory circulated in the popular ether during the 1970s, few clinical studies on exercise's psychological benefits were actually performed during this period, justifying to some degree the medical profession's lack of interest in exercise as a psychological remedy. Psychiatrists conducted much of the research on exercise and mental health, mostly on psychotics, alcoholics, and the mentally retarded, but rarely on depressed patients. A few large-scale prospective studies showed that exercise lowered depression scores in sedentary people, but whether these people were depressed because they were inactive or inactive because they were depressed was unclear.

In 1979, shortly after the discovery of endorphins, John Greist, a psychiatrist at the University of Wisconsin, penned a landmark article titled "Running as a Treatment for Depression," the first systematic exploration of exercise's role in depression, with a particular focus on minor depression. Greist divided patients with minor depression into three groups: a running group, a group treated with ten sessions of time-limited psychotherapy, and a group treated with ten sessions of unlimited psychotherapy. After twelve weeks he saw significant reductions in depression in all groups, with no significant difference between groups, implying that exercise worked as well as psychotherapy for minor depression. Without a control group of untreated patients, Greist couldn't say for sure whether patients needed either of the two therapies (i.e., whether patients might have improved on their own, without exercise or counseling). Nevertheless, his article had great impact, especially in primary care, for although primary care doctors couldn't perform psychotherapy they *could* prescribe exercise. Greist had put the treatment of minor depression within their reach.

After Greist's study came out, a few primary care doctors began advising their unhappy patients to exercise—a definite change, since exercise medicine had traditionally been the preserve of specialists like cardiologists and orthopedic surgeons. These doctors ("exercise doctors") aroused little suspicion among the medical establishment, since they simply did as other doctors did, although for a different purpose. However, the high level of psychotropic drug prescriptions during the 1980s disturbed these mavericks, who protested angrily. In hospital corridors they scolded colleagues for giving antidepressants out like water and recommended exercise as the safer option. One exercise doctor at my medical school, influenced by Marxism, accused colleagues of keeping unhappy patients in the dark about exercise so they could make more money treating them with drugs. From this distrust of psychotropic drugs arose exercise ideology, the belief that unhappiness is an engineering problem best treated with exercise.

Inherent in exercise ideology was a new worldview regarding the medical profession's role in preventive medicine. Exercise doctors believed that good medicine knew no boundaries and that the barrier separating prevention and cure was a relic from the irrational past. Lifestyle counseling, including exercise, was the hammer they used to collapse this barrier, one wielded at their own cost since no money was to be made in telling people to exercise. Since exercise was neither strictly preventive medicine nor curative medicine but both (curing unhappiness as well as preventing heart disease), it symbolized the incoherence of the century-old barrier and made exercise doctors feel especially justified in smashing it up.

Populist in spirit, exercise doctors also wanted patients to become more involved in their care. For too long the motto of American patients had been "I hear and obey," with doctors assuming that nothing could follow their commands but obedience. Exercise doctors believed patients needed to become more involved in their health and happiness, that this was not only necessary but also honorable, and the price to be paid for being competent human beings. Psychotropic drug safety was also a concern of theirs, although largely a theoretical one since these drugs were fairly safe. Still, many exercise doctors instinctively distrusted these pills, believing people who took them could hardly escape unhurt, although they couldn't characterize the hurt with any specificity.

Exercise ideology rested on a tripod of strength: first, doctors' fears that antidepressants were being overprescribed; second, a new worldview uniting preventive and curative medicine; and third, endorphin theory. Endorphin theory gave exercise therapy crucial scientific gravitas, turning a commonsense observation about exercise into a doctors' ideology. Certainly no self-respecting doctor, even the most generous-minded, would have pushed exercise on unhappy patients had he believed such advice could have come from a gym teacher. Endorphin theory made exercise for the treatment of unhappiness complex and biochemical, something worthy of a doctor's attention, letting doctors feel like doctors when hyping exercise's psychological benefits. It also let doctors think in ever more systematic ways about unhappiness, making exercise ideology part of an emerging order that paradoxically included psychotropic drugs. With the appearance of endorphin theory, the medical language of unhappiness was not only growing—first norepinephrine, then serotonin, and now endorphins—but increasingly easy to share. This common medical language let primary care doctors think about unhappiness in terms of mutually understandable components, thereby facilitating their control over the problem. Each doctor had his own favorite neurotransmitter and treatment, but the underlying assumption was always the same: unhappiness is an engineering problem.

Although endorphin theory raised exercise from gym play into a serious scientific phenomenon, thereby clearing the way for doctors to get involved, it was exercise ideology's democratic nature more than any questionable science that resonated with public opinion. Appealing to the American public's nascent distrust of authority, exercise ideology showed people how to create their own Artificial Happiness—just go for a jog—signifying a shift of power away from physician elites and toward the people. Emphasizing independence, perseverance, and hard work, exercise ideology even appealed to everyday American sociology, encouraging people to rely on their own resources to solve emotional problems rather than wait pathetically for a drug handout from a doctor, thus making it something even the Founding Fathers could have supported. For almost a century, the medical establishment had draped the practice of medicine in complexity to shield it from public scrutiny. Now, to the public's glee, exercise doctors were tearing holes in that drape and encouraging people to learn more about medicine so they could self-treat.

At first the medical establishment found exercise doctors extremely droll. What did exercise have to do with serious medicine? they asked, rolling their eyes. One of my medical professors, making light of what exercise doctors preached, boasted dryly that whenever he felt the urge to exercise he would go and lie down. Nor was it lost on the medical establishment that many exercise professionals were actually PhD exercise physiologists rather than "real doctors." Establishment physicians, many of whom drank, smoked, ate liberally, and lounged on their sofas after dinner just like their patients, laughed at this sudden intrusion of a band of amateurs into the hallowed halls of medicine.

Over time, as exercise doctors kept pushing, ordinary doctors grew annoyed, especially when exercise doctors accused them of practicing bad medicine by not encouraging their unhappy patients to exercise. Still, the medical establishment showed none of the counterrevolutionary fury it showed toward alternative medicine doctors. Establishment doctors hated alternative medicine doctors for advocating a mentality that seemed almost un-American, one that threatened the basic principles of allopathic medicine. At least exercise doctors worked within the allopathic system, like proper reformists. Biomechanical solutions to problems are the essence of allopathic medicine and endorphins are a biomechanical solution. True, exercise doctors represented a visionary force that threatened the old ways of doing things. They also appealed to "the people," an exercise in democracy that would have naturally disturbed any group of professionals, and they consorted with PhDs. But the exercise doctors spoke the same language as mainstream doctors, which softened the backlash against exercise therapy.

Nor were exercise doctors as obnoxious as alternative medicine doctors. When the alternative medicine movement began, some of the movement's idealists called Western medicine a tragedy; a few of them were rabid revolutionaries willing to destroy the whole health care system so they could triumph on the ashes of destruction. Their militancy sprang in part from fear, as alternative medicine doctors saw themselves leading a tiny movement threatened with extinction by the vast medical establishment. Historically, even public opinion had snubbed them. Living under siege made many of these doctors sarcastic and rude. Exercise doctors also formed a minority within organized medicine, yet outside of medicine, in the public realm they enjoyed enormous public support from the beginning. While the medical establishment ignored exercise, the average American embraced it, and had done so since the 1970s; exercise was enormously popular, so much so that by 1980 a total of 56 percent of Americans exercised twice weekly. With public opinion on their side, exercise doctors knew that no matter how puny their movement might be within organized medicine, their power and significance far exceeded their numbers; consequently, they had to be taken seriously. An inner confidence spawned a more businesslike demeanor and a more businesslike task: not destroying established medicine, but winning it over to an already popular idea.

Exercise doctors had no reason to be bomb throwers. In the 1980s, they knew, like many doctors in the medical establishment knew, that the grand era of medical breakthroughs was coming to a close; that new drugs increasingly were variations on older ones; and that the best way to manage illness—perhaps the only way—was to prevent illness in the first place. In addition, every shred of common sense indicated that a growing number of Americans were living with chronic disease, in part because fewer cures were being discovered, but also because the country was aging. These people suffered numerous psychological problems, including minor depression. Unless the medical establishment planned on treating every one of these individuals with antidepressants, a new, less invasive, modality was needed, and exercise filled the bill. A plateau in medical research combined with changing demographics to present a golden opportunity for exercise doctors, who knew they would soon be playing leading roles. All they needed to do was bide their time and wait for the overripe fruit to fall to the ground.

Although exercise doctors pushed the concept of healthy living under an accepted label and showed proper respect for allopathic medicine, the medical establishment vacillated. Diffident more than alarmed, many doctors remained passive toward exercise, content to leave it alone. Even psychiatrists looked the other way. Although psychiatrists had performed the initial studies on exercise and mental health in the 1960s and '70s, passion for exercise hovered mainly on the specialty's fringes. In accordance with their interests, psychiatrists naturally gravitated toward modalities they could control—medication, for example—and exercise lay beyond their control. Besides, psychotherapy was already suspected of being a placebo; although exercise-induced happiness had at least some biochemistry behind it, psychiatrists weren't eager to champion another questionable activity.

Despite resistance from the medical establishment, exercise ideology soon carried the day, in part because of internal inconsistencies within the establishment's position. Exercise counseling violated the rigid division between prevention and cure, but hadn't the medical establishment already set things in motion by calling unhappiness a disease? After all, this was what was driving the antidepressant prescription rate upward. And if unhappiness was a disease that exercise cured, then exercise naturally belonged to curative medicine rather than preventive medicine. The medical establishment had to agree. Faced with this internal contradiction, even the most conservative physician could see how preventive medicine and curative medicine were hopelessly intertwined and that the rigid division between the two disciplines no longer made sense, if it ever had. As for psychiatrists, they simply shrugged their shoulders and let exercise doctors have their way; after all, exercise had no proprietary value. If exercise had value and if it had been something they could control, psychiatrists would probably have contested it, but it didn't and it wasn't, so they let it go. Perhaps most important, latent forces of public opinion began to assert themselves in the debate: people believed in exercise therapy. Doctors saw no point in breaking with the American public on the matter of exercise-induced happiness when exercise had already demonstrated salutary physical benefits.

The medical establishment assimilated exercise ideology during the 1980s, with an explosion of exercise-depression studies following on the heels of acceptance, more in primary care than psychiatry. Most of the studies reaffirmed the association between exercise and happiness that the medical establishment now blessed. Although poorly designed, with inadequate population samples and bad follow-up, these studies prompted little criticism since their purpose was not to elicit truth so much as to confirm belief. These studies sustained doctors' beliefs and supported exercise therapy for unhappiness, although none of the studies would have made it possible for the FDA to clear exercise as therapy had exercise been a drug. To this day, only one well-designed clinical study examining the relationship between exercise and depression has been performed: in 1999, Dr. James Blumenthal of Duke University showed that a sixteen-week course of exercise therapy effectively treated depressed seniors, although antidepressants worked better.

Exercise ideology's popularity spread so quickly among primary care doctors that some physicians, eager to prescribe exercise for unhappiness but unsure what to prescribe, simply extended their prescription for heart patients to unhappy patients, recommending exercise to 80 percent of capacity for twenty minutes three times a week. No science underlay this prescription; doctors basically made it up as they went along.

By 1991 a total of 87 percent of American doctors agreed on the importance of exercise and more than 50 percent routinely prescribed it in both mental and physical illness. As a consequence, millions of Americans found Artificial Happiness through exercise. Starting in the late 1980s, health club membership in the United States soared; by 2003 it had nearly doubled, drawing from across the demographic spectrum. More important than this growth rate is the question of why Americans exercised. According to one study, the majority of Americans in the 1980s worked out to achieve the "hard look." Beginning in the 1990s, they did so because of the positive effect on stress levels, or because exercise made them feel good about themselves. Although some of these people ameliorated their stress for reasons of physical health, evidence suggests that improving mental health was also an important goal. An example is that a major marketing shift in the U.S. health club industry occurred during the 1990s, toward the idea of *wellness*, a word with definite mental health connotations. With their doctors' encouragement, Americans jogged, biked, or swam, searching for a "high" that made real life seem far away.

THE RISE OF FITNESS CULTURE

Jim Scott is a forty-year-old hospital orderly who works long hours in the operating room. Because the surgical theater is windowless, denying him a view of the sun, his only knowledge of time comes from a clock on the wall. Outside the surgical theater, he wanders through windowless halls under long fluorescent bulbs that radiate a constant light. It's as if the earth had stopped spinning on its axis, causing the sun to stand still in the sky. Inside the hospital, the only way Jim knows when it's morning instead of evening is that the cafeteria serves breakfast instead of dinner.

Disconnected from nature and unable to feel time's progression, Jim became depressed. Exacerbating his shrunken sense of time, and his depression, was a lack of movement in his career.

His work never varied. His chances for advancement were meager. Jim saw himself performing the same drudgery, scrubbing floors and picking up trash, ten years from now.

Looking for relief, Jim found Artificial Happiness through obsessive exercise. However, it is the culture of exercise—fitness culture—and not exercise per se, that makes him happy. Jim doesn't seek runner's high. Instead, he finds happiness by working toward fitness goals, which enhances his sense of time. After a workout, Jim ponders his exercise program. He doesn't know how much weight he'll lift in the future but he knows it will be more, which excites him since so much about his real life is fixed and predictable. Lifting more weight each week represents to Jim a steady stream of accomplishment—of change—letting him imagine layers and layers of time and giving him a sense of time's fullness. What Jim lacks in the real world—an awareness of time's progression—he creates artificially at the gym through self-improvement.

Jim also derives happiness from his excellent physique. He rarely passes a full-length mirror without glancing at his image, an image that boosts his self-esteem. When he sees overweight doctors climbing up the stairs at the hospital, panting and with little beads of sweat glistening on their sideburns, he swells with pride and thinks he's the better man.

Although millions of Americans experience Artificial Happiness through exercise, probably only a small fraction of them ever achieve runner's high. But exercise offers an alternative route to Artificial Happiness in the form of fitness culture, which is probably the route most exercise enthusiasts take. Fitness culture is not about exercise; it is about overexercise. It is not about health; it is about pride.

Within fitness culture, exercise enthusiasts live, work, and achieve just as people in the real world, but their milestones are athletic ones. Real life is chopped into holidays, work goals, and family celebrations. Gym life is chopped into athletic accomplishments. In both cases, people look forward to events and remember them afterward, an experience that imparts weight and depth to the passing hour and helps people feel an expanded sense of being. Although pursuing a counterfeit rhythm of life, exercise enthusiasts enjoy the same sense of achieving and advancing as people in real life. They experience the drama of life—the whole gamut of pomp and solemnity, passion and triumph—that kindles Artificial Happiness.

Fitness culture also gives people a reason to feel proud. Because the measures of success in fitness culture bear no relation to those in real life, the happiness that fitness culture induces is artificial. In real life, people succeed if they are rich, famous, powerful, or glorious. In fitness culture, people succeed if they are trim.

For this alternative source of Artificial Happiness to work, people must believe in it. Unless exercise enthusiasts think their goals are respected, useful, and significant, they won't feel proud when achieving them; they won't feel as if they're spending their time in a sensible way. If people don't feel proud and respected, they won't feel Artificially Happy. Thus, fitness culture's viability as a method of Artificial Happiness depends on the public's respect, which in turn depends on a well-respected institution vouching for it.

In most cultures people look to a higher authority before judging the value of other people's activities, seeking reassurance and guidance from leaders who preach some divinely inspired message about the world, man, and the difference between right and wrong. In the past, churchmen and politicians played this leadership role, telling people how to live and what constituted proper conduct. Doctors, at most, aspired to reach the apex of a scientific or administrative structure, like a medical school or a hospital department, worrying more about their own professional interests than about people's virtue.

When exercise doctors gave obsessive exercise their approval they thrust themselves onto the apex of an emerging cultural structure: fitness culture. Although people overexercise for different reasons, their activity gained respect after exercise doctors defended it and endowed it with a moral purpose. Talk show hosts and Hollywood actors played a role in the rise of fitness culture but not the pivotal one. They made obsessive exercise a "fad," even a lifestyle, but a fad or a lifestyle is not a culture. A culture is something more enduring and with greater consequence; it has a moral purpose. People arrange the whole of their lives in a culture and when they do they feel themselves to be walking along the road of duty. For a culture to exist on a mass scale it needs educated, dignified voices behind it. This voice is what exercise doctors provided.

A brief history of the exercise movement in the United States illustrates this point. After Windship died in 1876, support for exercise continued along two parallel paths. On the first path, men overexercised to show how tough they were. College sports during the second half of the nineteenth century were often violent brutal matches designed to display male prowess. Older men who exercised obsessively took part in the fringe sport of bodybuilding, unrelated to health, or joined gritty, low-life boxing clubs, which grew popular at the turn of the twentieth century. At worst, these activities were freakish; more typically, they were hobbies for working-class men organized around male bonding. Without the public's respect, these activities failed to give participants a sense that they were doing something important and thus failed to achieve the status of "culture." They certainly were not cultures on a mass scale. The average Joe punching a bag after work probably never imagined his activity as having special significance.

On the second path, men, and later women, exercised for health purposes. At first, educators and public health experts took the lead because of the medical profession's lack of interest in preventive medicine. In the early 1960s, after cardiologists and orthopedic surgeons proved exercise's health benefits, medical specialists became more involved. Interest in exercise expanded rapidly, especially among women. By the 1970s, millions of American women practiced "fitness for health" in Jack La Lanne's gyms. Jim Fixx popularized the sport of running in 1977 with his best seller, *The Complete Book of Running*. It was, however, moderate exercise and not obsessive exercise that became enormously popular. Few Americans expected to run as much or as often as Jim Fixx. Most people exercised to maintain their physical health, not to look "cut" or have "washboard abs." Although exercise became a popular phenomenon, there was no virtue in the activity. All that Jack La Lanne, Jim Fixx, and medical specialists hoped for was that people might become a little less sedentary.

The "toughness" path led men to overexercise to prove themselves, but without the public respect needed to make the activity a mass cultural phenomenon. The "healthy" path led many people to exercise moderately, which the public respected, but it lacked a higher purpose. Moderate exercise was like brushing one's teeth—an important hygienic measure but nothing worth bragging about and incapable of kindling Artificial Happiness.

Popular attitudes changed when some exercise doctors began aggressively policing people's lifestyle. These doctors praised people's commitment to exercise, especially when that commitment included a healthier diet and a cessation of smoking and drinking. A healthy lifestyle was no longer just healthy; it was moral. This represented a change from the physical fitness movement of the 1960s and '70s, when physicians told patients to get off their couches and walk twice a week. The goal in fitness culture was no longer exercise, but obsessive exercise. Obsessive exercise became a testament of piety and rectitude; going to the gym regularly became medicine's Sunday school version of life. Exercise doctors had infused exercise with a moral purpose.

Exercise doctors articulated a new and potent vision that combined science with morality. Sociologist Franz Schurmann describes a vision as a form of prediction. If the prediction is important enough and strikes people as true, it will be taken seriously. As scientists, for example, doctors know from experience that if they inject a patient with poison the patient will die. This is one kind of vision and it is real, although there's nothing in the vision worth following. Religious leaders predict at another level: their prediction, or vision, carries moral weight. They claim to know who will go to heaven and who will go to hell, making their vision something people pay attention to. The problem for religious leaders is that their prediction, although conveyed by powerful imagery, is impossible to verify, since no one really knows who goes to heaven or hell. Nor do clergymen have the power to make one scenario come to pass or the other; in a way, they have less predictive power than a simple country doctor. Exercise doctors say people who live unhealthy lifestyles not only die but also get what they deserve, because a bad lifestyle hinges on free will. Since everyone inevitably dies and few people live perfect lifestyles, the conditions of the doctors' vision are always being met, which lets doctors take credit for predicting that people with bad lifestyles will die. In reality, the link between lifestyle and death is not so clear-cut and doctors can't say for sure whether a certain lifestyle *caused* a certain person to die. But when people see fat people dying and think such a thing wouldn't have just happened anyway, they assume both that the tragedy has moral overtones and that it was decreed by science. Doctors combine the practical reality of science with the mysterious quality of myth, which mesmerizes patients and leads them to take the vision of exercise doctors very seriously.

Not all exercise doctors pushed the new view that health was a moral matter hinging on free will, but enough did to influence other physicians. I find myself influenced by their prejudice, tending to look at morbidly obese people who come for surgery (and whose obesity tremendously complicates the anesthetic) with a kind of resentment. *What's wrong with you!* I think to myself while staring at them. *Why did you let yourself get like this?* Some anesthesiologists view the complicated and painful procedures that sometimes have to be performed on obese patients almost as just punishment for getting so fat. At the very least, these procedures teach obese patients the hard way that things can't go on like this and that after their operations they will simply have to live healthier lives.

Several years ago, while I was taking care of a ninety-year-old obese man with heart disease, another doctor looked over my shoulder and shrugged. "Well, he has only himself to blame," the other doctor observed. To be sure, a connection sometimes exists between lifestyle and disease among the elderly, but it seems almost perverse to emphasize bad habits in a ninety-year-old fatty dying of heart disease who, had he not overeaten, might have lived to ninety-three. By fixating on lifestyle this doctor gained an explanation, even a justification, for the patient's suffering. When the ninety-year-old man died the following week, the doctor's facial expression read, "See, I told you so." From the doctor's perspective, the man was not only dead but also damned.

Exercise doctors moralized in different venues. At a hospital meeting, I listened warily as one exercise doctor explained why no beer should be served at the annual crabfest for the medical staff. "We need to set a good example for our patients," he opined. Special occasions demanded special sacrifices. With the rest of the medical staff too embarrassed to openly attack such high-mindedness, the doctor's motion almost passed without challenge, until, fortunately, one older physician, contemptuous of the whole lifestyle movement, uttered straightforwardly, "I want beer with my crabs." Cheers rang out, the doctor's motion was defeated, and beer was put back on the menu.

The new morality diffused throughout the medical profession and the public at large, expressed most commonly in contempt for fat people and an elevation of trim people to sainthood. In one case, I anesthetized a man with colon cancer who had a perfect physique, well-defined muscles, and as much fat on him as a Diet Coke. After he was asleep the rest of the operating room staff protested how incredibly unfair it was that a man so committed to a healthy lifestyle should suffer from such an awful disease. Their protests were analogous to the wails of people who cannot understand why God lets innocent, sinless children die.

Many doctors and laypeople refused to accept the new morality, but enough did to inspire exercise enthusiasts, especially on the country's two coasts. Instead of viewing themselves as "gym rats" or "exercise kooks," exercise enthusiasts saw themselves as existing on a higher plane. Their rapid rise in social status recalls that of artists, who during the eighteenth century occupied a low position on the social scale, and then during the nineteenth century, when the Romantic movement glorified self-expression, suddenly found themselves closer to the top.

When healthy "lifestylism" became a moral movement, exercise became serious and important business, almost a matter of the soul. Exercise enthusiasts grew convinced that if important professionals like doctors praised what they did, then obsessive exercise had to be worthy. Many nonfitness people in the general public agreed. Although they themselves lacked the willpower to become fit, they admired those who did. During the 1990s I noticed personal trainers being invited to elite dinner parties for no other reason than their handsome bodies. Treated reverentially by the other guests, they could have passed for members of the clergy.

With the support of both the medical profession and the public, exercise enthusiasts walked proudly and imagined themselves doing so among the heathen. They felt special; they saw their activities as having vital import; and those feelings were translated into Artificial Happiness.

THE END OF THE THIRD ACT

The rise of exercise ideology cemented doctors' control over unhappiness. Doctors now dominated the field, able to attack unhappiness with three big guns—drugs, alternative medicine, and obsessive exercise. Yet, all during the medical practice revolution, doctors received help from businessmen in the insurance industry, without which they could not have succeeded. From the 1970s to the 1990s, as the three doctors' ideologies gathered steam, managed care rose to dominance. Seemingly an independent variable, a system run by insurance people according to business principles and with little or no connection to idealism of any kind, managed care actually complemented at each stage what the physician revolutionaries were trying to accomplish, making it a crucial part of the Artificial Happiness story, as I will now show.

SIX

HAPPINESS HITS
THE ASSEMBLY LINE

IN 1993, WHILE working on the health policy committee of a Maryland gubernatorial candidate, I attended a meeting to discuss our candidate's position on managed care. Tensions ran high, since money was involved. A surgeon spoke first, blaming managed care for his declining income, then harping on the threat of managed care to patients and citing the case of a patient who died because an insurance company refused to cover his operation. When the surgeon finished his speech, the room fell silent. The air was thick with reverence for the medical profession, while the surgeon himself looked grave. A second doctor, equally determined to throw managed care out of the state, described another case gone bad because of managed care. He, too, looked solemn—and confident, expecting the steady stream of horror stories to bring everyone around to his point of view. A doctor's wife went third, railing about how managed care had cut into her husband's income, causing her lifestyle to suffer.

Wearing a light green pantsuit with matching toenail polish, she begged the campaign to join the fight against managed care, as she had already been forced to sacrifice her membership at the local country club.

Those in support of managed care spoke next. Several small business owners expressed sympathy for the victims in the doctors' stories, but they then explained how runaway health care costs were killing their businesses. For them, it was either managed care or bankruptcy. Meaning no disrespect to the doctors, they recommended a wait-and-see approach, that managed care be given a chance to work out the kinks. Finally, the vice president of a managed care company rose to speak, with audible grumbles from the doctors' corner. The executive proved extremely adept, paying respect to the various interests involved before transcending interest politics altogether and appealing to "the people," explaining how managed care made health insurance more affordable and improved people's health through innovative preventive medicine and wellness programs. His speech swayed the campaign operatives, who understood that if managed care had some public appeal their candidate needed to be careful about attacking it.

Clearly, the managed care executive had his own interests at heart, but for the purpose of understanding the great changes in American health care over the last twenty years, including the rise of Artificial Happiness, his high-minded speech needs to be taken at face value. The rise of managed care was not merely a business event; it was also a cultural one. Managed care executives tapped into the business community's desire for cheaper medical insurance, but also into the public's desire for a new direction in health (for example, in the area of prevention and wellness). Although many health care subscribers had no insurance option other than an HMO, managed care companies frequently emphasized wellness clinics and preventive screening (at least in their brochures) to make their product seem less like a prison.

In this respect, managed care executives, like all revolutionaries, were ideological. Although they shared the businessman's belief in the market system and showed themselves to be especially greedy during contract negotiations with doctors and hospitals, they also sensed the public mood and factored people's anxieties into their calculations. In the 1960s and 1970s, primary care doctors responded to people's fears that no one cared about their unhappiness; in the 1980s and 1990s, managed care executives responded to people's fears of getting sick—and not just getting sick without insurance. As life expectancy increased during the second half of the twentieth century, Americans feared missing out on living longer, or perhaps living longer but in a debilitated state. As one doctor writing for the *New York Times* put it, patients now wanted to die comfortably in their sleep at age ninety after playing two sets of tennis followed by sex with their spouses. People's expectations for a quality life had shifted.

Much of managed care is about cutting costs, taking the pressure off employers, and making money for shareholders; this is how managed care operates in the realm of interests. But another part is about giving people a sense of hope and optimism that they will live longer and healthier; this is how managed care operates in the realm of ideology. True, as a practical matter it's easier to guarantee people medical coverage when they're sick than to promise them a long and healthy life. Yet sustaining people's belief in the future is an essential role of all ideologies. The sense that someone is looking out for them and will make things go well makes people feel better, an intangible sensation that may or may not be warranted but that is nonetheless vital to peaceful living. By advertising preventive medicine and wellness, two concepts traditionally ignored by the medical profession, managed care executives touched a nerve among the public, enabling them to leverage control over health care while fattening business profits.

The rise of managed care aided the Artificial Happiness movement on both the level of interests and the level of ideology. On the level of interests, managed care executives reorganized health care to award more power to primary care doctors at the expense of psychiatrists, securing the new and aggressive policy toward psychotropic drugs. They also adapted Artificial Happiness to the principles of mass production, making it available to millions of people at the lowest possible cost. On the level of ideology, managed care executives supported the new worldviews of the physician revolutionaries: among psychotropic drug doctors, the belief that unhappiness is a disease; among alternative medicine doctors, the belief in the mind's impact on health; and among exercise doctors, the belief in preventive medicine.

What separates the managed care executives from physician revolutionaries is cynicism. Unlike the physician revolutionaries, the managed care executives didn't really believe in their ideology and certainly didn't act on it. Managed care executives were shrewd. They knew that insecure people would support almost any new policy that promised health and longevity, especially if the only sacrifice involved was a cut in doctors' salaries.

In this respect, managed care executives were better at playing with the realm of ideology than were their physician opponents. Warning against managed care's shoddy approach to medicine, many doctors also claimed to represent "the people." But the public perceived that doctors worried more about their own interests, including their salaries and professional autonomy, than the people's interests—something I also sensed while working on the health policy committee. Managed care executives were no less attentive to their own interests, but they radiated more sincerity in their popular appeals, perhaps in part because they envisioned health care as a democratic and capitalistic enterprise rather than an elitist and feudal one. Emphasizing medicine's complexity, doctors told the public to butt out and let the experts (meaning themselves) run health care; they imputed a transcendent merit to the medical profession, as if it were some kind of priestly caste. Managed care executives, on the other hand, saw health care like any other human activity, amenable to market principles and comprehensible to people without professional training, with the job of doctor no different than any other honest way of making a living. Their antielitism resonated with the American people.

Managed care arose in America because existing health care interests showed themselves incapable of safeguarding their own livelihood. With double-digit inflation in medical costs and the system creaking under its own weight, the interests themselves—meaning the doctors and the hospitals—were endangered. Taking advantage of the crisis, managed care executives spoke eloquently to people's concerns while coldly implementing a divide-and-conquer business strategy. In the process, they gave Artificial Happiness an institutional base, including the resources and bureaucracies needed to change Artificial Happiness from an ideological movement within the medical profession into a national structure with organizational power.

KEEPERS OF THE GATE:
SOLIDIFYING THE HOLD OF PSYCHOTROPIC DRUGS

As an anesthesiologist, I often go to dinner parties thrown by surgeons, but until the mid-1990s the parties consisted mostly of surgeons and anesthesiologists—no surprise, since a common surgical theater gives these doctors the chance to become friends. Occasionally I saw gynecologists or internists with subspecialties, the former because they also work in the operating room, the latter because they provide surgeons and anesthesiologists with preoperative consultations, both leading to close contact. But I never saw a family practitioner, a general internist, a pediatrician, or a GP.

Three reasons account for the pattern. First, specialists who work in the surgical theater rarely encounter primary care doctors, who usually spend all day in their offices across the street. Lack of close contact makes for less chance of becoming friends. Second, surgical theater doctors and primary care doctors often harbor feelings of contempt toward one another. Surgeons and anesthesiologists pride themselves on being doers, not just thinkers; they view primary care doctors, with their tedious, undramatic outpatient responsibilities, as weak and effeminate. In turn, primary care doctors see surgical theater doctors as dumb—"strong hands, weak minds"—with the standing joke in primary care being that to become a surgeon one's knuckles have to touch the ground while walking. Third, primary care doctors have traditionally been envious of surgical theater doctors. Until recently, the latter made much more money, which showed up in bigger houses and nicer cars. To defuse the tension, surgical theater doctors told primary care doctors that they had only themselves to blame for their relative poverty. "You knew what you were getting into," I reminded one primary care doctor after he complained about the income differential. Yet the tension persisted and many surgical theater doctors thought it best not to inflame the jealousy of primary care doctors by showing them the insides of their houses.

Starting in the mid-1990s, primary care doctors were routinely invited to these parties. Managed care accounted for the abrupt change. In the past, when indemnity insurance dominated, patients went to specialists whenever they wanted, bypassing cheaper primary care doctors in search of more expert care. Under managed care, a patient had to see a primary care doctor first, then get a referral to see the specialist. Suddenly, primary care doctors controlled the flow of patients to specialists. Surgeons, psychiatrists, and internists with subspecialties were enormously vulnerable; careers tottered; making nice with the primary care doctors became imperative. Hence, primary care doctors found themselves invited to the surgeons' dinner parties, although the old prejudices lingered.

Managed care took over American health care with astonishing rapidity. Industrialist Henry Kaiser, in 1937, created a prepaid health plan to cover his employees; eight years later the plan opened up to non-Kaiser employees, becoming the Kaiser Permanente Health Plan. For the next thirty years, managed care showed little growth. Even as late as 1970 only thirty managed care plans existed in the entire country. Rising health care costs paved the way for managed care's explosive growth. In 1975, federal legislation required all companies with more than twenty-five employees to offer a managed care plan. Subsequent legislation encouraged Medicare patients to join managed care. With employers eager to trim costs, and pushing employees into these plans, managed care quickly expanded. By 1997 over 600 managed care plans existed, covering more than 80 percent of Americans.

Of all the specialists, psychiatrists were the most vulnerable to managed care. Unlike other specialists, psychiatrists lacked a signature procedure that only they could do (e.g., endoscopy, angioplasty); their most high-tech activity involved prescribing pills, which primary care doctors could do just as well. Naturally, primary care doctors referred fewer patients to psychiatrists once their own salaries varied inversely with the number of referrals they made. Even subspecialists in psychiatry were threatened by managed care. Pediatricians, for example, created a new subfield called "behavioral pediatrics" that replicated child psychiatry, again cutting down on the need to refer. Finally, the stigma attached to seeing a psychiatrist caused many Americans to prefer a primary care doctor when dealing with emotional trouble. The restrictions managed care placed on seeing a psychiatrist simply reinforced their natural inclinations.

To cut costs, managed care reorganized mental health care, using either an "integrative" model or a "carved-out" model, with both models shuffling psychiatrists into obscurity. The integrative model set primary care doctors up as gatekeepers. In the carved-out model, mental health was split off from the main body of health care and handled separately, even subcontracted out to other business entities, which shielded it from the full force of managed care's reorganization. Still, even with traditional mental health care intact in the carved-out system, psychiatrists lost out, as less expensive nurse practitioners, social workers, and psychologists took on the gatekeeping role played by primary care doctors in the integrative system.

Faced with looming disaster on both fronts, psychiatrists found themselves with few options. Some psychiatrists scrambled to become gatekeepers themselves. They advocated changing the residency training programs to teach psychiatrists how to manage not only mental illness but also basic medical problems like asthma, back pain, and hypertension, thereby turning psychiatry into a specialty within primary care and letting psychiatrists function as both psychiatrists and primary care doctors. The problem was that a century of separation between psychiatry and the main body of medicine made this an unrealistic option; psychiatrists couldn't retool so quickly. In the end, managed care worked its damage and psychiatry faded. Today, psychiatrists care for less than a third of all mentally ill Americans. With primary care's ascendancy in mental health, some community hospitals have even disbanded their psychiatry departments.

Critics blame managed care for forcing doctors to treat depressed patients with cheaper psychotropic drugs rather than costlier long-term psychotherapy. Although managed care executives deny the charge, circumstantial evidence supports the accusation. An explosion in psychotropic drug prescriptions happened on managed care's watch, and managed care puts restrictions on psychotherapy, including a cap on the number of sessions it pays for.

But I argue that managed care played less of a role in rising psychotropic drug prescription rates than the doctors themselves. After all, in the late 1960s and early 1970s managed care was still only a regional phenomenon, with a presence in certain cities like Los Angeles, Minneapolis, and Rochester. Even then, minor tranquilizers such as Valium and Librium were being massively prescribed across the country. Managed care could not have been the driving force behind psychotropic drug overprescription during this era.

Instead, managed care empowered primary care doctors who had been pushing psychotropic drugs on unhappy patients for over a decade. Before the managed care era, psychiatrists exerted a restraining influence on primary care doctors; during the managed care era, that restraining influence waned, giving primary care doctors free rein to implement their ideology, while they also fought for more turf.

Managed care's restructuring allowed for the systematic implementation of psychotropic drug ideology. A nation of solo doctors, each operating independently of one another, made any coordinated policy toward unhappiness impossible. Unhappy patients going for an office visit before the managed care era couldn't count on getting a drug prescription from a doctor; it all depended on the doctor's unique practice style. Managed care institutionalized the doctors' ideology, harmonizing the practice patterns of vast numbers of doctors on a statewide, even nationwide, scale. A few doctors high up in HMO management created official policies that went far and deep into the various communities, coordinating the doctors' practices and making the drug solution to unhappiness a reliable and predictable response at the office level.

In addition, individual doctors were emboldened to medicate unhappiness once they discovered through the managed care network that other doctors were doing the same thing and that some higher force countenanced it. Although managed care didn't explicitly order doctors to prescribe drugs for unhappiness, it made doing so a reasonable option, one consistent with the prevailing standard of care in the community that managed care now defined. Even primary care doctors ambivalent toward aggressive drug therapy found it easier to prescribe psychotropic drugs once inside the managed care organization. With business executives, utilization review specialists, administrators, and doctors in the managed care organization so conjoined that the responsibility for any particular therapy never fell on any one of them individually, these doctors suffered fewer pangs of conscience when behaving in a way they had mixed feelings about. They could always say that management had "forced their hands."

Guidelines for treating depression in primary care, published by the federal Agency for Health Care Policy and Research (AHCPR) in 1993, offer an example of how managed care took advantage of federal guidelines, crafted in accordance with psychotropic drug ideology, to implement a preference for psychotropic drugs on a nationwide scale. Physician experts at the federal level created an algorithm for diagnosing and treating depression, which many managed care plans adopted. Through the various managed care networks, a brief educational pamphlet published by the AHCPR, titled *The Quick Reference Guide for Clinicians*, found its way to thousands of primary care doctors, who read it and fell in step. The pamphlet, in the words of one psychiatrist, "encouraged primary care doctors to provide pharmacotherapy to their depressed patients as the first line of treatment." More precisely, the pamphlet suggested that primary care doctors hold back referring depressed patients to psychiatrists until two trials of antidepressants had failed.

The pamphlet indoctrinated doctors in psychotropic drug ideology in two more ways. While discussing at length the problem of underdiagnosing depression, the pamphlet failed to mention the equally serious problem of overdiagnosing depression. Although receiving less publicity, several studies had shown that primary care doctors wrongly diagnosed healthy people with depression at a rate of 10 and 20 percent, which given the size of the primary care population in the United States translated into huge numbers of false positives being treated with psychotropic drugs. Second, by telling doctors to focus more on depression's signs and symptoms rather than on the life circumstances surrounding and possibly causing the depression, the pamphlet encouraged doctors to treat unhappiness out of context, as if it were solely a problem of neurotransmitters—the sine qua non of psychotropic drug ideology. The approach meshed perfectly with managed care's practice model, which had primary care doctors working in large groups and patients seeing a different physician during each visit. Under such conditions, doctors couldn't keep track of every patient's unique life circumstances, but they could follow a short checklist of signs and symptoms.

Managed care didn't command the drug approach to

unhappiness, but it did routinize it, creating an environment allowing it to thrive. Because physician-engineers like routinization, managed care increased the likelihood that these doctors would enforce the psychotropic drug solution, especially when so many of them were already straining at the leash to do so.

Although Artificial Happiness under managed care acquired a kind of industrial or factory character, ideology played a role in its transformation. Under managed care, primary care doctors medicated unhappiness efficiently and cheaply, in fifteen-minute intervals, working on volume to make the whole thing pay, the way Henry Ford built cars. Yet the assembly-line approach to happiness would have failed had there been insufficient consumer demand; it was vital that psychotropic drug ideology appeal to broad sections of the American population. Fortunately, many unhappy Americans wanted these drugs, seeing in medication the quickest and surest route to happiness and with the imprimatur of science giving the drug solution legitimacy.

Popular support for psychotropic drugs gave managed care executives the advantages of economies of scale, making the reorganization of mental health care possible. If doctors had needed antidepressants to treat just ten thousand unhappy Americans, the drug companies' price per pill would have been enormous, making individualized psychotherapy the more financially attractive option. If such conditions had applied to automobiles, it would have been cheaper for Henry Ford to make every car by hand. Fortunately, millions of unhappy Americans wanted medication, or at least acquiesced in drug therapy, which lowered the unit price of these drugs and made the assembly-line approach to Artificial Happiness both possible and profitable. Thus, psychotropic drug ideology and the popular force behind it generated a health care organization that managed care executives alone could never have achieved.

Ideology springing from popular social forces helped managed care executives in another way. A peculiar aspect of the American character is its belief in the "perfectibility of man." During the nineteenth century, when Alexis de Tocqueville first coined the phrase, Europeans believed that man had pretty much reached the limits of what he, with his imperfect nature, could aspire to. Americans, on the other hand, constantly strove for progress, always trying to make life a little easier, inching humanity toward a better existence, and putting their faith in two forces to do so: science and capitalism. Both forces mesh perfectly in Artificial Happiness. Psychotropic drugs are quick, clean, and scientific, at least compared to psychotherapy, with the latter's irrational pessimism, opaque language, and long counseling sessions that seem to go nowhere. Moreover, drugs make people happy, while in psychotherapy the most a "big neurotic" can aspire to is to become a "little neurotic." Managed care is equally optimistic. From their perspective, managed care executives liberated mental health from the psychiatrists, who, with their monopolistic practices and miserly attitude toward psychotropic drugs, subverted the market economy and prevented the have-nots in the system—meaning millions of unhappy Americans—from getting their share of happiness through unrestricted commerce. Idealistic in a capitalistic sense, these executives envisioned limitless happiness once they brought competitive market forces to bear on health care, and patients (now consumers) got the drugs they wanted.

PLAYING THE PUBLIC OPINION CARD: SOLIDIFYING THE HOLD OF ALTERNATIVE MEDICINE AND EXERCISE

Life expectancy for American men and women in 1900 was forty-seven and fifty, respectively. In the 1980s, life expectancy for American men passed seventy. For American women, it was close to eighty. Americans not only expected to live longer but also to live in a style once reserved for the very rich. Golf, tennis, and intercontinental travel beckoned, with Social Security benefits increasing at a faster rate than inflation to pay for them all. The only thing Americans had to do to enjoy these things was to stay alive and healthy. If alternative medicine and exercise conferred some advantage in this area, no matter how remote, then Americans wanted them.

During the 1980s alternative medicine and exercise appealed more to the public than to the medical establishment, which refused to yield to popular pressure and support these activities. Instead, the medical establishment counseled patience among its members, arguing that when a society loses its mind the only thing sensible people can do is bide their time and wait for the insanity to pass. In this environment, alternative medicine doctors and exercise doctors faced an uphill battle trying to implement their respective visions for medicine, but they had valuable allies: managed care executives who possessed an uncanny sense of the people's mood, who could identify themselves with major currents in American society, and who could bring popular pressure to bear on the medical profession's weakest point. Although the medical establishment presented the façade of being in control of health care, it was *not* in control. The health care system wobbled dangerously, buffeted by rising medical costs. Seizing an opportunity, managed care executives leveraged public opinion to capture the support of two groups that did respond to democratic pressure: legislators and employers. Legislators and employers had good economic reasons to support managed care, but the executives clinched the deal with their rhetoric about wellness and preventive medicine, rhetoric that appealed to the American people. With medical costs exploding, howls coming from the business community, the media crying "something must be done," and the American people eager for modalities promising longevity and improved quality of life, legislators and employers took the path of least resistance and signed on to managed care.

From the outset, managed care offered so much rhetorical support to alternative medicine and exercise therapy that it grew identified with these revolutionary causes. In support of alternative medicine, managed care promoted wellness, a mind-body concept that joined optimal physical health with inner peace. In stark contrast with the medical establishment's hostile attitude toward alternative medicine, managed care executives spoke sympathetically about this upstart field, praising it as a way for patients to feel more in control of their health. In support of exercise, managed care touted preventive medicine, including not just exercise but also diet control, antismoking campaigns, and lifestyle counseling. When pitching these concepts to legislators and employers, managed care executives predicted not only huge financial savings but also a healthier and happier population. In a parting shot against doctors, these executives noted how the medical establishment had not only brought the health care system to the brink of bankruptcy but had also, in its contempt for wellness and preventive medicine, showed itself incapable of innovative thinking.

Some legislators remained uncommitted, at which point managed care executives stoked the fires of public opinion, holding forth the benefits of wellness and prevention, then intimidating legislators with the threat of arousing the people's wrath against them. Having already convinced the public that doctors opposed prevention and wellness programs for financial reasons, the executives conjured up an image of disgruntled doctors conspiring with reactionary politicians to keep the American people unhealthy. One rumor that made the rounds had legislators opposing preventive medicine and wellness programs so as to kill people off at a young age to take pressure off the Social Security trust fund.

During this period, the phrases "wellness" and "preventive medicine" achieved popular resonance, much like the phrase "neurotransmitters" had a decade before, revealing the workings of a significant ideological current. No longer just medical concepts, wellness and preventive medicine were symbols of a new worldview that expressed people's aspirations. Millions of Americans wanted to live longer and healthier; wellness and preventive medicine became sloganistic shorthand for what they were trying to accomplish. Managed care executives spoke these words all the time, legitimizing alternative medicine and exercise in the public consciousness despite resistance from the medical establishment, which persisted in calling these modalities gimmicky. In addition, these words solidified managed care's public image as a progressive force in the health care debate. A residue of this view persists to this day: although the American people have long since turned against managed care, the one nice thing they continue to say about managed care is that it supports wellness and preventive medicine.

But managed care executives showed no intention of turning their ideology into operational reality. In his critical review of managed care, Richard Dean Smith notes that "prevention in managed care ended with marketing" and that "'wellness' appealed to members in consumer surveys, even though most managed care plans had no health risk-reduction programs whatsoever." In his study of managed care and alternative medicine, Dr. Kenneth Pelletier observes, "Although the popular media report that an increasing number of insurers are offering CAM [complementary and alternative medicine], the current status of CAM coverage is quite limited."

Pelletier's review article is illustrative. Even as late as 1997, managed care companies rarely covered what would be considered true alternative medicine. In Pelletier's study of eighteen managed care companies, most alternative medicine coverage was restricted to psychotherapy, physical therapy, acupuncture, and chiropractic, with the first two modalities rarely grouped under alternative medicine and the second two modalities alternative medicine's most respectable examples. Coverage for herbal medicine, aromatherapy, meditation, yoga, and naturopathy was rare or nonexistent. In addition, what little coverage was available was geared toward purposes other than health maintenance. Pelletier writes: "The majority of insurers interviewed do not offer CAM coverage to enhance wellness or prevent disease. Rather, like conventional therapies, CAM therapies are covered only if treatment is medically necessary for a specific diagnosis."

Activists pushing for mandated alternative medicine coverage exposed managed care's devious strategy. Washington State passed a comprehensive state health insurance program in 1993 that included such coverage. Two years later, legislators attacked it and the coverage survived only through the efforts of an insurance commissioner sympathetic to alternative medicine. During the drama, managed care showed its true colors, fighting to eliminate alternative medicine coverage rather than maintain it. To this day, state mandates are the second major reason other than consumer demand that managed care covers any alternative medicine at all. In essence, state governments *force* managed care to cover a field that managed care supposedly supports.

Managed care executives had every good reason to avoid funding alternative medicine: other than for chiropractic, few studies had proven alternative medicine's clinical efficacy or cost-effectiveness. Still, the public wanted alternative medicine, especially managed care's most profitable clients. Alternative medicine coverage attracted healthier members to join managed care plans, including highly educated and high-income Americans between the ages of twenty-five and forty-nine, who conveniently paid money into the insurance system while taking less out. From an executive's perspective, the best strategy was to offer "token" coverage, meaning just enough coverage to preserve managed care's image as an alternative medicine supporter and thereby attracting these enrollees, but not enough to cost real money.

Similar logic applied to exercise medicine. Managed care's "health maintenance" theme implied that managed care would do everything it could to keep people healthy—first, because it was good medicine, and, second, because it saved money. However, the truth surrounding preventive medicine threw a monkey wrench into the plan. Only three preventive services really paid for themselves: prenatal care for poor women, tests in newborns for some congenital disorders, and childhood immunizations. Preventive services that lured baby boomers to managed care with the promise of greater longevity did not. For example, screening for cancer cost more than cancer therapy. Screening for high blood pressure cost more than treating the heart attacks and strokes that resulted from high blood pressure. Even if the initial investment in prevention could be recouped down the line, the managed care company making the investment wouldn't see it, since plan members shifted from one managed care company to another on average of every two years. Managed care's two reasons for pushing prevention were in conflict: although inspirational and good medicine, preventive medicine didn't actually pay. Confronted with this truth, executives resorted to their old system of dilatory behavior—prolonged bargaining, sly maneuvering, the making and breaking of promises—the end result being little funding for preventive medicine programs.

To this day, managed care's support for alternative medicine and exercise continues to drift along in complete ambiguity. Still, that support has revolutionary significance, for, during the late 1980s and 1990s, it tipped the balance in the conflict between the medical establishment and the physician revolutionaries and forced the medical establishment to assimilate alternative medicine and obsessive exercise into the medical mainstream. Used to docile businessmen, such as hospital presidents who deferred to physicians and did what they were told to do, establishment doctors were broadsided by the managed care executives. Although public opinion by itself couldn't force the medical establishment to change its policy toward alternative medicine and exercise, the managed care executives had cleverly manipulated public opinion to affect the balance of power within the health care debate, swaying legislators and employers to their side. For many doctors it was the last straw. The specter of managed care executives, employers, and legislators allying together to solve the health care crisis at the medical profession's expense forced them to abandon their strong opposition to alternative medicine and exercise therapy. The medical establishment needed to pacify the public and show people how doctors were as sensitive to their aspirations for a better life as the managed care executives. Through a chain reaction of steps, managed care compelled the medical establishment to embrace alternative medicine and exercise therapy.

Even if their ideological impulses were disingenuous, the managed care executives proved immensely helpful to the physician revolutionaries pushing for change. Their actions show what a powerful force ideology can be. Even when serving a selfish purpose, ideology can open the way for public opinion to enter a battle between competing interests and decide the outcome.

NEW WORLDS TO CONQUER

Managed care's rise filled the minds of primary care doctors with hopes, calculations, and fears. Relative to other physicians, primary care doctors gained real power under managed care; at the same time, an alarming situation stared doctors in the face. Managed care robbed all doctors, including primary doctors, of their professional autonomy. In addition, primary care doctors were burdened with a staggering amount of paperwork because of their new gatekeeper status, without extra income to pay for more secretaries. In addition, a new medical malpractice liability associated with gatekeeping arose—in bad patient outcomes, primary care doctors could be sued for not referring patients to specialists—with no money to pay for higher malpractice insurance premiums. Finally, primary care doctors lived in constant fear of being removed from an HMO panel (a process ominously called "deselection") if their practice patterns cost the HMO too much money. Not surprisingly, as managed care ascended, the mindset of primary care doctors passed from elation and confidence to distrust, hostility, and gloom.

The unease felt by primary care doctors toward managed care is ironic, given that managed care was the result of new attitudes these doctors themselves had popularized. In the past, when doctoring hinged on thoughtfulness and inspiration—for example, when doctors talked to patients about their everyday unhappiness—the notion that insurance executives could "manage" doctors using fixed rules and procedures would have been inconceivable. It would have been like telling ministers to sermonize with one or two words or telling painters to paint with one or two colors. Doctoring, like preaching and painting, was an art requiring a broad grasp of humanity and subtle intelligence.

However, physician-engineers are easy to manage. Their tools are predictable. Their thinking is predictable. Their output is predictable. Insurance executives like to manage workers whose decision trees follow a few simple pathways. When doctors became engineers of the body and began treating unhappiness according to a preset algorithm—to drug or not to drug—they paved the way for insurance executives to come in and manage them, too. Primary care doctors led the medical practice revolution, but the physician-engineering mindset they had adopted inevitably led to their oppression under managed care. Primary care doctors hoped to remake medicine in their image; in the end, managed care executives remade primary care doctors in their image. The sad fate of primary care doctors offers another example of a revolution consuming its own.

Still, as the takeover by managed care dragged on by virtue of its own momentum, perplexing and frightening doctors, the vague outlines of a new field of conquest for the Artificial Happiness movement began to appear. By putting primary care doctors in control of medical practice, managed care executives obliterated the distinction between physical health and mental health. A single physician type now cared for both the body and the mind. Along with rhetoric about meeting people's spiritual needs in the form of "wellness" therapy—again with primary care doctors in charge—managed care covered all the likely trouble spots in a person's life: body, mind, and spirit. Managed care was about more than managing disease; it was about managing life.

For centuries, a fundamental contradiction had kept doctors from thinking they could care for all of life's dimensions. Doctors couldn't unite their scientific definition of life with the more popular definition of life. According to doctors, the body's organs "live" as separate units, yet each person understands himself or herself as a single, indivisible being searching for happiness. Is a person's "life" in his or her organs, or is it in his or her consciousness? If life is in the former, then consciousness is all an illusion, a mere by-product of brain activity; if life is in the latter, then organs are not alive; in which case, what are they? Doctors couldn't answer these questions, let alone solve the contradiction, so they focused their scientific expertise on the body's organs and put their general knowledge toward the problems of consciousness, advising unhappy people in their capacity as educated laymen rather than as scientists. Sometimes they just let clergymen handle the problem of unhappiness.

Managed care's rise symbolized a change in doctors' thinking: medicine could tackle the question of life—the life of the body's organs plus the life of human consciousness, including the desire for happiness. Brewing on the horizon was another revolution that would go forth on a scale dwarfing the medical practice revolution, one that years from now may be reckoned the most fateful historical phenomenon since the Enlightenment. In this second revolution, primary care doctors didn't fight psychiatrists, the medical establishment, or insurance executives; nor were their objectives turf or money. Instead, primary care doctors found themselves side by side with other doctors in a common struggle to give life a new meaning. The Artificial Happiness movement was about to enter the big leagues.

MORE REVOLUTION

I FAINTED ONLY ONCE during my medical career, as a third-year medical school student during the early 1980s caring for a young woman named Cindy Dimas. Unmarried and poor, Cindy came to the outpatient clinic complaining of stomach cramps, learned she was pregnant, then broke down crying. She knew abortion was an option, but she also confessed a secret terror: that if she had the abortion, she would go to hell. Dr. Fernandez, the attending physician on duty, spoke impatiently with Cindy, coaxing her toward abortion, saying that everything in this life has its price and that abortion was the most sensible solution given the circumstances. Cindy weakly agreed, although her ambivalence portended trouble. When she returned for the procedure two days later, the noises and odors of the strange hospital world made her uneasy. She howled each time she thought it was her turn to go back to the operating room. At one point, the moving spectacle was too much for me and I looked away.

Once Cindy was on the table and anesthetized, Dr. Fernandez methodically dilated her cervix with a metal rod, inserted a suction catheter into her uterus, then moved his arm back and forth furiously, causing significant bleeding. The gold chains around his neck flopped about each time he thrust his suction instrument into her. Upon finishing, he winked at me, dropped his instrument, smiled, shouted "Merry Christmas, everyone!" (it was December), and walked out of the room, leaving the rest of us to move Cindy onto the stretcher. Cindy lay on her back, her legs crossed like scissor blades, as if frozen in that position by the cold operating room air.

I felt a sinking, gnawing sensation grow inside me. Then I felt lightheaded. Unsure what was happening, I excused myself and briskly left the operating room. By the time I made it outside, the world was spinning; had I not squatted immediately, I would have fainted right away. Dr. Webb, the chief resident on the case, followed me out into the hall and asked me what the problem was. I said I didn't know. Then, while I was still in the squatting position, she leaned over me and asked me in a severe tone, "But you still believe it's a woman's right, don't you?" Holding up my hand, palm facing outward, I cried, "Yes! Yes!" (which was true). Still, doubt is a contagious thing and my unease over Cindy's care spread rapidly to Drs. Webb and Fernandez, for whom abortion was a bit of sore spot. While Dr. Webb anxiously invoked women's rights, Dr. Fernandez growled about being the only doctor on staff who helped the little people, although his nervous manner belied a strange, inward fear that maybe he had been too aggressive with Cindy. Like Dr. Webb, he seemed insecure.

In the early 1980s, a feeling of restlessness and agitation commonly surrounded abortions. With their consciences cloaked in hurried behavior, doctors feigned to make abortion seem inconsequential; but underlying their matter-of-fact attitude was a well-screened uneasiness and a general feeling that the whole abortion thing was messy. Their self-assurance in performing the procedure reflected mostly the degree to which they became reconciled to it all. Doctors confidently operated on diseased organs because they knew their science justified it, but they felt less secure about abortion because their science took no position on the question of when life begins; they relied on the arguments of lawyers and philosophers to defend the procedure. Not surprisingly, although many individual doctors were pro-choice, the medical profession as a whole resisted speaking with one voice on the matter. In 1973, the year abortion was legalized in the United States, neither the *New England Journal of Medicine* (*NEJM*) nor the *Journal of the American Medical Association* (*JAMA*) commented on the Supreme Court ruling the week after it came down. Equally silent were the general science magazines, including the flagship journal *Science*. It was as if the debate over when life begins was none of medical science's business, even though doctors were directly involved.

Over the next twenty years, a sea change occurred in the medical profession's attitude toward the question of life. Doctors showed surprising new confidence on the issue. They saw abortion as just another procedure; only the fear of retribution by religious activists weighed on their minds. Their confidence reached a high point in 2001, when journalists caught doctors at the Jones Institute for Reproductive Medicine at Eastern Virginia Medical College mixing human eggs and sperm together like so much straw on a threshing floor to create embryos for stem cell research. With perfect frankness, doctors called these embryos "nonlife." A few weeks before the Jones Institute story broke, scientists at Advanced Cell Technology, a Massachusetts-based firm, announced they were ready to clone human embryos for research, a process that would destroy embryos. Doctors and scientists at both places were so obstinately sure of themselves that they resented any effort on the part of religious conservatives to stop them. Physician organizations like the American Society for Reproductive Medicine and the American Medical Association defended them.

Even the professional journals rallied around. Rather than duck the debate over the human embryo the way it had in 1973, the *NEJM* published two long essays in support of research cloning, almost as a direct challenge to organized religion. *Science* magazine also published an article in support of human embryonic stem cell research, citing the lack of continuity in the Catholic Church's position, including the Church's relatively recent embrace (in 1869) of the idea that "life begins at conception." This was bold. Three decades before, none of the science magazines with wide public appeal dared to point out the apparent inconsistencies in the Church's position. It was a far cry from the medical profession's mincing posture toward human embryos in the early 1980s, when doctors, reluctant to speak its name, referred to abortion by its numerical code in the insurance manual, and occasionally the gynecologist and anesthesiologist avoided eye contact during the procedure.

It is no coincidence that the sea change in the medical profession's attitude toward the question of life came at around the same time as the medical practice revolution. To launch that revolution, primary care doctors needed to fight—mostly psychiatrists, but also neurologists and anesthesiologists. Alternative medicine doctors and exercise doctors even had to fight the entire medical establishment. Primary care doctors won every battle, yet each struggle took place within organized medicine and against other doctors. All the while, a more dangerous enemy lurked beyond: religious people, especially the nation's clergymen. Organized religion had its own approach to unhappiness, one that carried moral weight. If clergymen fussed loud enough, they could turn the whole country against psychotropic drugs, alternative medicine, and obsessive exercise, thereby derailing the Artificial Happiness movement. To neutralize organized religion, primary care doctors needed to launch a second revolution in tandem with the first, a revolution that defined *life* in medical terms, not unhappiness. Clergymen derived their power to manage unhappiness from their unique vision of life. To check that power and sustain the medical practice revolution's momentum, doctors had to create their own vision of life to rival and ultimately supplant religion's vision.

In the next three chapters I will be speaking in very broad terms about two heterogeneous groups of people: doctors and religious people. Although I recognize the diversity of opinion within these two groups, and I may misrepresent any given individual, my personal experience and research tells me that I am describing their evolution accurately. Sociologists often speak of large groups to account for the behavior of many people; it is in this spirit that I do so here. In this chapter I even rely on the characterizations of sociologists to put the evolution of doctors and religious people in historical context. At different moments in American history, sociologists noticed large numbers of people expressing new attitudes and opinions, which they used to define new character types. Not every American fit one of the new character types; in some ways, the new character types were idealized versions of people. Nevertheless, the sociologists who lived during those periods observed a cultural shift that was real, and to communicate that shift to readers they gave it a human face. I use their character types to show how the Artificial Happiness movement brought doctors and religious people into conflict.

In the effort to create a new vision of life, primary care doctors led the way. Although medicine's ranks included both clinicians and research scientists during the struggle against organized religion, the medical profession spoke for both groups. And because primary care doctors comprise the bulk of the medical profession, forming that profession's center of gravity, the revolution to redefine life, like the revolution to redefine unhappiness, became associated with primary care. Certainly, when the media wanted to interview a physician on the question of abortion, assisted suicide, or the role of spirituality in daily health, they didn't call a dermatologist or a plastic surgeon; typically, they called a primary care doctor.

The whole history of the medical profession, the whole bent of doctors' personalities since they adopted the outlook of engineers, seems to disqualify them from such a big task. If anything, turning unhappiness into a cut-and-dried business suggests a complete lack of imagination on their part, one that would discourage doctors from tackling a problem of even greater complexity—like the question of life. Yet if doctors were alien to life's subtleties their initial success in managing unhappiness as an engineering problem convinced them that their solution was efficacious for all ills, including life. Had they been given half a chance, they would have turned politics into an engineering problem. And ironically (given the public's fury toward doctors in the late 1960s), this engineering bent worked for doctors rather than against them. Unlike some clergymen, who hovered near the far aerial boundaries of fancy and philosophy when talking about life, doctors radiated a no-nonsense quality, confining their ideas to the solid earth. Realistic and hyperpractical, doctors were hard to excite, which made the public feel secure; their lack of imagination made them seem trustworthy and without a secret agenda, since no one with such a lack of imagination could have a secret agenda. Unlike clergymen, doctors were neither subtle nor profound nor impassioned, yet their complete flatness and stolid plainness inspired confidence and respect. People distrustful of clergymen were only too happy to take their cue from doctors.

The revolution to redefine life took place in three phases, with each phase covered separately in the next three chapters. In the first phase, during the early 1980s, doctors defined when the life of the body begins and ends. In the second phase, during the late 1980s, doctors who now ruled the body grabbed control of the mind. In the third phase, during the 1990s, doctors who now ruled the mind and the body grabbed control of the spirit. Once doctors controlled all three—mind, body, and spirit—they controlled the question of life and, derivatively, the question of unhappiness.

Ultimately, it was a contest of ideologies. Both the medical profession and organized religion pushed their respective points of view, not because any government contract hinged on the outcome but to enlighten the nation. For both sides, faith lay at the living core of what they fought for. Each side thought itself useful, beneficent, and disinterested; each side believed its worldview would most help Americans.

Still, throughout the struggle doctors lacked any sense of the grand strategy that I impart to them with hindsight. In other words, the revolution to redefine life, unlike the revolution to redefine unhappiness, lacked a specific policy outcome. During the struggle, doctors knew they were fighting and whom they were fighting—religious people—but, other than in abortion and stem cell research, not necessarily *what* they were fighting for, except to build a vision of life that governed the country. In the 1970s and '80s, when primary care doctors battled psychiatrists over the unhappiness problem, they had a specific goal in mind—to treat unhappy people with drugs. In the 1980s and

'90s, when doctors and scientists strove to understand how the brain worked and then found themselves in conflict with religious people, they envisioned no specific course of action. They certainly didn't envision bringing unhappiness under tighter medical control.

Nor were the three phases of the revolution coordinated in any serious way. Doctors pushing a woman's freedom to choose, for example, lacked any connection with scientists probing the mind. Even if doctors knew these scientists, they probably wouldn't have understood half the stuff they were doing. To this day, most doctors fail to recognize that a medical revolution to redefine life has even occurred, let alone the fact that it occurred under their auspices.

Nevertheless, while neither calculated nor planned, an alternative vision of life flowed out of the medical profession starting in the 1980s, which stymied organized religion and cleared the way for doctors to assume total control over unhappiness in this country. The medical profession's determination to manage unhappiness fueled this confrontation and made a medical vision of life both necessary and inevitable. More revolution was the only way Artificial Happiness could assure its own survival.

The origins of this contest stretch deep into American history. By the time the medical profession and organized religion met in battle, trouble had been brewing for decades. Let's take nineteenth-century America as our starting point.

THE NINETEENTH-CENTURY AMERICAN

Every Sunday morning during the 1890s Corra Harris rode through rural Georgia in an old wagon sitting next to her husband, who was a "circuit rider," a title given to ministers who traveled great distances to preach in remote parts of the country. With sun-battered faces and work-stained hands, the mountain people on the Harrises' circuit seemed to grow out of the very soil they tilled, spending their days in unceasing drudgery, sacrificing their lives just to stay alive. Rather than tempt these people with pretty stories of an afterlife, however, Corra and her husband delivered a stern message about *this* life. They explained why this world is the way it is and how people should live amidst hardship. Life's goal wasn't happiness, but passing God's test, Reverend Harris declared, and the mountain people took his message to heart. In her autobiography, *A Circuit Rider's Wife*, Corra observes:

> They [mountain people] were not happy nor good [sic], but they were Scriptural. The men were in solemn bondage to Heaven. Religion was a sort of life sentence they worked out with awful diligence. And the women seemed "born again" just to fade and pray, not as these women of the world fade, utterly, but like fair tea-roses plucked for an altar, that wither soon.

Mountain people were not the only Americans to see life through religion's prism; many Americans during the nineteenth century did the same. Although reasons for worshipping varied across the continent, enough Americans approached religion the same way Corra's mountain folk did to produce a distinctive American personality: calmly stoical; detached from others; ambitious, but with scruples; pleasure-seeking, but with an underlying seriousness; enterprising six days a week, but thoughtful on the seventh, when the American rested from his exertions, went to church, and pondered the eternal.

Visiting Europeans commented on this odd personality of

the nineteenth-century American and religion's role in creating it. As you read through some of their firsthand accounts, sentences appear that give you a sense of what many nineteenth-century Americans were like: Alexis de Tocqueville in *Democracy in America*: "Even in their zeal there generally is something so indescribably tranquil, methodical, and deliberate that it would seem as if the head far more than the heart brought them to the foot of the altar."; James Bryce in *The American Commonwealth*: "They have an intelligent interest in the form of faith they profess, are pious without superstition, and zealous without bigotry."; Max Weber in *The Protestant Ethic and the Spirit of Capitalism*: "This [Protestant] asceticism turned with all its force against one thing: the spontaneous enjoyment of life and all it had to offer."

The medical profession in nineteenth-century America adopted a similar approach to unhappiness. Most doctors, like most clergymen, saw everyday unhappiness as a normal fact of existence, like bad weather, something to be faced forthrightly and not just tricked away. As a general rule, neither clergymen nor doctors paid much attention to everyday unhappiness because people's lives were difficult and there was little that could be done. However, individual doctors, like individual clergymen, could rise to the occasion. My grandfather, born in the nineteenth century, had a sanguine temperament and a genial disposition; he was subtle and worldly-wise, warm but firm when dealing with unhappiness. His sympathy had the great merit of being practical, a quality acquired not through any professional training but in the course of everyday life. His strength in dealing with unhappiness lay in his ability to put unhappiness in perspective.

Unhappiness wasn't a disease in nineteenth-century America. Although some Americans treated unhappiness with laudanum, a mixture of opium and alcohol, laudanum was a general remedy, not a specific treatment for unhappiness. (People used it for coughs and back pain as well). Doctors did not prescribe laudanum for unhappiness, though a subgroup of unhappy people abused the drug in private and in shame. Even psychiatrists expended little energy on people's unhappiness, spending most of their careers in asylums caring for the insane. Some psychiatrists called depression a brain disorder ("melancholia"), yet melancholia included far too much pathology to ever be confused with everyday unhappiness; today, melancholia would include depression, schizophrenia, and obsessive-compulsive disorder. Even "simple melancholia," the most likely counterpart to today's "minor depression," bore symptoms more akin to major clinical depression.

Dr. George Beard moved nineteenth-century American medicine closest to the problem of everyday unhappiness, but not that close. Having already gained notoriety for promoting electricity as a tonic, Beard invented the diagnosis of "neurasthenia" to describe a common form of anxiety. Yet Beard used biology merely to explain how the body manifested unhappiness—"an exhaustion of nerve force"—and not why unhappiness occurred. Unlike contemporary psychotropic drug ideology, which credits unhappiness to a neurotransmitter imbalance, Beard blamed unhappiness on culture—for example, the fast pace of modern life, the roar of the steam engine, and society's obsession with punctuality. Comparing the unhappy American with the contented preindustrial savage, he says:

> The savage has no property and cannot fail; he has so little to win of wealth or possessions, that he has no need to be anxious. If his wife does not suit he divorces or murders her; and if all things seem to go wrong he kills himself.

In 1875 a second American doctor, Silas Weir Mitchell, devised the rest cure for neurasthenia, which included total isolation, a long stay in bed, no reading, and no speaking. The rest cure was expensive, and both it and the diagnosis of neurasthenia were reserved for upper-class individuals. By the end of the nineteenth century, a subculture of neurasthenics arose among the international elite, with members traveling back and forth across the Atlantic looking for relief. Doctors treating these patients grew rich (Dr. Mitchell made $70,000 a year, an enormous sum for the time) but touched relatively few lives.

Because both clergymen and doctors in this era distanced themselves from the problem of everyday unhappiness, tension over the issue was rare. Tension over any issue was rare, since doctors cared for the body, clergymen cared for the soul, and people managed unhappiness on their own. By keeping to their respective spheres, doctors and clergymen lived together in order and peace.

Occasionally, scientific progress thrust clergymen and doctors into sensitive confrontation. The discovery of the reflex arc in 1823 proved that nerves could fire without brain input, which meant that some human behavior occurred reflexively—without input from the soul. Clergymen believed insanity was proof of the soul's derangement and a moral issue; to their consternation, the reflex arc made it possible to uncouple human behavior from the soul, potentially robbing mental illness of moral content. Some clergymen resisted the inevitable logic; a few ministers even trespassed the asylum to warn inmates that God was their only salvation.

The fact that psychiatrists barely protested these intrusions is highly significant. The balance of power between organized religion and the medical profession during this period, to the extent that a balance of power existed, tilted toward organized religion, and doctors knew it. The public respected organized religion more than they did the medical profession. In their weakened state, psychiatrists were sometimes even forced to share authority over their science with clergymen. In 1840, Harper and Brothers, responding to popular demand for a book on mental illness, hired a minister rather than a psychiatrist as the author. Five years later, when a doctor published a book linking excessive religious zeal with insanity, the press and the clergy attacked him so vigorously that he had to declare his belief in God and religion to save his reputation.

In the nineteenth century, organized religion told many Americans to make the best of life. As Edwin Hubbel Chapin, a popular preacher of the era, declared, "Not in achievement, but in endurance, of the human soul, does it show its divine grandeur and its alliance with the infinite." Messages like his shaped many people's response to unhappiness. Clear and steady, the idealized version of the nineteenth-century American credited God and his own hands when things went well. When things went badly, he blamed no one, muttering, "Things just didn't turn out for me," or "I had bad luck in life." His approach to unhappiness was fairly simple and the situation remained unchanged until the 1950s.

THE FIFTIES

During the 1950s, many Americans anxiously soaped up the windows of their houses to keep the neighbors from looking in until the better furniture arrived. It was enough to be in any one of these houses to know what the furniture would be like in all the other houses, even to know how the furniture would be arranged; yet these Americans couldn't rest until their house shared an amazing similarity with all the others. Something in the American character had changed. Although the new character type went by several different names—the "Organization Man," the "other-directed person," and the "status-seeker"—each name captured the same phenomenon: how Americans felt about themselves now depended less on religious belief and more on how other people saw them. Americans craved peer approval, hence the new obsession with conforming.

The rise of the modern corporation hastened the change. Unlike the older free-market ethos, which stressed individualism, the new corporate climate in businesses like Ford and IBM emphasized the group. Executives wore company faces, while personnel managers administered tests to prospective employees to predict whether they would follow the company way. Businessmen in general learned that conforming and being well-liked advanced their careers. Yet a change in American religion also played a role in the new order's development. Writing in the 1950s, journalist William Whyte, author of *The Organization Man*, devoted an entire chapter in his book to the decline of the traditional Protestant Ethic and the rise of what he called the new Social Ethic. Instead of being fortified by an inward faith in God, the Organization Man looked outward toward his peers for guidance; this was the Social Ethic. Subscribing to this new ethic, the American church became just another place for the Organization Man to fit in and belong. Although being popular was irrelevant to eternal salvation, it was essential for happiness. Old sectarian disputes over the best way to heaven gave way to a more nondenominational idea that the church should be socially useful and win people friends.

In the 1950s religion stopped being the determinant factor in the American character. Religion just followed the popular culture. Whatever the popular culture preached, so, too, did the churches and synagogues. Clergymen conformed as eagerly as everyone else. Writing in 1958, C. Wright Mills, sociologist and author of *White Collar* and *The Power Elite*, noted, "If there is a safe prediction about religion in this society, it would seem that if tomorrow official spokesmen were to proclaim XYZ-ism, next week 90 percent of religious declaration would be XYZ-ist. . . . As a social and as a personal force, religion has become a dependent variable. It does not originate: it reacts."

Because religion stayed popular, the change was subtle. Like the America that preceded it, 1950s America was still Christian America. Religious affiliation in the United States actually shot up to an all-time high in 1958, with 48 percent of Americans going to church or synagogue regularly. What changed was *why* people worshipped. Rather than to fulfill some holy duty, many Americans went to church to relieve themselves of anxiety, whatever the anxiety's cause—a crumbling marriage, loneliness, a lost job, or the looming Communist threat. Popular clergymen told people how to find happiness, or at least reassured them that things would go well. Norman Vincent Peale declared, "Our happiness depends on the habit of mind we cultivate. So practice happy thinking every day. Cultivate the merry heart, develop the happiness habit, and life will become a continual feast." Billy Graham, evangelist and author of the 1955 best seller *The Secret of Happiness*, said, "I've read the last page of the Bible. It's all going to turn out all right." Bishop Fulton Sheen, author of the 1954 best seller *Way to Happiness*, told unhappy people to go to confession, which he called "the key to happiness in the modern world." For organized religion, helping people find and experience happiness had become a major purpose.

Although some Americans truly believed in religion, many others contrived to be seen as faithful in the hope of receiving happiness as if it were a special gratuity. Rather than question the motive behind this new religiosity, churches encouraged it. Clergymen told parishioners that God would reward them with happiness so long as they worshipped. As one bulletin put out by the Protestant Council of New York City read, "Come and enjoy our privileges, meet good friends, and see what God can do for you!"

In the country at large, religion became a kind of "national talisman" to ensure continuation of the economic expansion, an insurance policy against the end of affluence. Much of religion was more sentimental and patriotic than it was Christian.

For organized religion it was a fatal error—an error from which it never fully recovered. During this period the medical profession also entered the unhappiness field, through psychotherapy, causing organized religion and the medical profession to converge on a common mission: happiness. The convergence not only locked organized religion and the medical profession in competitive rivalry but also brought religion down to medicine's level. Before, religion stood apart from medicine the way it generally avoided meddling in politics; nothing that happened in either medicine or politics (e.g., a discovery, an election) threatened the sanctity of religion because religion operated on an entirely different plane. It was timeless. Its veracity depended not on empirical proof or poll numbers but on faith, and no change on earth could perturb that faith. It was precisely because religion stood apart from earthly endeavors that religion endured despite change. Once organized religion and the medical profession embarked on a common mission, it was only a matter of time before people started asking which discipline did the better job and researchers crunched the numbers to prove it. Suddenly, religion's value depended on outcomes. Although religion soared high in the 1950s, it could also sink low. The medical profession only had to work a little harder at making people happy.

Although doctors in the 1950s entered the unhappiness field to meet the new public demand, they also rode a larger trend in American medicine. In the early 1900s European and American psychiatry went their separate ways. European (especially German) psychiatry followed the path of Kurt Schneider, who built a model of mental illness that set the sick apart from the merely chronically unhappy. In contrast, American psychiatry, under the influence of Adolf Meyer, put mental illness and everyday unhappiness on a continuum. Small neuroses dismissed by past generations of doctors loomed large in Meyer's psychotherapeutic model. Not surprisingly, as the line of demarcation between real pathology and everyday unhappiness blurred, American psychiatrists grew increasingly involved in the care of unhappiness. The management of middle-class neurotics became a staple of American psychiatric office practice. Although unhappiness was not yet an official disease (at most, it was a psychological disease, not a biological one), many American psychiatrists saw unhappiness as a problem worthy of their attention.

Although the convergence of doctors and clergymen put both groups on the road to competitive rivalry, a spirit of collaboration actually prevailed during the 1950s. One of the earliest examples of collaboration was the creation of the Midwest Christian Counseling Center in Kansas City. Opened in 1957, the center mixed Christian counseling with psychotherapy to help unhappy people without forcing them to choose between psychotherapy and faith; thus, clergymen and psychiatrists were pursuing the same goal and creating a common means to get there. Still, psychiatrists and psychologists were junior partners in the new alliance. Although faith-based counseling resembled psychotherapy, the public looked suspiciously on the latter as something foreign and strange. Only if clergymen put a religious face on therapy would the public accept it; thus, clergymen became the front men, translating psychotherapy into religious language for popular consumption. Some psychiatrists resented having to suffer the indignity of watching clergymen corrupt their technique, but public opinion favored religion and there was little psychiatrists could do about it. Drug therapy for unhappiness wasn't yet an option. One of the first psychotropic drugs, Thorazine, introduced in 1952, treated only schizophrenia, while Miltown, a popular antianxiety aid during this era, caused muscle weakness and drowsiness, invalidating it for long-term use. To reach the unhappy masses, psychiatrists had no choice but to play second fiddle to churchmen.

Norman Vincent Peale was a leading exemplar of the new collaborative effort, with his book, *The Power of Positive Thinking*, second only to the Bible in book sales from 1952 to 1955. Peale started out in the 1930s writing guides to happiness that mixed Christian ideas with psychiatry, with one of his earliest tracts written jointly with a Freudian psychoanalyst. He promised Americans happiness, emotional security, and self-assurance if they just took "God in as a partner" and followed some easy five-step programs. Peale's message, that we "manufacture our own happiness" and "nearly all basic problems are personal, the result of inner conflicts," was right out of the psychology handbook, but he creatively weaved these ideas into his sermons at his popular Marble Collegiate Church in Manhattan.

What Peale did for white, middle-class, mainline Protestants (the "organization men" of Whyte's book), Billy Graham did for lower-middle class and working-class Evangelicals and Fulton Sheen did for American Catholics. All three ministers mixed a lot of religion with a little bit of psychology to service people's everyday psychological needs. Americans of all backgrounds, caught up in the new impulse to feel happy, turned to religion and medicine, with a bias toward religion. For clergymen, the

1950s represented the best of all possible worlds, when medicine was effective enough to assist them but also weak enough to be their pliable tool. Little did they know that by allying with doctors to fight unhappiness they were slipping down an inclined plane, at the bottom of which lay one thing and one thing only—medicine's triumph. The only question was how long it would take to get there.

THE SIXTIES AND SEVENTIES

The 1967 movie *The Graduate* dramatically exposed the rot in the Organization Man's life. In the movie's climactic wedding scene, Elaine sees Benjamin hovering in the distance, a man with an uncertain future whom she loves. She turns to her repressed, teeth-clenched fiancé, then to her repressed, teeth-clenched, alcoholic mother, then to her repressed, teeth-clenched father, and finally to Benjamin, at which point she screams out his name—an eruption of intense feeling that her peers try to repress—and runs toward him. For many viewers, the scene was a defining moment. They learned that sacrificing individual feelings and obsessing about status didn't bring happiness; following one's inner voice did.

At first, the new idea thrived on the margins, in the counterculture, especially among hippies, who preached free love, danced in the streets, and took drugs to feel in new ways. Hatred of the Vietnam War and capitalism fueled the hippie phenomenon, but just as the rise of the Organization Man had a religious dimension, so, too, did the rise of the hippie. Best-selling books like William Braden's *The Age of Aquarius* and Timothy Leary's *The Politics of Ecstasy* documented the new spirituality. In *The Greening of America*, Charles Reich praised the counterculture's spiritual goals, including a more liberated individual and an end to the loneliness and emptiness of American life. Although Reich also attacked the pernicious Corporate State, economic change ranked low on the list of what the hippie movement wanted to accomplish. Over time, counterculture ideas went mainstream; by the 1970s the Organization Man was no more.

Many Americans, however, had a rude awakening, as they discovered that free love and listening to one's inner voice didn't bring happiness. Life was still difficult and unfair, giving people plenty of reasons to feel down. Organized religion was a logical place to turn, since it had eased people's anxieties in the 1950s, but things had changed. Because organized religion mimicked the larger cultural trends in the 1950s, many Americans associated religion with repression and conformism. It is no coincidence that *The Graduate's* crucial scene takes place in a cold, sterile church, blindingly white, yet tasteless—like white bread—and a painful reminder to Elaine of what living with an Organization Man, playing the phony, and upholding the status quo is like.

Sensing their vulnerability, some clergymen fell in step with the new counterculture and changed their emphasis. Influenced by the writings of German theologian Dietrich Bonhoeffer, who spoke of a "religionless Christianity" and social action, they threw themselves into the civil rights struggle and the war on poverty. But when these clergymen adopted the progressive agenda many believers just felt abandoned; religion's vision of life became less a reality with everyday consequences and more just a pious wish. Soon, organized religion was in free fall. Weekly church and synagogue attendance in the United States fell to around 40 percent, with some studies putting the number closer to the mid-thirties. Mainline Protestant denominations were particularly hard hit, suffering actual drops in membership. In this unstable environment, some clergymen contented themselves with people worshipping out of habit or for the organ music. With their popularity hanging by a thread, these clergymen adopted a new, more tolerant attitude toward faith, surmising that if organized religion couldn't give people happiness, at least it shouldn't undercut the feeling by making lots of demands on people.

One thing organized religion had going for it during this period was its alliance with the medical profession—more specifically, psychotherapy. But now medicine was no longer the junior partner in the alliance; the relationship had grown more equal and began tilting toward medicine. By the 1970s the American people were so comfortable with psychotherapy that they began talking casually about their odyssey through life in psychological terms (what historian Edward Shorter calls "psychologizing"). Concepts like "personal growth" and "self-actualization" became popular. The religious cover that ministers like Peale gave psychotherapy in the 1950s was no longer necessary.

Even more significant, clergymen began to doubt their own paradigm, putting psychology ahead of theology. In the 1960s, psychology and counseling techniques began appearing in the training curricula for ministers, priests, and rabbis. Many clergymen were enthusiastic about the new approach, with their new interest in psychology balanced by a declining interest in traditional religious practices and convictions. Meanwhile, the Christian mental health industry took off. Preachers James Dobson, Tim La Haye, and Larry Crabb set up entire ministries around psychotherapy, telling believers that God cared as much for their mental health as for their souls. In the 1950s, clergymen used psychology to further core religious ideas; by the 1970s psychology was a core idea, as many clergymen exchanged traditional notions of sin, evil, and damnation for psychology's odyssey of self-discovery, reinforcing psychology as life's organizing principle for millions of Americans.

But psychology didn't make people happy, whether the care-giver was a psychiatrist or a minister, with growing evidence showing this to be the case. By the 1970s, sociologist Christopher Lasch, in his best-selling book, *The Culture of Narcissism*, described a new American character type: the self-absorbed narcissist. Plagued by anxiety, unhappiness, vague discontents, and a sense of inner emptiness, the narcissist tries different forms of psychology (e.g., *est*, gestalt therapy, and analysis) but happiness remains beyond his grasp. The narcissist is bland and submissive but seething with inner anger. In the late 1970s, America was full of narcissists, and their unhappiness was fast becoming a national tragedy.

The Culture of Narcissism still makes for interesting reading; nonetheless, it is a period piece. When Lasch wrote in the 1970s, psychotherapy's wide public appeal was relatively new. Although some psychiatrists had already lost heart over therapy's promise, the public had just begun to take the discipline seriously. Today, with psychotherapy almost passé among doctors and the public, Lasch's criticism of psychology, even his use of psychological categories to frame arguments, is outdated. Some critics still think it worth the effort to attack the "therapeutic culture." Examples of the attack are James Davison Hunter in *The Death of Character* and, more recently, Christina Hoff Sommers and Sally Satel, MD, in *One Nation Under Therapy*. These authors see psychotherapy as religion's main rival and the tension between therapy and religion as a crucial fault line in American society. But in the 1970s, the first stage of the medical practice revolution—a revolution in which psychotherapy plays no role—changed the dynamic between organized religion and the medical profession altogether. With its emergence, the war between religion and psychotherapy became yesterday's war. The war between religion and real medicine had begun.

In the 1970s an immense antagonism grew up between clergymen and psychiatrists, replacing the good feeling that had surrounded their earlier collaborations. The turnaround among clergymen was understandable: as early supporters of psychology, imagine their rage when Freud, not Jesus, gained ascendancy in America. Nonetheless, the hostility between the two groups had little time to mature, for the medical practice revolution had begun. Clergymen and psychiatrists had a new common enemy: primary care doctors wielding psychotropic drugs.

A TITANIC SHIFT

Sometimes a tiny entry in a boring textbook offers the best indication that a social upheaval has occurred. In this case, the textbook is the *International Classification of Diseases* (*ICD*) and the entry is "life."

As discussed earlier in this book, the *ICD* was created for the purpose of assigning every medical disease a numerical code and has a long history. The coding of diseases actually dates back to seventeenth-century England, where statistics were collected through a system called the London Bills of Mortality. By 1937 the system had evolved into the International List of Causes of Death. The World Health Organization took the project over in 1948, publishing causes of morbidity and mortality in its slender *ICD* and making revisions every ten years. The book grew thicker over time, giving such a complete account of all the bad things that can happen to people that by the 1980s, I, along with other doctors-in-training, amused ourselves at night by imagining obscure conditions, then checking to see if the *ICD*'s authors had enough foresight to imagine the same conditions and assign them codes. The authors usually won, remembering to assign codes for such rare maladies as getting lost at sea and hit by lightning; they even thought up a code for being denied a room at a hotel. But at no time between the seventeenth century and the 1970s did the *ICD* have a code for "everyday life trouble." Nor was there a code for "unhappiness." In a 1978 edition of the *ICD*, based on a 1975 revision, code V62 makes its first appearance ("anxiety caused by unemployment"). Then, in 1989, code V62.89, or "life circumstance problem," appears. A code for "unhappiness" appears for the first time in the same edition.

It is no coincidence that codes for "life" and "unhappiness" make their first appearance in the same edition, and in an edition compiled during the 1980s. Religion and psychotherapy's failure left many Americans confused. Chaos reigned, and into this chaos rushed primary care doctors, not because these doctors actively conspired to fill the void with a vision of their own—at least, not at first—but because Americans craved a practical solution to unhappiness, and clearly there was only one party able in terms of power and prestige and willing in its strength to provide such a solution: primary care doctors prescribing psychotropic drugs.

The motives for the medical practice revolution have already been described. By pushing psychotropic drugs, primary care doctors arrested the medical profession's decline. Yet, for many Americans, fixing unhappiness fell short of what was needed. Religion's decline left people without a vision to answer the fundamental questions of existence, questions such as when life begins and when it ends. People sensed an intellectual void that even Artificial Happiness couldn't fill. Even doctors sensed a void, since the decline in religion's vision brought confusion to their own practices, including, for example, whether to terminate a pregnancy or when to cut off life support. Amidst the public's restlessness and religion's ruin, doctors felt compelled to fill the void with their own vision of life. Having already succeeded on the unhappiness front, they mobilized for this much bigger task, starting with the question of when life begins and ends.

Doctors proceeded confidently but cautiously. Confidence grew out of their reputation for scientific accomplishment. Although many physician-engineers lacked bedside manner, medicine's engineering feats, including its most recent triumph over unhappiness, had attained an almost magical prestige among the public; a mysterious glamour lingered about doctors. While it was possible to politely ignore a philosopher on the question of life, it was impossible to ignore the medical profession. In addition, political liberals possessed a reflexive negative attitude toward religion, to the point that whatever religion wanted they would oppose. Doctors, quite rightly, sensed the wind at their backs.

Yet doctors remained understandably cautious. Organized religion, after all, hadn't collapsed altogether. A precipitate debate between doctors and clergymen over the existence of God would only arouse unnecessary resistance from the general public. Therefore, doctors couched their arguments about life in technical terms, which played to their strength, anyhow. They paid lip service to the accepted doctrine that religion knows best about life's purpose—a convenient ploy, as will be shown—and stuck to the matter of life's beginning and end.

In 1981 Dr. Clifford Grobstein, an experimental biologist and my professor in medical school, wrote a book about abortion ethics called *From Chance to Purpose*. This was around the time of Cindy Dimas's abortion, when most pro-choice doctors, reluctant to call the fetus nonlife, defended abortion by arguing that women with unwanted pregnancies were at risk for clinical depression, or by going outside of medicine altogether and appealing to women's individual rights. Dr. Grobstein's book signaled a change in the medical profession's thinking. He argued that abortion's rightness hinges on the fetus's capacity for consciousness and not on any risk to the mother's health. By all scientific measures, a fetus during the first two months of development lacks the rudimentary nervous system to make self-awareness possible, thus making abortion during the first trimester moral.

The medical profession adopted Dr. Grobstein's syllogism: self-awareness is felt inside the mind; since there can be no self-awareness without a mind and doctors know when the mind begins, it follows that doctors know when life begins. Dr. Grobstein's model dominates the medical profession's thinking on abortion and embryonic research to this day. Liberals also support the model. They argue that because women have self-awareness, which embryos lack, the balance tips in women's favor.

Nothing in liberal philosophy compelled liberals to embrace Dr. Grobstein's model. If anything, liberalism preaches the sanctity of the individual, especially disadvantaged individuals who can't speak for themselves—such as embryos. Liberalism alone can't have pushed embryos out from underneath their protective umbrella. True, the women's movement in the 1960s and 1970s championed women's rights, which influenced people's thinking on abortion, but it affected only one part of the equation. Although strong on women's rights, the women's movement failed to develop a philosophy that devalued a fetus's rights. Minus that philosophy, abortion remained one person trampling on the rights of another.

Nor, for that matter, was there anything in medicine's tradition driving the new model. On the contrary, doctors like to think in discrete categories. Because the moment of conception draws a clear line between reproductive events compared to the onset of self-awareness, which is spread out over time, the former was a better fit for doctors. In addition, the original Hippocratic Oath carries a proscription against abortion.

Instead, both the medical profession and liberals accepted a defense of abortion that combined organized religion's new emphasis on happiness with psychotropic drug ideology. A major goal of organized religion since the 1950s had been happiness, whether in the form of well-being or contentment. Christian therapists counseled people to make them happier, or at least less anxious. Liberal clergymen grew absorbed in the details of public policy, fighting over a few percentage points in the tax code, even lending support to socialist movements abroad, such as Catholic liberation theology. As a presidential candidate, the Reverend Jesse Jackson was no different from any other politician promising to gratify people's wishes. At the other end of the spectrum, many religious conservatives saw religion as the faithful custodian of law and order. The conservative Family Research Council promoted "the Judeo-Christian worldview as the basis for a just, free, and stable society," the word "stable" a codeword for a society that protected private property. Some religious leaders even sold religion as a method of self-preservation: evangelist Pat Robertson claimed to have used the power of prayer to steer a hurricane away from his office, which was only a half step away from using prayer for less essential purposes. Whether by advancing the well-being of the individual, the family, the working class, or society as a whole, organized religion across the political spectrum had become seriously involved in helping people find or keep their happiness.

Doctors and liberals didn't need organized religion to see abortion as a question of happiness, but organized religion's own emphasis on happiness and on fostering those conditions conducive to people's greatest well-being confirmed them in their belief that they were right to do so. With growing confidence, doctors defended people who terminated unwanted pregnancies to preserve their happiness. "Life is short. Take what you can get from it," one doctor I know told a patient struggling with whether to have an abortion. The fetus itself was viewed through the prism of happiness, as doctors told expectant parents with deformed fetuses that their children, if born, would live hellish lives, unhappy lives, which was a sufficient reason to abort. Even healthy fetuses born into unhappy circumstances were destined for unhappy lives, doctors noted.

Still, there was the question of whether a fetus feels pain, or some kind of unhappiness, during the abortion. Although desiring happiness for themselves, few people felt comfortable enjoying happiness at another person's expense. Their dilemma mirrored the larger one born in organized religion's new emphasis on well-being: how much personal well-being should an individual sacrifice for the welfare of society, family, or another individual? Reconciling the contradiction between the desire for personal well-being, now lauded by organized religion, and religious teachings that demanded that an individual sacrifice his well-being for the well-being of the larger group or of another individual seemed impossible. Dr. Grobstein's model, working in concert with psychotropic drug ideology, solved this dilemma as it pertained to abortion.

Dr. Grobstein equated the onset of life with the capacity for consciousness. But that aspect of consciousness that really concerned people in the abortion debate was happiness. When did the fetus develop the capacity for happiness, which would be sacrificed in an abortion? In some Christian theology, for example, a fetus ensouled at the moment of conception was capable of living happily with God if a miscarriage occurred during the first trimester. This capacity for happiness made the developing fetus a person and abortion a form of murder. Although Dr. Grobstein's model spoke only of the development of consciousness, leaving unresolved the question of whether a fetus feels happiness, doctors applied psychotropic drug ideology to Dr. Grobstein's model to tilt the debate against the fetus. Because unhappiness turns on neurotransmitters and because the existence of neurotransmitters requires the existence of basic neural machinery, a fetus cannot feel unhappiness before such machinery exists. Although doctors didn't know when the capacity for happiness appears in a developing fetus, even common sense dictated that no chance of unhappiness exists before the capacity for consciousness.

Once this connection was made, no further explorations in fetal development were needed to justify abortion. The syllogism was now complete: the larger culture prizes happiness and unwanted pregnancies lead to unhappiness. The question is whether a first trimester fetus feels unhappiness during an abortion; by anchoring unhappiness in neurotransmitters, psychotropic drug ideology rules out this possibility because a first trimester fetus's neurology is unformed.

Before the rise of psychotropic drug ideology or the change in organized religion's mission, doctors could not have made this intellectual leap. Their engineering model extended no further than an understanding of the body. They assumed unhappiness was cultural in origin rather than a product of neurotransmitter imbalance. Even the question of whether people should strive for happiness in this life or the next was beyond medicine's comprehension. However, once organized religion made happiness in this life a major priority and once doctors turned that happiness into an engineering matter, the engineering analogy became the basis for all theory regarding life's onset. A distinction arose between a mere collection of cells that lacked the machinery to feel happiness and a human being fully equipped to do so. By making this distinction, doctors stripped the first trimester fetus of personhood, including its rights, broke the stalemate between a fetus's rights and a mother's rights, and swayed the debate in favor of abortion.

Doctors naturally extended their logic to encompass the end of life. The same year that Dr. Grobstein published his book, other doctors changed the definition of death. The 1981 report of the President's Commission for the Study of Ethical Problems in Biomedical and Behavioral Research is a milestone in medical ethics. Previously, death was seen as the cessation of circulation and respiration. The 1981 report codified a new idea called "brain death," which was first proposed at Harvard Medical School in 1968. The report said that brain death equals human death, even when circulation and ventilator-assisted respiration continue. Death no longer turned on whether the person had "given up the ghost," but on whether the person retained any capacity for thought and therefore self-awareness. By 1989, some bioethicists were already promoting the idea of "higher brain death" to complete the revolution begun by the 1981 report. Their criteria for death were even looser than in the earlier report, though more precise in regard to what medical science was trying to accomplish. They argued that death occurs when only the cerebral cortex, that part of the brain necessary for consciousness, permanently ceases to function. Without a capacity for consciousness there was no capacity for happiness, and without a capacity for happiness there was no life.

Applying psychotropic drug ideology, doctors succeeded in framing life between two new points—between the onset and end of consciousness—giving them complete rights to the life of the body: beginning, middle, and end. More important, their vision touched people's imaginations, producing palpable change in public opinion. The majority of Americans began to view abortion in the first trimester as moral. Attitudes toward end-of-life issues also changed: five decades ago, only 37 percent of Americans supported physician-assisted suicide; today, the number is 67 percent. Medicine suddenly became an indissoluble part of people's whole scheme of things. The fact that doctors already played an important role in people's lives explains their considerable influence, but not this strange and momentous change, which was in no way inevitable.

The doctors themselves learned something important about organized religion during the debate: although outwardly zealous, some religious people seemed inwardly hesitant and unsure. Obsessing about abortion, religious people acted as if they had been disoriented by a tremendous blow, and, now, fighting for their lives, flailed wildly at the nearest thing. Religious people fought doctors on abortion not just because their tradition com manded them to—on the contrary, Christianity and Judaism have a complicated history in regard to abortion policy—but in part because they were afraid of doctors. Religious people already took it for granted that doctors could do anything, like some demonic force; whenever public opinion turned against religion's position on beginning-of-life and end-of-life issues, religious people blamed doctors for orchestrating the shift. Lacking any grand strategy, religious people dared not cede any ground.

But the tenaciousness with which these religious people fought doctors over the definition of life's beginning and end only convinced doctors that the future favored them. The doctors smelled weakness, and they moved into the next two battles with more confidence than ever.

A USEFUL DIVERSION

Several years ago, I participated in a conference on medicine and society attended mainly by religious conservatives. Most of the panelists called embryonic stem cell research and physician-assisted suicide the two great terrors of civilization. At one point I rose in disagreement, noting that millions of Americans take psychotropic drugs to boost their spirits, wreaking havoc on their lives; and I asked why the panelists ignore this problem. In regard to medicine and society, I continued, Artificial Happiness poses a far greater risk to the social fabric than the destruction of embryos or the eagerness of a few dying Americans to see what lies on the other side. My remarks were received with a politeness that only faintly concealed a total lack of interest. The panelists simply didn't see Artificial Happiness as a problem.

Medicine's vision of life filled religious people with alarm. They saw quite rightly that doctors threatened them in an ideological and systematic way. Yet religious people (mostly religious conservatives) decided to focus on beginning-of-life and end-of-life issues instead of on doctors' subsequent efforts to redefine the life of the mind and the spirit. The life of the body became their field of action; abortion, stem cell research, and physician-assisted suicide became their issues. To this day, Artificial Happiness barely registers on their list of fears, many of them just as eager as doctors to help people find happiness. Although the ideology that gave rise to Artificial Happiness provides an important defense of abortion, religious conservatives fail to see this connection, let alone see how the change in organized religion itself contributed to the new state of affairs. Instead, they put all their energy toward reversing court rulings. Even then, religious conservatives have accomplished little, other than to prevent medicine's understanding of life's onset and end from being carried to excess, for example, joining with many liberals to beat back infanticide and euthanasia. They remain in the minority on abortion and stem cell research.

Religious conservatism's focus on life's onset and end actually smoothed the medical profession's path to victory on Artificial Happiness. To neutralize organized religion's role in unhappiness, the medical profession needed to grab control of the mind and the spirit, where unhappiness manifests itself. Grabbing control of the body was just a preparatory step. Looking back on medicine's war against organized religion, the fight over the question of life's onset and end turned out to be a useful diversion, one that soaked up the attention of religious conservatives. It caused conservatives to pay less attention to the next two battles—the most important ones—and gave doctors easy victories.

EIGHT

THE PLIGHT OF SIR JOHN ECCLES

T HE MUSIC BLARED every Friday night, playing to a crowd of scientists trying to get their minds off their cat experiments. In between dance numbers, guests gathered around their host, Dr. John Eccles, who told stories about his Oxford days studying under the great neuroscientist, Sir Charles Sherrington. One story that made the rounds had Sherrington closing up his lab for the day and leaving the test animals behind to roam freely among the benches and sinks. This was common practice at the turn of the twentieth century: after a hard day's work of being experimented on, the test animals would get the night off just like the scientists. On this particular evening, Sherrington locked the door, then peered through the keyhole, wondering what the animals did with their free time. On the other side was a chimpanzee looking back. Apparently, the chimpanzee had wondered the same thing about Sherrington.

For Eccles, the 1940s and early 1950s, spent at the University of Otago in New Zealand, constituted the most fertile period of his career, when his experiments on the motor neurons of cats revolutionized neuroscience and earned him the Nobel Prize in Medicine. Had he died at midcentury, his reputation would have been that of a courtly genius who advanced the world's understanding of the brain, not an overbearing fanatic who pushed a dying idea. But, as a matter of fact, Eccles lived for another half century, and during most of that long period he slaved away on behalf of a hopeless cause called "dualism." Dualism was the fulcrum on which he hoped to move the world. Everywhere he went, he worked its lever, trying in vain to keep people from going over to the dark side of "monism," lecturing people with stern piety. Toward the end of his life, his desire to convince people of his ideas could barely be distinguished from mania. Most poignant, Eccles lived long enough to witness his own failure: the age of dualism, an era that covered more than three centuries, ended under his watch.

Ironically, the subtext of Sherrington's funny story alludes to what the fight was all about. Human beings and chimpanzees are amazingly similar creatures; their bodies share 99 percent of their genetic makeup. Even their brains are similar. Nevertheless, according to dualism, human beings and animals are fundamentally different. Dualists like Eccles believed that the human mind was unique and set apart from the physical world of the brain; it was an independent reality that obeyed supernatural principles, a corridor to a mysterious divine world where the laws of chemistry and physics did not hold. Monists, on the other hand, argued that the human mind emerged from the physical structure of the brain; it obeyed scientific laws just like everything else in nature. The monists accused dualists of peddling a ridiculous disjunction between mind and brain out of religious belief. From their perspective, the mind was just an appendage of the body; what distinguished human beings from chimpanzees was not any special mental conduit to God but a little extra gray matter that made human beings smarter.

The plight of Sir John Eccles crosses paths with the story of Artificial Happiness in the late 1980s, when monism triumphed over dualism, giving the medical profession total control over the human mind. Before then, doctors controlled only the body. True, in the early 1980s doctors earned the right to decide life's beginning and end, but so long as dualism was viable they shared control of the mind with religious people, thereby exposing Artificial Happiness to attack. Psychotropic drug ideology, a monist application, blamed unhappiness on neurotransmitters—in other words, on the brain's physical structure—making drug therapy the most logical solution. Dualism challenged this ideology. God rules remotely but with omnipresent force, dualists warned, making unhappiness not a problem of neurotransmitters but a manifestation of God's will. The key to happiness, religious dualists claimed, was getting in right with God.

Even some psychiatrists attacked psychotropic drug ideology from a dualist perspective. As dualism's secular branch, psychotherapy also saw the mind as an independent reality; but, in its model, subconscious forces rather than divine intervention caused unhappiness. These subconscious forces wandered around the mind according to their own laws—laws that had nothing to do with chemistry and physics. Psychotherapy, not drugs, was the best treatment for unhappiness.

With high-toned muster, both psychiatrists and clergymen—especially clergymen—raised doubts in the public imagination as to whether drug therapy for unhappiness was the right answer. Doctors fought back, but with the mind-brain debate unsettled it was impossible to disregard dualism's invisible world, with its tempting image of God the savior, especially when dualists painted their opponents as wicked. When Eccles spoke of monism, a frown deepened on his forehead and his lips pursed; "Don't succumb to materialism!" he warned audiences, as if doing so meant making a pact with the Devil. To continue the medical practice revolution, dualism needed to be thoroughly discredited, which it was finally in the late 1980s.

Although many doctors have never heard of monism or the mind-brain debate, they benefit from monism's triumph. The story of the Artificial Happiness is a story of competing ideologies. Because the medical profession's ideology was rivaled only by religion, any retreat by religion affected the doctors' position. Monism's triumph over dualism signified not only religion's loss but also medicine's gain. True, the direct effect of monism's victory on medical therapy was nil, but important ramifications occurred elsewhere. When neuroscientists showed how the mind could spring from the brain, doctors reaped an overarching conceptual framework to supplement psychotropic drug ideology, thereby boosting Artificial Happiness's legitimacy. The triumph of monism was a moral victory for doctors, who could now deduce Artificial Happiness from the most abstract principles.

ECCLES DISCOVERS DUALISM

Sir John Eccles's life tracks the rise of neuroscience. He was born in Melbourne in 1903, around the time Santiago Ramon-y-Cajal, Spain's most famous scientist, wrote the *Histology of the Nervous System of Man and Vertebrates*, establishing the nervous system's general architecture and identifying neurons (nerve cells) as the system's basic signaling units. A shy man who disliked social interaction, Cajal dreamt of becoming an artist, but his father, a doctor, pushed the young Santiago toward medicine, punishing his resistance by sending him to a school for unruly youths, then forcing him to work as a barber's assistant and a shoe repair boy until Cajal relented. Once in medicine, Cajal turned his love of art toward the world under the microscope; late at night, while lying in bed, he would draw pictures of the brain cells he had studied in the lab that day, creating in the process neuroscience's foundation.

Eccles's future teacher, Sir Charles Sherrington, follows Cajal in neuroscience's pantheon. Doctor, philosopher, and poet, Sherrington worked out the mechanism of spinal reflexes; he even coined the terms "neuron" and "synapse." When Eccles arrived at Oxford in 1925, Sherrington's career was almost at an end, but Sherrington groomed the tall, athletic Rhodes scholar to become neuroscience's third hero. While Cajal discovered the neuron and Sherrington discovered that neurons communicated with one another, Eccles showed how it all worked on the cellular level. In a critical experiment in 1951, Eccles demonstrated that individual neurons communicate through chemicals—neurotransmitters. His pioneering work earned him a knighthood in 1958 and a Nobel Prize in 1963.

Eccles began publishing on the mind-brain problem around the time of his critical experiment. The subject had long interested him. His mentor Sherrington was a dualist, and when Eccles converted to Catholicism to marry his first wife, growing quite devout, his dualist convictions only intensified. Yet a new era in the mind-brain debate dawned during this period, making it a logical time for Eccles to step in.

Descartes' view of mind and brain as two separate realms (known as "Cartesian dualism") had dominated people's thinking on the subject for three centuries. Several monist theories had existed in one form or another since ancient times but had little support. One theory repudiated the mind altogether and argued that only the brain existed; La Mettrie, a French materialist of the eighteenth century, said, "The brain secretes thoughts like the liver secretes bile." A second monist theory granted the mind existence but maintained that feelings and emotions were by-products of random molecular collision. Naturally, the public rejected these theories since they reduced vital life experiences like love and friendship to waves, pulses, and electrons. They also invalidated free will. In the first part of the twentieth century, the psychologists joined the debate, but they were as reductionist as the monists. Behaviorism dominated the field of psychology during the first half of the twentieth century; the school's subscribers ignored consciousness altogether, viewing people as nothing beyond their bodies, and behavior as a mere mechanical response to stimuli.

Two influential books written toward the middle of the twentieth century radically changed the mind-brain debate. First came Erwin Schrodinger's *What is Life?* A Nobel Prize–winning physicist and founder of quantum mechanics, Schrodinger believed science could tackle the question of life without resorting to crude materialism, possibly through a new quantum physics. His book electrified the scientific community. Explaining life—including the mind—within the closed system of chemistry and physics suddenly seemed feasible. The second book, British philosopher Gilbert Ryle's *The Concept of Mind*, criticized dualism for equating the mind with an inner "ghost." No ghost exists inside the body, Ryle said, just because the act of thinking lacks physical expression. Clever and with a good catchphrase (he coined the phrase "ghost in the machine"), Ryle forced a second look at monism. By the time Eccles published his defense of dualism in 1952, many scientists had already joined the monist side.

Eccles hewed closely to the dualist line with only a slight

deviation. He argued that the mind is located within an alternative universe that interacts with matter at a special receiving device inside the brain's cerebral cortex called the "liaison," where EEG activity is most intense during thinking. (Descartes thought the pineal gland was the liaison.) Eccles proposed that the mind thinks a thought, which penetrates the brain at the level of the cerebral cortex, causing neurons to fire, while sensory perceptions flow from the brain into the mind through the same corridor.

The monists laughed, calling Eccles a "cultist" and a "crank," although Eccles cared little for their opinions. Nothing would break the immovability of his faith in dualism; such was the peculiar character of the man. Nevertheless, Eccles accepted the monists' criticism that dualism had a hole that needed to be plugged: it violated the first law of thermodynamics, which states that energy is neither created nor destroyed in a closed system. If the mind lies outside of the matter-energy system, as dualism suggests, yet moves brain matter, then energy will have been created out of nothing. Conversely, if brain matter lies inside the matter-energy system, yet acts on the mind outside that system, then energy will have been destroyed by going nowhere. Both acts violate the first law. To stimulate neurons in the brain, the mind must be part of the matter-energy system, not of another universe.

Eccles wrestled with the energy issue, even flirting with the paranormal to explain it, citing experiments in telepathy where concentrated thought had reportedly moved a pair of dice. But how can a mind move dice if dice lack a cerebral cortex and therefore a "liaison" with the mind? The monists asked this question gleefully. Eccles hesitated, then backtracked, never to mention the paranormal again.

In the 1960s, Eccles opened up a new front against monism using Darwin's theory of evolution. He accepted evolution as applied to the human body but not to the human mind. First, he said, there were too many differences between humans and animals to think that human consciousness evolved from animal consciousness. (For example, only human beings show concern for their dead and only human beings use complex verbal language). Second, he said, each of us experiences selfhood in a unique manner that has nothing to do with his or her genetic inheritance. Twins, for example, share a common gene structure, yet each twin feels selfhood differently. Evolution works on the principle of natural selection: favorable genes are more likely to be passed down to the next generation than unfavorable ones. If the feeling of being an individual isn't tied to some genetic inheritance (i.e., if twins think differently), then it can't be derived from evolution. Eccles called this feeling of selfhood part of the alternative universe and a miracle that evolution couldn't explain.

Eccles's tactic was shrewd. By the 1960s, behavioral psychology, which had ignored the mind-brain problem, had given way to cognitive psychology, which welcomed the problem. Some cognitive psychologists saw the brain as a kind of computer, with the mind as the computer software. Just as software can run on any computer, so can the processes and algorithms called mind run on any brain, insisted the psychologists; if mind and brain are independent, then the brain can be ignored when studying the mind. But cognitive psychology's computer analogy had serious weak points. First, if human mental "software" can run on any brain, then why can't it run on a chimpanzee's brain, which shares 99 percent of the human brain's genome? Second, if the brain is irrelevant to the working of the mind, why do brain lesions change one's personality?

With each side simultaneously paralyzing the other with its tactics, the mind-brain debate stagnated. By the 1960s the sense of expectation aroused by Schrodinger and Ryle had waned, the debate lost its dynamism, and educated laymen left the issue for theorists to dispute in their obscure academic backwaters.

Nevertheless, Eccles had changed the balance of political forces involved. As both a world-famous neuroscientist and an extremely devout Catholic, his presence injected organized religion into the proceedings. Although Eccles's advocacy of dualism received no official support from organized religion, participants in the mind-brain debate saw Eccles as religion's man in science, and Eccles never disabused them of the notion. While some monists were content to let religion have its share of the pie in spiritual matters, other monists relished knowing that the stakes had increased and that taking Eccles down also meant taking Christianity down. Conversely, Eccles believed a dualist victory would vindicate religion, possibly leading to a renewal of faith. Although the mind-brain debate barely changed over the next ten years, with move leading to countermove and all advantages only temporary, both sides felt an apocalyptic excitement, knowing that whoever won would rule not just over the academy, but perhaps over the entire culture.

MEDICINE UNDER A DUALIST REGIME

"A psychoanalyst has no place in an undergraduate medical school," the dean of Cornell replied, turning away a young doctor seeking a position in the neurology department. The doctor had just returned from Vienna, where he had spent five years training in psychoanalysis under the great Freud himself. Yet in 1922 his training worked against him rather than for him—a consequence of dualism. All the medical specialties cared for a body part, including neurology, which cared for the brain. But psychiatry cared for the mind, putting it on the wrong side of the tracks. Three centuries before, Cartesian dualism had divided mind and body into separate realms to free science from religious interference. Henceforth, doctors studied the body; clergymen and philosophers studied the mind. Although Cartesian dualism kept the peace between the medical profession and organized religion, within medicine it made psychiatry a permanent outlier and perennially suspect. The more psychiatry distanced itself from material science—such as Freudian psychoanalysis, which required no understanding of the brain to be performed—the more suspect it became.

Albeit just a theory, dualism manifested itself in American medicine in concrete ways, reaching its greatest expression in the rigid division between neurology and psychiatry. To some degree, the separation arose naturally from the logistics of medical practice. In the late nineteenth century, psychiatrists enjoyed an institutional base as superintendents of public asylums. Neurologists, on the other hand, lacked any such base, since most general hospitals had not yet designated beds for patients with neurological disorders. Neurologists worked mostly as consultants in private practice. In the early twentieth century the division deepened. Neurologists identified with scientific medicine, emphasizing anatomy, physiology, and the laboratory, while psychiatrists moved in the direction of psychoanalysis and emphasized the couch, causing them to resemble philosophers more than scientists.

Even when the two specialties converged on the general hospital, with psychiatrists leaving the asylum and neurologists gaining ward privileges, the division remained intact. Dualism inspired the canonical division between "organic" and "functional" mental illness: neurologists handled diseases with objective physical evidence—with "signs"—while psychiatrists treated illnesses defined by people's subjective feelings—with only "symptoms." Nevertheless, the demarcation line between brain illness and mind illness lacked clarity, just as the division between brain and mind lacked clarity in the realm of theory, tempting neurologists and psychiatrists to poach on one another's turf. Neurologists threatened to take over a psychiatric disease after discovering a brain lesion associated with that disease, setting off alarms among psychiatrists that neurologists harbored an insidious scheme to conquer all psychiatry. Psychiatrists, in turn, claimed to have a better working knowledge of the brain than neurologists had of the mind, which neurologists took as a cannon shot across their bow.

To cut down on these border conflicts, both psychiatrists and neurologists walled themselves off. The status of psychiatry and neurology varied across American hospitals in the first half of the twentieth century: in some hospitals, psychiatry was a separate department while neurology was a subdivision of internal medicine; in other hospitals, only neurology was a separate department; in still others, psychiatry was a subdivision of neurology. A desire for professional security as well as a casual belief in dualism pushed these specialties to create their own separate departments, their drive to do so dominating much of the medical profession's politics at midcentury.

During the 1960s and 1970s, with dualism still influential, the division between neurology and psychiatry held and even intensified. In 1965, to hermetically seal the division at its most remote points, the Residency Review Committee for Psychiatry and Neurology deleted psychiatric training as a mandatory experience for neurologists. Five years later, the psychiatrists took the drastic step of abandoning the medical internship as a prerequisite to specialty training in the field (a decision reversed in 1978). Many physicians supported this deepening separation, for it both conferred protection on neurology and psychiatry and preserved the general medical order. Although some doctors consciously supported dualism, a dualist policy became part of a larger strategy within the medical profession to contain trouble spots and maintain peace within the ranks.

In the 1950s, some doctors deviated from dualism, pursuing a policy more akin to monism. David McKenzie Rioch, a psychiatrist trained in neuroanatomy, brought neurologists and psychiatrists together at the Walter Reed Army Institute of Research to study the nervous system. His efforts led a decade later to the establishment of the nation's first neuroscience research program at MIT, the goal of which was to bring chemistry and physics to bear on the study of both behavior and the nervous system. The term "neuroscience," coined during this period, became a catch phrase symbolizing the monist worldview in medicine: when doctors spoke it, they asserted the global unity of mind and brain. Some physicians in the medical establishment saw the trend toward neuroscience as provocative, but as long as the discipline remained confined to the nation's research labs they looked the other way.

BREAKING THE STALEMATE

In 1966, Eccles found himself an important man but soon to be unemployed. Since 1952 he had been Professor of Physiology at Australian National University, but now mandatory retirement loomed. To compound matters, he suffered a serious financial setback after divorcing his first wife, who reportedly "took him to the cleaners." Desperate for another post, preferably outside of Australia to get away from the gossip surrounding his personal life, he joined the Institute for Biomedical Research in Chicago. Several years before his divorce he had met a woman destined to become his second wife—a much younger postdoctoral student from Czechoslovakia. The two hooked up in Chicago and the following year traveled to Buffalo, where Eccles took a position at the State University of New York. Money remained a problem so he embarked on a busy speaking career, talking about the mind-brain problem at different venues, including a Moonie convention, despite the risk to his reputation. As he confided to a friend, he needed the thousand-dollar lecture fee.

Dressed like an elegant English gentleman and charming in his wit and humor, Eccles fascinated audiences. Yet many established scientists saw him as conceited and stubborn, one of the breed of men who imagine they alone possess the truth. They especially resented going to an Eccles lecture on neuroscience and then listening to him plug God and religion during the last twenty minutes. Religious people thought Eccles a noble and God-fearing man, a fighter, an enthusiast, and an international asset; his colleagues found him overbearing, obnoxious, already famous but now wanting to be glorious.

Eccles's climactic moment in the mind-brain debate came in 1977, when he teamed up with philosopher Sir Karl Popper to write *The Self and Its Brain*. A dualist but also an agnostic and slightly uncomfortable with Eccles's strong belief in God, Popper had befriended Eccles in New Zealand three decades before. At that time, Popper impressed on Eccles the idea that all science proceeds on the basis of a provisional hypothesis. Hypotheses are formed before, not after, long periods of observation, despite what scientists say. Popper's idea had emboldened Eccles to announce his dualist hypothesis in 1952 before he could firmly defend it; now Eccles was teaming up with the man who first inspired him. At the very least, by allying himself with a well-respected professional philosopher, Eccles gained new legitimacy for his dualist views.

Popper and Eccles divided life into three worlds. World 1 is the outer world of matter, including the human brain. World 2 is the inner world of self, ego, thought, feeling, memory, and the soul, which, according to Eccles, was God's creation. World 3 is the world of culture that evolves over time, including language, intellectual accomplishments, and all the treasures housed in the world's museums. Worlds 1 and 2 are on the same level, linked by way of the liaison in the brain; people access World 3 through World 2.

To explain the link between World 1 and World 2, Eccles envisioned the cerebral cortex subdivided into power units like columns, vertical to the brain's surface and interacting with the mind when they reached a certain level of activity (neither too much, as in a seizure, nor too little, as in sleep or coma). Although the model was elegant, monists still raised the matter of thermodynamics. World 2 working on World 1 implies a force outside of the matter-energy system acting on matter: didn't this violate the first law of thermodynamics?

Eccles found refuge in a controversial theory in quantum physics. In unrelated work, theoretical physicist Robert Margenau had argued that a system with small enough parts functions like a "probability field," which means that it carries neither matter nor energy, such that when a change takes place in the system, the system somehow furnishes the energy automatically. Eccles theorized that the mind-brain works like a quantum probability field. When the mind changes the brain, the mind is not called upon to furnish the energy; instead, the neurons inside the brain furnish their own energy. More precisely, a mental intention momentarily changes the probability of certain neurons firing without causing any change in the mass or energy of the mind-brain system. All this happened, Eccles claimed, at synaptic units called "microsites" with "transcendental properties." Like secret passages in an enchanted castle, microsites were the channels between Eccles's two universes.

The monists dismissed the notion of probability fields, saying that even if such fields existed, a problem remained. Let's say the mind tells the body to raise its leg, changing the probabilities of certain brain cells firing, except that something else is involved. Whenever the mind tells the body to raise its leg, it virtually always gets the body to do so; thus the mind doesn't simply change the probabilities of certain brain cells firing, it changes them in a *regular* way. What is the power that makes the change in probabilities regular as opposed to random? Eccles couldn't say. He conceded that his mechanism for mind-brain interaction stood outside conventional quantum physics. But the monists knew the truth: some additional force had to shape the probabilities of certain brain cells firing, and for some additional force outside the matter-energy system to do so violated the first law of thermodynamics. It was the same old problem.

Eccles grew anxious, collaring anyone in his lab willing to listen, although most people refused to do so. Shortly after publication of *The Self and Its Brain* he retired to Switzerland, but still his fanaticism grew. Dr. Vernon Mountcastle, a distinguished neuroscientist, muses, "The best day I ever spent with Jack [Dr. Eccles] was rowing in a canoe on a lake in Switzerland. It was a beautiful summer day. Our wives were with us, and the whole time Jack didn't bring up religion once."

In response to monist criticism, Eccles sent messages around the world, telling his confederates to hang tight, that another experiment would soon even the score just as it always had. But time was running out for dualism. In the 1980s the sword of Damocles poised above every dualist's head for three centuries—including Eccles's own—suddenly dropped. The monists had found the key to victory, a way to crush dualism for good.

Well into the 1970s monism had changed little since the era of Schrodinger and Ryle. The two men had pointed the way to serious monism, but monism had yet to develop any convincing model of mind-brain interaction. Materialists still saw the answer to the mind-brain problem in the brain's cellular components: knowing the neuron, they believed, was enough to know the mind. Their philosophy lives on in Nobel Prize–winner Francis Crick's *Astonishing Hypothesis*: "Your joys and your sorrows, your memories and your ambitions, your sense of personal identity and free will, are in fact no more than the behavior of a vast assembly of nerve cells and their associated molecules." Although Eccles failed to prove dualism, monism's picture of thinking as a blind, purposeless activity so horrified people that they were willing to suspend reason and sympathize with his theory.

However, in the 1980s, a new monist concept arose: emergent materialism. Emergent materialists like philosopher Mario Bunge, neuroscientists Gerald Edelman and Vernon Mountcastle, and neurologist Antonio Damasio saw the mind as an extension of the brain, but they also saw the brain as more than just a bunch of cells and the mind as more than just a by-product of cellular activity. They called the mind-brain a "biosystem": consciousness emerges from special cellular systems, they said, thereby enjoying physical properties that no one cell has alone, similar to the way a city consists of thousands of people while enjoying properties that no one individual has alone. A molecule, for example, lacks temperature or liquidity but when molecules combine, temperature and liquidity are possible: temperature and liquidity are emergent properties.

The concept amazed scientists. Suddenly monism was palatable. With confidence, emergent materialists fielded any question that came their way, knowing they were winning both the intellectual war and the public relations war. Is there a difference between cellular life and the life each person feels? Yes. All life obeys physical laws, but because each person's inner life emerges from a biosystem, it is richly endowed in ways that a cell's life can never be. Do we have free will? Yes. Atoms lack free will, but people have free will—people and atoms are different—and since self-movement is commonly observed in nature (in the form of inertial motion and the spontaneous self-assembly of molecules) free will is perfectly consistent with science. Is each person's feeling of selfhood just an illusion? No. The feeling of selfhood is real; it is an emergent property representing an advanced state of consciousness. Is there a difference between man and chimpanzee? Yes. A brain needs not only the right genome but also the right shape to yield the complex neural system known as mind, which explains why consciousness is only a recent evolutionary development. Is life a part of the purposeless winding down of the universe? No. Life is the evolution of an ever more complex neural system revealing itself in consciousness.

Emergent materialism's popularity spread rapidly beyond science, producing a deluge of literature. Professors in the humanities and the social sciences embraced the idea and used it in their research, including classicist Martha Nussbaum in *Upheavals of Thought* and philosopher Craig DeLancey in *Passionate Engines*. Antonio Damasio's *Descartes' Error* became a best seller. Books written outside the emergent materialist tradition but still "new monist" in spirit, like psychologist Steven Pinker's *How the Mind Works*, also became best sellers. The public sensed great change was afoot, that science had made a tremendous discovery.

For Eccles, matters grew worse. Applying emergent materialism to dualism, Roger Sperry, awarded the Nobel Prize in Medicine in 1981 for his split-brain experiments, proposed a new kind of dualism, one that explained the origin and existence of

mind in dualist terms but without appealing to any supernatural source. Like the emergent materialists, Sperry saw mental
phenomena as emerging from neural systems; only then these
phenomena exerted downward control on the very brain tissue
that gave rise to them. Mind came from brain, then was separate from brain, then ruled brain. Although only a few scientists
agreed with Sperry, Sperry's quasi-dualist model eclipsed Eccles's
religious dualism. True, mind still commanded brain, but now
it sat politely within the closed system of chemistry and physics
to do so. Gone were the soul, the spirit, and the divine universe.
Eccles called Sperry a religious dualist at heart. Sperry denied
it. Much of the scientific community sided with Sperry. It was
the final humiliation for Eccles. Outwardly he exhibited a vague
mixture of consternation and contempt toward emergent materialism, but inwardly the movement's success cut deep into his
heart. Says a former coworker, "Dr. Eccles spoke and debated at
conferences; then quietly went home. Later, I heard how he had
been 'torn to shreds,' but he would never admit to it."

At one mind-brain conference in Venice in 1990, Dr. Piergiorgio Strata, a neuroscientist and emergent materialist, asked
the following hypothetical: A woman goes to Mars in a spaceship
but on her way back the ship malfunctions. She is going to die,
but a special device makes an exact copy of her body's molecular
structure, preserves it, and then returns it to physical form when
the ship reaches earth. Will the woman keep her memories of
Mars? The emergent materialists said yes. Not only her brain
molecules but also the relationships between her brain molecules
will have been preserved, which is all that is needed to reproduce
mind. Eccles refused to answer the question: the man who had
spent a lifetime talking about the supernatural suddenly groused
that he had no time for "fantasies."

Eccles didn't doubt himself, but he was tiring and sorely

lacking in allies. He commanded an army of one—himself. At any mind-brain conference, he was often the only dualist in the room. Under such conditions, he found it hard to keep slogging. Fortunately, help was on the way.

THE CHRISTIANS RISE

Emergent materialism's ascendance and Eccles's subsequent flap with Sperry flushed organized religion out of hiding. Previously content to let Eccles represent them unofficially in the mind-brain debate, religious people sensed the enormous seriousness of the new threat and decided to fight. They represented a broad alliance, since most members of organized religion share dualism as a common ideology. Although the Catholic church's official account of the soul rejects dualism (preferring to call the soul "the substantial form of the body" rather than an independent reality), Catholic clergy rarely disabuse lay Catholics of their dualist prejudices, since dualism cultivates faith in a world beyond the senses. In addition, dualism confers protection against evolutionary theory, for even if human beings and apes share a common physical heritage the human mind's "alternative universe" creates a permanent gap between the two species. Many Catholics see the papal notion of the soul "infusing" the body as code for the mind-brain split. In the mind-brain wars, these Catholics joined forces with Protestants who had long viewed traditional monism as their mortal enemy.

Regardless of dualism's shortcomings, which some Christians conceded in private, Christians saw monism as a threat to the doctrine of the soul. Although a few Biblical scholars and liberal Protestant theologians maintained that dualism lacked scriptural support, most Christian leaders equated the mind with the soul, which meant that to concede the monist position risked the soul's existence. Traditionally, these leaders had preferred to downplay the whole mind-brain issue, fearing that exposing doctrinal inconsistencies would confuse believers. In the 1980s, faced with the menace of serious danger, religious leaders saw no alternative but to fight for their turf. But weakness showed in some of their faces; more than a few dualists had a premonition that things would go badly. While marching into battle, one Catholic priest pleaded with me: "Can't you [the scientists and doctors] leave us something?"

The religious opposition broke down into three factions. The first faction advocated bold action. Telling other Christians not to lose heart, the members of this faction never tired of quoting the Bible or belittling monists. They defended dualism in its purest form: the idea of a human being as a unity of two distinct entities—body and soul—with the soul capable of entering a disembodied state upon death, eventually to be reunited with a resurrected body. In "Restoring the Soul to Christianity," theologian J. P. Moreland writes: "Under the pressure of scientism, physicalism is an inappropriate revision of biblical teaching that is central to the core of Christian theology." Raising the stakes in the debate, these religious people threatened the monists with hell. In addition, they vigorously policed their own ranks. It was precisely because dualism seemed conditional and fluctuating and open to compromise, the traditionalists argued, that the emergent materialists were winning. The point was to stand firm and fight—the way Eccles had—and never give in.

The second faction was the party of extreme compromise. The goal of the people in this faction was to salvage the soul doctrine by making peace with the monists as soon as possible. Some of them hoped to embed the soul concept within emergent materialism; others prayed that the emergent materialists would be magnanimous in victory and let organized religion pretend the soul still existed. Sensing science's strength and their own weakness, they were eager to cut a deal. They warned extremists in the first faction that only humiliation and defeat could follow from a frontal assault on emergent materialism.

The third faction adopted a middle course. Giving tacit support to the field of "parapsychology," which investigates phenomena like telepathy, out-of-body experiences, and apparitions, the people in this faction hoped to ground the soul's existence in a parallel science run by renegade doctors. The people in this faction rejected any compromise of dualism's basic tenets, but they knew that the word of a doctor on the spiritual universe's existence was far more valuable to their cause than the word of any minister.

The dualists in organized religion launched their counterattack in the 1980s through books, magazines, and conferences. The battle for control of the human mind was joined. To honor the occasion, Eccles came up with a new model for dualism but few scientists even bothered to comment on his theory. It was the same old stuff, they said: the whole business of conjuring up mental entities and meddling with an imaginary universe was nonsense.

During the battle, the two sides intensely distrusted one another, finding evil intention in the most innocent behavior. When I asked a neuroscientist a simple, but critical, question about monism, he accused me of being a "closet dualist." When I denied the charge, noting that I was just interested in the debate as an academic exercise, he looked surprised. In his world, people chose sides; no one was indifferent to what was going on.

Despite straining every effort, the dualists failed. Monism had won. Although there was no way to measure monism's victory, emergent materialists had the more coherent argument. Educated people supported it, some by reasoning through things, others because of inherent sentiment. Religious dualists, on the other hand, were powerless. Their shrill warnings about the danger of living without a soul fell on deaf ears. Although still fielding a formidable force, religious people knew the game was up and that dualism was bound to perish.

Within scientific circles, being a dualist—once a respectable position in the mind-brain debate—became a source of embarrassment, like being a racist. Educated people shunned dualists, who took refuge in their conservative churches. Their ideas lived on in tabloids that support the existence of an alternative universe, along with UFOs and politicians impregnated by aliens. Dualism's collapse was a watershed event in American culture, one that marks the end of organized religion's command of the mind and the beginning of a new era in which science enjoys undisputed control.

THE WORLDVIEW OF MONISM

Old and feeble, Eccles put his armor on one last time in 1994, writing *How the Self Controls Its Brain*, although by now his work was largely ignored. His health continued to deteriorate; still, he refused to surrender, fighting monism from his bed. His New Year's message, read out loud at the 1997 annual meeting of the Japan Neuroscience Society, gave this warning: "As the situation is now very much serious, I wish you to reconsider all of your neurophysiological work in terms of dualism. It is the question of truth and meaning in life. There is no other way to go."

On May 2, 1997, Sir John Eccles died. Five days before, as he lay in bed near death, he suddenly opened his eyes and cried, "Life is a mystery, it's a mystery, it's a mystery and I will get it.

I've spent my life looking for the mystery, now I am sure I'll get it." He never did. Although Eccles had thrown his whole life onto one side of the scale, the opposite side outweighed him.

Almost immediately after monism's triumph, the realities of the new situation assumed a visible shape. Neuroscience's prestige rose dramatically. The barrier separating neuroscience from other sciences collapsed; neuroscientists gained access to any field thought helpful to furthering their understanding of the mind. Interdisciplinary activity, once dismissed and later tolerated, became the norm. The number of neuroscientists in the country skyrocketed from six hundred in 1968 to over twenty thousand in the mid-1990s. The union of cognitive psychology and neuroscience in the late 1980s made monism's triumph official. Cognitive neuroscience merged the study of mental activity with the biology of the brain and became a symbol and an inspiration, a message transmitted to the outside world that monism was now medical science's official creed.

Within clinical medicine, the division between neurology and psychiatry crumbled. Although the two specialties remained separate, a spirit of reconciliation replaced the old hatred. With neuroscience forming a bridge between the two specialties, whether one trained in neurology or psychiatry mattered less than whether one possessed the relevant neuroscience background to apply scientific methodology. A common approach to problems like schizophrenia, autism, and manic depression arose. Only psychotherapists lost out in the growing neurology-psychiatry rapprochement. As dualists, their point of view now seemed archaic, even quaint, causing their influence in psychiatry to wane.

Yet monism's triumph had its greatest effect on primary care doctors building a new world of Artificial Happiness anchored in neurotransmitters and drugs. A three-tiered empire in medicine emerged: on the bottom, specialists and primary care doctors caring for the body's ailments; in the middle, primary care doctors caring for everyday psychological trouble with drugs, alternative medicine, and obsessive exercise; and on top, scientists and theoreticians unifying body and mind, sanctioning the primary care doctors' activities and giving the whole enterprise moral force.

For the first time in the modern era an age-old dream had been fulfilled, that of bringing the two halves of life under one dominion. With organized religion losing its centrality on matters of the mind, the medical profession alone now ruled both mind and body. This new circumstance added vital momentum to the medical practice revolution. If before monism's triumph doctors anchored their aggressive approach to unhappiness in questionable psychotropic drug ideology or endorphin ideology, *after* its triumph they did so with the full faith and backing of the entire scientific establishment. Before monism's triumph, the medical profession was one among several professions (including clergymen and philosophers) managing unhappiness. After its triumph, the medical profession became the sole active agent in the psychological affairs of millions of Americans. Taken together and all working under monism's umbrella, alternative medicine, obsessive exercise, and the loosely joined alliance of doctors prescribing psychotropic drugs became the axis on which the entire country's mental health revolved.

For doctors, only one more battle needed to be fought, the battle for the spirit. Although doctors controlled the body and the mind, they needed to control the spirit to unite all of life's domains. It was organized religion's last autonomous realm, the last place from which clergymen influenced the direction of people's everyday psychology. Doctors advanced in full force, but with a different strategy from the one guiding them during their campaign for the mind. In the battle for the spirit, doctors lured organized religion to its destruction.

NINE

THE LAST BATTLE

TWO YEARS AGO I watched a nurse answer a quiz in a magazine to see if she and her boyfriend were compatible. She paused for a moment over the question of religion. I asked her what the choices were. She replied that they were Catholic, Protestant, Jewish, Muslim, or spiritual. In the end, she checked spiritual. "What does that mean?" I asked. "Well," she replied, "it means that I don't like organized religion, but I still think about humanity. And sometimes, when I do yoga, I have this incredible feeling of peace. I know I'm not just the same old me."

The medical profession nurtured the split between religion and spirituality that began in the early 1990s. Curiously, its role in that split is rarely mentioned, as people assume that medicine has little influence on religion's internal workings. In fact, the medical profession helped generate the split, with the split representing the final act of the Artificial Happiness story. Doctors pried religion and spirituality apart, then turned spirituality into a medical concern.

The medical profession acted in the face of a looming threat. In the early 1980s, doctors won control of the body; in the late 1980s, they won control of the mind; still, Artificial Happiness was vulnerable. Although doctors convinced people that unhappiness turned on brain activity rather than on God's will, they conceded that culture influenced the relationship between neurons and therefore how people think and feel. Dr. Gerald Edelman, a leading monist and Nobel Prize winner, told me, "Science has to do with relations amongst matter and energy. Relations aren't material. [These relations are] a product of the activity of neurons, your phenotype, *and your environment* [author's emphasis]." In other words, how a person feels depends not only on his neurons but also on how those neurons react within a system—a condition affected by culture and life experiences.

Religious leaders saw an opening: so long as people held erroneous views about life, they risked unhappiness in the form of a spiritual crisis. Even if unhappiness expressed itself biologically, through neurotransmitters, culture affected brain geometry, therefore creating the possibility of unhappiness. This idea squared with all the notions then current in monism. Rather than argue that God moved the human brain, as Eccles had, religious leaders said that just believing in God changed the neuronal firing pattern. Actually, believing in anything changed the firing pattern, since ideas feed back on each other in the complex loop that forms a person's consciousness. By emphasizing a belief in God rather than God's direct control over the mind, religious people had found a key to the mind's backdoor, a way to remain influential without resorting to dualism. Worse for doctors, these people showed every intention of finding more and more keys to more and more backdoors.

When doctors admitted that ideas affected brain geometry, they opened themselves up to competition. Ideas were a threat. Of course, doctors couldn't neutralize every idea, but not every idea was dangerous; doctors were content to let laypeople counsel other laypeople with homegrown ideas. The danger to Artificial Happiness emanated from professional disciplines that pushed a *system of ideas*, ideas that might substitute for psychotropic drugs, alternative medicine, and obsessive exercise. Only two disciplines boasted of such a system: organized religion and psychotherapy. Doctors had neutralized psychotherapy in the 1980s, especially when psychotherapy's original proponents—the psychiatrists—conveniently lost interest in the field. Although PhD psychologists continued to pose a threat, they were too attached to doctors (sometimes even working under doctors) to deviate from the doctors' ideology. If anything, psychologists challenged doctors, not by pushing ideas over psychotropic drugs but by demanding for themselves the right to prescribe these drugs.

Organized religion posed the major threat to Artificial Happiness. In the form of religious spirituality, its system of ideas dangled before unhappy people as a serious alternative to medical therapy. Religious leaders could advise unhappy people to find God rather than to take drugs or resort to alternative medicine or exercise obsessively.

Another confrontation between the medical profession and organized religion was inevitable. This time, however, doctors responded with a different tactic. Rather than attack religion the way they had over abortion and dualism, doctors praised religion, even feigned an alliance with religion, all the while stealing

spirituality for themselves. For doctors, it was a precision operation, since spirituality—and only spirituality—was the trouble
spot; doctors were more than content to let organized religion
retain its autonomy and integrity on matters of morality.

If doctors had consciously contrived to rob religion of spirituality, one could almost call them shrewd. But doctors lacked
any such agenda. They simply pushed their ideology to its logical
conclusion, which meant redefining spirituality as an engineering
problem. Because they found their approach to life so compelling,
they couldn't imagine anyone else thinking differently; even religious people, they assumed, would sooner or later come around.
As long as religious people refused to deal with unhappiness on
the doctors' terms they constituted a threat, which necessitated
bringing spirituality under medical control. However, doctors
consciously expanded into spirituality not to checkmate organized
religion but because it seemed like the logical next step. If ideas,
including a belief in God, affected brain geometry and therefore
the chance of unhappiness, well, then, ideas had to be accounted
for by the doctors' ideology. In other words, the doctors' ideology
had to expand to cover contested areas like spirituality, not simply
to preserve Artificial Happiness against threats from organized
religion but to preserve the ideology's integrity.

Hence, most doctors failed to see their takeover of spirituality as a hostile act, especially when so many religious people
applauded what they did. Eager to do business with doctors,
many religious people foresaw in a religion-medical axis a way
to bring religion out of its isolation. Afterward, when spirituality became a wholly owned subsidiary of medical science, a few
religious people recognized the disaster for what it was, at which
point the doctors' outward signs of respect for religion only
made the inward truth of religion's position more intolerable.
Yet most religious people remain oblivious to the disaster, just

as most doctors remain oblivious even to the fact that a battle occurred, in part because doctors continue to flatter religion but also because many religious people now see spirituality from the medical point of view. In the end, the medical profession gained control of the life of the body, the mind, and the spirit, turning organized religion into a high-minded nonentity on the matter of unhappiness, a cultural appendage without influence or power.

RELIGION PROVES USEFUL

A not-so-bright man I know jogs three times a week. During the week, his course varies but on Sundays he always jogs to church and back. When I asked him if the church lets him wear shorts and running shoes to services he said he didn't know, he wasn't religious, he jogged to church but never went in. I asked him why he never went in. He said he had read somewhere that religious people live longer and healthier lives. By jogging to church—on Sundays—thereby retracing the steps of religious people, he hoped some of religion's health benefits might rub off on him.

Prior to the 1990s the medical profession and organized religion had no common goals save for improving people's everyday psychology. Except for Christian Scientists, religious people showed little inclination to get involved in health matters, while doctors, faithful to older habits, deferred to religious people on the question of transcendent experiences. For all their interest in everyday unhappiness, doctors (especially physician-engineers) were materialists and believed devoutly that real medicine existed where there was matter and energy. Thus, real medicine concerned itself with the body and the mind, not with any so-called realm of the spirit.

An article in a 1972 issue of the *Journal of Chronic Diseases* heralded change. The authors described an association between weekly church attendance and lower rates of heart disease, emphysema, and cirrhosis. More articles followed in the 1980s and '90s, all pursuing the same line. One study, for example, showed a relationship between religious commitment and lower blood pressure. A second study showed that religious belief helped heart transplant patients recover faster, a third study tied religious activity to lower cancer mortality rates, and a fourth study showed religious people needed fewer visits to the dentist. Tens of such studies were performed during this period, each demonstrating a favorable correlation between religion and morbidity, mortality, or the ability of patients to cope with chronic illness.

The reason behind religion's health benefits remained a mystery. Since physical health can never be totally divorced from moral behavior (e.g., monogamy lowers the risk of AIDS and other sexually transmitted infections), some doctors theorized that clean living explained the phenomenon. Other physicians cited organized religion's dietary practices. A third group of doctors, emphasizing the social implications of church attendance, anchored religion's health benefit in the church's network of support and friendship. A fourth group called spirituality the active beneficial ingredient. But the reason behind religion's health benefits didn't really matter. What mattered was that doctors, once so critical of religion, now spoke nicely of religion, and religious people lapped it up. In the age of modern science, nothing could be calculated to please religious people more than for doctors to announce that religion made sense. Suspicious of medical science and accustomed to being mocked by doctors and scientists, religious leaders increasingly distrusted the medical profession. After the mind-brain debacle more than a few religious leaders saw medical science as an evil force—of which they lived in dread fear. With doctors, once so smug and condescending, now praising religion for its health benefits, many religious leaders were overjoyed. They quickly regained the self-confidence that had been slipping away from them. Religion's fortunes, it seemed, were on the rise.

The new interest in religion's health benefits extended to the sphere of mental health. In the mid-1980s, articles began appearing in medical journals showing a positive correlation between religious faith and psychological traits like sociability, self-control, and responsibility. An entire literature subset documented how religion helped people cope with stress. Cross-disciplinary activity exploded as religious people and doctors teamed up to study the phenomenon. Organizations like the American Association of Christian Counselors and the Christian Association for Psychological Studies thrived.

The new alliance between religion and medicine differed in important ways from past collaborations. In the 1950s, clergymen and psychiatrists applied various shadings of psychotherapy to combat unhappiness; in the 1980s, clergymen and primary care doctors collaborated, with more of a focus on physical health than mental health. To the extent that mental health was an issue, another crucial difference existed. In the 1950s, clergymen and doctors met each other halfway, coalescing around psychotherapy, which was neither religion nor medicine but a kind of hybrid—a secular movement with scientific trappings that emulated religion's style. In the 1980s, clergymen were under no obligation to compromise. To the contrary, doctors told religious people to keep doing what they were doing, such as walk to church, light incense, pray, and ring bells. Doctors didn't know *why* such practices helped people cope with stress but they knew that they did, which was enough. In the 1980s, doctors showed greater respect for religion's peculiar way of doing things than psychiatrists had shown three decades before.

On the surface, the relationship between the medical profession and organized religion appeared to have taken a step forward. Eager to cement the new union was Sir John Templeton. Born in rural Tennessee in 1912 and later a Rhodes scholar at Oxford, Templeton founded his own investment management company and created some of the world's largest mutual funds, growing enormously wealthy in the process. With a longstanding religious interest, he set up the John Templeton Foundation in 1987 to fund research in the area of religion and science, with a special emphasis on religion's health benefits. By working this territory, Templeton believed he changed religion's image into something more modern and forward-looking. His foundation supported, either directly or indirectly, many of the scientific studies performed on religion during this period.

Religious leaders of all stripes hoped that when people found religion through health concerns they would eventually embrace religion for the right reasons. Their task, as they saw it, was to launch a vast public relations campaign around faith's tangible benefits. The Templeton Foundation moved into high gear. Television shows, newspapers, and magazines trumpeted the relevant studies from medical journals. On Sundays, clergymen told parishioners that church was good for their health. Although clergymen never ceased to point out heaven as the great object of a believer's hopes, they wryly observed that going to church postponed the inevitable meeting with God just a little bit. (According to one study, attending religious services once a week as opposed to never attending added eight years to life.) In private, one minister bragged to me, "Jesus is as good for blood pressure as any of your pills."

Doctors and religious people had found common ground on

which to build a new alliance. However, each camp differed fundamentally in their understanding of the nature of that alliance, which, as the battle for the spirit progressed, proved especially dangerous to religious people, who dropped their guard. The disagreement was on emphasis. For doctors, the health benefit superseded all other relevance religion might have in people's lives. Their priority concern was fighting disease. Since they were better equipped to do so, they imagined religion lower down in the hierarchy, with themselves as the real leaders. Privately, many doctors lacked respect for religious people. They assumed that they had the advanced consciousness and that religious people should be grateful for the chance to serve under doctors and finally do something productive in the modern era. At the very least, doctors didn't expect any more lip from religious people on medical matters.

Religious people, on the other hand, saw the new alliance quite differently. They thought harnessing religion to fight disease was only the first step in an ascending spiral of success and that religion might flourish in new and unexpected ways. Religious people thought they, not the doctors, sat at the top of the hierarchy, since religion saved souls and fought disease, while medicine only fought disease. On mental health, for example, religious people felt particularly strong, since they had the greater experience in dealing with spiritual crises. At the very least, they envisioned the new association between themselves and doctors as an alliance of equals, each respecting the other's independence to conduct an agenda as they saw fit. Neither side, they assumed, would take any action that compromised the interests of the other.

The superficial declaration of common purpose among doctors and religious people brushed under the carpet profound differences between the two parties. Doctors saw religion as a kind of broken-down appliance; they would salvage the useful parts and junk the rest. Religious people failed to understand this and their assumption proved disastrous as the battle for the spirit progressed. At every step doctors penetrated deeper into religion and grabbed whatever they thought useful, while religious people assumed that doctors had religion's best interests at heart. Religious people failed to see that the new climate of sympathetic understanding masked a deeper competitive struggle and a determination on the part of doctors to control everything.

SUGARCOATING EVOLUTION

Psychologist Barbara Fredrickson thinks positive feelings help people endure hard times. For her, such feelings are not only pleasant but also a matter of survival. Because they allow people to think more creatively, feelings like joy and happiness represent a major advantage from an evolutionary standpoint, increasing the chance that a person will recover from adversity. In an interview with the Templeton Foundation's magazine, *Science and Spirit*, Dr. Fredrickson talks about the importance of positive feelings, although she gives negative feelings their due. Without feelings like sadness and fear, she notes, emotions in general would lose their authenticity, while positive feelings would lose their credibility. Dr. Fredrickson concludes that the perfect ratio of positive to negative feelings—the one most associated with a flourishing mind and therefore the one with the best chance for survival—is 2.9.

In the 1980s and '90s, research like Dr. Fredrickson's mushroomed as scientists tried to put the inner life of human beings in evolutionary perspective. Gratitude, altruism, friendship, and love were just some of the behavioral traits examined for the advantages they conferred on human beings in their struggle to survive as a species. Scientists even applied the concept of natural selection to artistic ability. Evolutionary biologist Geoffrey Miller theorized that artistic talent among human males attracts human females, as some male birds lure female birds with ornate nests. The impression of energy, skill, and overall fitness associated with artistic talent communicates a greater likelihood of being a solid mate, rendering genes for artistry more favorable within the gene pool.

Inevitably the debate over what did and did not have evolutionary significance extended to religion. This evolutionary perspective on religion was new. In the nineteenth century social anthropologists saw religion as a product of evolution but they meant cultural evolution, not biological evolution. Calling Christianity a marker of "civilization," Western anthropologists imagined themselves occupying an advanced stage of cultural evolution compared to "primitive" people in Africa, who worshipped bundles of sticks and mud or seemed to have no religion at all. At the turn of the twentieth century, anthropologists turned away from evolution, viewing religion as a purely cultural phenomenon with no connection to "progress." With the rise of evolutionary biology in the middle of the twentieth century, some anthropologists revisited evolution—this time biological evolution—and concluded that religious faith improved people's chances of reproduction and survival. However, they persisted in tying religion to culture, calling it a higher brain function.

In 1985, psychiatrist Eugene d'Aquili stripped religion down to its base components and argued that religion evolved in human beings as a way to promote group solidarity through rhythmic sensory stimuli. Subsequently, researchers studied religion without the earlier prejudice that religion sprang from the brain's higher-reasoning, culture-producing centers. Henceforth, religion was just a biological phenomenon, conferring benefits similar to those realized from standing erect or the oppositional thumb. Religion had nothing to do with exalted thoughts or poetic sentiments; it was simply a matter of how the human brain was wired.

An alarm should have gone off in religious circles, but it didn't. Some religious leaders even embraced the new evolutionary paradigm. For over a century Darwin's theory had threatened religion, not just by exploding the myths surrounding man's creation but also by calling religion a useless fantasy. With science increasingly dominant it grew harder to oppose evolution, to the concern of religious people everywhere. Stanley Beck of the American Lutheran Church noted: "To call himself reasonably well-educated and informed, a Christian can hardly afford not to believe in evolution." When religion found a connection with evolution many religious leaders from across the denominational spectrum sighed with relief: a compromise had been achieved. True, religious leaders had to show respect for evolution and surrender their literal interpretation of Genesis, including their dreams of man being created in the Garden of Eden, but in return they received recognition from scientists that religion was no silly thing, that nature designed human beings to believe, and that believing enjoyed a solid utilitarian basis.

Some religious leaders called the new compromise philosophy "theistic evolution," which admitted that evolution unfolded as the Darwinists said except that God played more of a role in the process than the Darwinists realized, as evolution itself revealed signs of God's existence—including, for example, the human capacity for religion. Others called it "Intelligent Design." The new philosophy differed significantly from "creation science," pushed by Christian fundamentalists, which repudiated evolution altogether and argued that God created man in his current form ten thousand years ago.

By 1991 a Gallup poll showed 40 percent of Americans believed in theistic evolution. Another 45 percent believed in creation science, while the rest believed in classic Darwinian evolution. On the surface, this looks like a victory for religion over science but, since the vast majority of Americans at mid-century had repudiated evolutionary theory altogether, some movement in the direction of science had occurred. The majority of Americans now believed in some form of evolution.

More relevant to the story of Artificial Happiness, the triumph of medicine over religion in the treatment of everyday unhappiness didn't require victory on evolution. Many Americans believe in creation science or theistic evolution but still rely on medicine for treatment of their everyday unhappiness. By leveraging the evolution debate, doctors could prevail over religion on the matter of unhappiness even as the larger scientific community failed to convince the majority to believe in Darwinian evolution.

With evolution now appearing to work for religion rather than against it, theistic evolutionists imagined a new era of peaceful coexistence with science. After all, scientists could no longer just condemn religion, since that would be like condemning the oppositional thumb. Evolutionary theory had pushed religion beyond the scientists' reach into the realm of fixed biological nature. Science would have to learn to live with religion, if not to like it.

In reality, religious leaders had propelled themselves into an ideological trap. With evolution now the accepted litmus test for the value of all human activity, religion ceased to be special. The notion that religion made health sense had already exposed religion to danger, reducing religion to the same trivial level as eating right and exercising daily. When religion made evolutionary sense, religion fell even lower—to the level of animal behavior. Even if believing in God were "a positive evolutionary development," it was no different than the wolf's keen eyesight or the lion's strength—merely a comparative advantage of human beings in the animal kingdom.

In their hearts, people supporting theistic evolution still believed religion was higher and special, a concept so self-evident to them that only ignorance, they assumed, inhibited doctors from sharing their view. However, when organized religion found safe harbor within evolutionary doctrine, any romantic belief surrounding religion became intellectually unsustainable. Although the theistic evolutionists continued to see a higher purpose to their lives, the doctors knew better. According to evolution, the primary purpose of all animal species is reproduction and survival; if evolution encompasses religion, then survival must be religion's purpose, too. Like children playing tag, theistic evolutionists countered by saying that God encompassed evolution, preserving religion's higher purpose; yet their cleverness was only too apparent, causing doctors to dismiss their argument as a rhetorical ploy. With crushing brevity, doctors noted that just because religious people believed in their romantic notions about religion didn't make them true. Still, doctors avoided pressing the issue, eager to keep their relationship with organized religion running on a smooth and even course. Again the two parties buried the contradictions to keep the peace.

Neither doctors nor religious people recognized that evolution was the kiss of death. Even when doctors equated religion with a healthy lifestyle, religion had retained its independence. When religion merged with evolution, it lost that independence, becoming a cog in the great machine of science. Biological in origin, hardwired into the brain, religion was now scientific property, not a cultural phenomenon.

Die-hard creation scientists like Henry Morris, who had revived the creation science movement in 1961, warned against the new approach, fearing the finesse would be interpreted as a sign of weakness, which it was. In response, theistic evolutionists counseled optimism and patience while continuing their scientific egg dance. Even if what the creation scientists feared was true, religious life would go on as before: holidays would be celebrated, children would be baptized, and clergymen would continue to counsel parishioners suffering from spiritual crises. Nothing would change except that, now, educated Christians would be able to hold their heads high among doctors and scientists, something that the creation scientists could not do.

They were wrong. By their nature, doctors could not live without certainty on all points of their doctrine regarding Artificial Happiness. Now that religion had entered the scientific system, it had to be made compatible with that doctrine. Spirituality was especially problematic because it muddied the doctors' engineering worldview. How could doctors call unhappiness an engineering problem when their own science accepted the validity of religion's existence and therefore the validity of spirituality, which blamed unhappiness on bad ideas, not on neurotransmitters? Spirituality threatened the doctors' ideology with contradiction. It had to be absorbed.

THE OPERATION BEGINS

Since the early 1980s, doctors had debated the mystery behind religion's health benefits, with spirituality repeatedly coming up as the most logical explanation. Studies showed that people who went through faith's motions enjoyed fewer health benefits than those who truly believed. In addition, atheists who meditated showed improved health scores, suggesting that active involvement in organized religion mattered less than a particular mode of thinking and feeling. Dr. Benson's work in mind-body medicine in the late 1980s showed a convincing link between attitude and health. Indeed, the whole PNI concept supported spirituality as religion's active ingredient.

Spirituality's rising importance intersected with another trend in medicine. Now that religion was biological rather than cultural, doctors had to make religion comport with immutable laws. Although each individual religion is unique because of its ideas, ideas are irrelevant from a scientific perspective. Because they vary from religion to religion, ideas cannot be deduced from general theory; they are not material for science. To assimilate religion and make it compatible with evolution, doctors had to find the essential biological ingredient in all religions—in other words, the one aspect of religion that remained constant across different religions. Finding this ingredient was not only important for therapeutic purposes but also vital to completing science's understanding of man and nature. When spirituality emerged as the most likely explanation for religion's health benefits and therefore the essential biological ingredient in all religions, doctors committed their resources to getting a handle on the phenomenon.

So long as spirituality was an idea, such as believing in God, it fell under religious control. However, if doctors redefined spirituality to mean a sensual phenomenon—a feeling—then doctors would control it, since feelings had long since passed into the medical profession's hands, the best example being unhappiness. Turning spirituality into a feeling would also help doctors square the phenomenon with their own ideology. If spirituality were redefined to mean a feeling rather than an idea, then doctors could group spirituality with all the other feelings, including unhappiness, thereby preserving their ideology's integrity. Spirituality, like unhappiness, would become a problem of neurotransmitters and a subclause of their ideology.

The doctors matured their plans. They described spirituality as an altered form of perception, or an enlightening trance. Meditating test subjects had to attain this peculiar state of mind before doctors agreed to call them spiritual. One doctor went so far as to lump spiritual people with other bizarre cases of perception, including amputees who suffer from phantom limb pain, or brain-damaged patients who believe their limbs belong to someone else.

A phenomenon is medically relevant only when it induces a measurable change. For doctors to accept spirituality as religion's active ingredient they needed to confirm that spirituality induced change. Working on the assumption that change occurred in the brain, they investigated using neuroscience. Neuroscience not only verified spirituality's effect on the brain but also ratified the doctors' conversion of spirituality from an idea into a feeling. Neuroscience cannot measure a change in ideas. For example, it cannot distinguish between a communist's brain and a monarchist's brain or between a Catholic's brain and a Protestant's brain. It can, however, measure a change in feeling—as in the brain of a person in love compared to the brain of a person not in love. By "measuring" spirituality, neuroscientists implicitly endorsed the medical profession's position that spirituality was a feeling, not an idea.

During the 1990s, neuroscience investigations into spirituality pursued three different paths. First, doctors investigated spirituality's general effects on the body. They discovered that the act of meditating lowered blood pressure, pulse rate, and serum cortisol, the body's stress hormone. Second, doctors performed brain imaging studies on people during "spiritual moments." EEG studies of meditating subjects showed alterations in brain wave frequency and amplitude; MRI, CT, and PET scan studies also showed deviations from baseline. In one study, test subjects read a psalm, which induced strong religious feelings, then a nursery rhyme, and finally the telephone directory. The feelings associated with psalm reading produced a unique blood flow pattern within the brain. Third, doctors showed how spirituality appeared to cause a change in neurotransmitters; in one study of Nidra Yoga meditation, doctors observed an increase in dopamine during the meditative sessions, especially in the area of the brain below the cerebral cortex.

Neuroscience implied that spirituality was religion's active beneficial ingredient. More important, and more relevant to the story of Artificial Happiness, it reinforced the definition of spirituality as a feeling. Spirituality, like love, hate, sexual arousal, and boredom, became one more feeling that brain imaging techniques could pick up.

Rather than protest this new definition, many religious leaders supported it and were almost eager to use brain imaging to corroborate what they had once taken on faith alone. On hearing reports that the temporal lobe might be the site where people experience God, the bishop of Oxford declared that God had purposely put an antenna in our brains to connect us to the divine. In a 1998 conference on religion and medicine sponsored by the Templeton Foundation, with John Templeton himself participating along with other representatives from religious-based organizations, participants issued a report defining spirituality as "the feelings, thoughts, experiences, and behaviors that arise from a search for the sacred." Religion became spirituality plus "rituals and prescribed behaviors," the latter being mere fluff from the medical point of view. Two glaring examples of spirituality's redefinition include a section in the report devoted to the study of "drug-induced" spiritual experiences—where the feeling experienced on a hallucinogenic drug is equated with spirituality—followed by a brief discussion on the feasibility of using animals to conduct spirituality research.

Many religious laypeople, especially theistic evolutionists, adopted the new definition. In casual conversation they praised the doctors' work on spirituality, calling neuroscience investigations into spirituality "progress," and bragging to nonbelievers how spirituality was a real phenomenon, after all. Not wanting to seem antiscience or antimodern, they went with the herd. With their tacit consent, spirituality in America became a feeling. It was a grave error, and one with enormous consequences.

Spirituality's redefinition divided Americans into two warring camps—"religious" and "spiritual." Before, when spirituality was an idea, it was impossible to separate spirituality from religion's larger message. Spirituality was just one idea among many ideas. When spirituality became a feeling, people could embrace the feeling and dispense with the larger message. Henceforth, people could be spiritual without being religious.

More important, spirituality's redefinition is wrong. True religious spirituality is not an abnormally intense feeling. Rather, it is an idea that connects human beings to God and the infinite, and in doing so explains certain routine aspects of life, such as one's obligation to others or one's purpose. In practice, spirituality is experienced day-to-day as a kind of vague consciousness. If a man believes he should love his neighbors as he loves himself and conducts himself that way, then that man is spiritual. If a man believes he has a covenant with God and that his duty is to adhere to that covenant, then that man is spiritual. Spirituality is rational and sensible, an idea clearly understood rather than an aura of sensations. Doctors wrongly confused spirituality with a funny feeling, such as the sensation one has while half asleep, looking at the world through a dreamy haze and most susceptible to suggestion.

Spirituality's redefinition threatens to undermine religion's entire belief system. For centuries organized religion layered one irrational belief over another to create a unified system of thought. Angels and demons, heaven and hell stretched the limits of the human imagination, but the whole enterprise seemed reasonable because everyone agreed beforehand that the existence of God constituted established fact. Belief in God formed religion's cornerstone, for it was the one "irrational" idea that most appealed to people's reason. It upheld all that was laid on top of it.

When doctors changed spirituality from an idea into a feeling and told people to look upon the perception of God (as opposed to the existence of God) as established fact, religion weakened considerably. God fell to the same level as all the other crude delusions. Doctors compensated religion for the loss by telling believers that their awareness of God was an authentic "hyper-lucid unitary experience" operating from special neural networks inside the brain. By conceding this ground, doctors thought they were doing religion a favor. But when the perception of God replaced the existence of God as established fact, religion's pyramid of belief tottered. With this new middle position available, many reasonable people refused to profess a belief in God, the cornerstone on which rested all the other irrational ideas in the religious system. Substituting a "funny feeling about God" for "belief in God" made all religion conjecture and ambiguity.

Ironically, given science's enormous influence on religion today, the one major trait that both religious and spiritual people share is superstition. The supernatural, the irrational, and the absurd increasingly form the basic characteristics of religious and spiritual life in America. One would expect science's involvement in religion to repress such tendencies but, in fact, the opposite has occurred. Spiritual people seek hypnosis, or a state of altered feeling, which they equate with spirituality. This makes supernatural delusions more satisfying to them than simple, intelligible ideas, especially when those delusions boast a connection with science, as in the form of alternative medicine. Religious people, on the other hand, must constantly balance supernatural delusions with intelligible ideas, since both form parts of the religious system. Doing so requires sense and subtlety. Yet science's heavy hand forces them to choose openly: either forsake religion's supernatural delusions or be called a philistine. Refusing to give up their myths and legends, some religious people forsake their reason instead. They start thinking everything is possible and dilate their imaginations to include ridiculous things, until, in the end, images of angels, demons, devils, and the Garden of Eden form the basis of their religious understanding.

Changing spirituality from an idea into a feeling neutralized the last remaining challenge to Artificial Happiness. Once spirituality stopped being a system of ideas and became a feeling, doctors neutralized it as a threat. Without novel ideas to help them see the world in a different light, unhappy Americans now had nowhere else to turn but medicine in all its forms: drugs, alternative medicine, obsessive exercise, psychotherapy, and medically supervised spirituality.

FINISHED

At a dinner party of mostly doctors I recently attended, a minister lavished attention on one doctor in particular, trailing the doctor around the room, laughing at the doctor's stupid jokes, all because he wanted something from the man. Trained as a

Christian counselor and trying to establish his psychology practice, the minister needed patients; the problem was that managed care had all the patients. A few insurance companies had just started paying for religious counseling, but only if primary care doctors within the managed care network made the referrals. Angling for these referrals, the minister talked up the role of combination therapy in depression—antidepressants combined with religious counseling—before thrusting a business card into the doctor's commanding hand. The doctor glanced at it out of courtesy then put it in his back pocket with all the confidence of a man who knows he's in control and all the contempt of a man who hates bootlickers.

Watching this minister sell himself was painful enough from a human perspective but even worse from an historical perspective. The tradition of Western religious training stretches back two thousand years. Over the centuries, millions of believers confused by their momentary, vacillating existences have unburdened themselves to clergymen, who in turn responded by inspiring these people to see life in a new way. Sophisticated, subtle, almost aristocratic, clergymen guided worshippers toward an idea that was clear and eternally significant. Yet here was this minister, heir to the tradition of Saint Augustine, Thomas Aquinas, Martin Luther, and John Calvin, pathetically begging a doctor for patients so he could teach them biofeedback and meditation. This minister had ceased to be the representative of a glorious tradition; he was now the emissary of a defeated and humbled power.

The medical profession now controls all three dimensions of life—the body, the mind, and the spirit—and clergymen have lost their relevance. Even religious people who refuse drugs, alternative medicine, and obsessive exercise can treat their unhappiness by meditating under a doctor's direction, imagining that they lead spiritual lives when they really don't and pretending that their therapy is more religious than medical. Because alternative medicine includes Eastern religions with extensive healing traditions, unhappy patients drawn toward religion can also dabble in religion under an alternative medicine doctor's guidance, again without a clergyman.

Some clergymen, having been struck dumb after fifty roller-coaster years of alternately colluding with doctors and fighting with doctors, unable to distinguish between the trivial and the essential and now confused about the meaning of spirituality itself, have fallen back on old tricks to regain market share. They paint a detailed picture of heaven to incite people's hope, or they talk about miracles to incite people's trust, thereby deceiving unhappy people into happiness the way alternative medicine doctors do, although with less science. Unhappy people drawn toward these measures accept on faith the hypnotism exercised over them. They dream that by fulfilling religious ceremonies or behaving a certain way they will get the happiness they desire. When happiness eludes them they view their failure as accidental or ascribe it to bad luck; with a peculiar mixture of devotion and boredom they continue to go through the motions of religion, waiting impatiently for the happiness they've been promised. It is this pattern within modern organized religion that repels so many Americans and drives them to define themselves as spiritual rather than religious.

The triumph of medicine's vision of life is the central turning point in the history of the relationship between medicine and religion. For the first time, doctors claimed to know life from all sides, even from its interior, relying on an engineering model with tremendous flaws to do so. The American people supported the doctors because their temper harmonized with the doctors' inmost proclivities. Clergymen and the modern era remain profoundly separated, while doctors and the modern era remain very much in synch. This explains why the titanic shift in the relationship between medicine and religion, something that in any other age would seem like a monstrous reversal of nature's course, has barely registered on the public's radar. Science has become such an important part of people's scheme of things—even for clergymen—that the new relationship scarcely evokes attention. Although doctors and religious leaders continue to fight over abortion and stem cell research, this fight is a mere epilogue to a drama that has ended. On the issue of greatest relevance to the American people—unhappiness—doctors rule supreme.

Two revolutions—the medical practice revolution and medicine's revolutionary vision for life—changed the way Americans feel, producing the experience that I call Artificial Happiness. In the course of this narrative I have focused mostly on the psychology of the revolutionaries—the doctors—to show how the medical treatment of unhappiness became a phenomenon, a business, and a faith. During this momentous period in American history the character of the scientist and the ideologue blended together so intimately in doctors' personalities that they formed an inseparable unity. It's impossible to say that one aspect was less genuine than the other; both were vital to the doctors' success. In their capacity as scientists, the doctors radiated power, ego, and intelligence. In their capacity as ideologues, they radiated vision, single-mindedness, and simplicity.

The doctors succeeded with Artificial Happiness because they were well-educated, but, even more important, because they were leaders: they gave the American people a system that not only promised the efficient management of unhappiness but also one that was consonant with the average person's worldview. All during the revolution the doctors' efforts to be scientific about

Artificial Happiness, at times ludicrous, were vital to their success with the public, not because science contributed to any real discovery but because it was the hook that captured the people's imagination.

Now it is time to examine the special psychology of the Happy American, whom the doctors created in their triumph, and to glimpse the dark side of the new happy class.

TEN

THE HAPPY AMERICAN

I KNEW KEVIN GRIMM when we were teenagers growing up in California. He was smart, bold, and quick-tongued, with a nice physique and a good sense of humor, working in his late teens as the manager of a McDonald's restaurant where he was surrounded by a harem of young, sexy cashiers. After we graduated from high school we both went on to college but he dropped out, enjoying life too much at the restaurant. By his midtwenties his outlook changed: a creeping anxiety seemed to grab hold of him. He sensed he was falling behind career-wise so he left McDonald's for a job at a department store. By his midthirties, with most of his friends establishing themselves in high-powered careers, Kevin began openly to regret the course he had taken. In conversation his voice seemed feeble; something of life seemed irrevocably gone. He called himself a failure and a nobody. Simply put, he was unhappy and afraid. Trying to joke him out of his doldrums, while also respecting the gravity of his situation, I told him that a man can't call himself a failure until he's at least fifty and that he still had time to succeed; then I encouraged him to go back and finish college. I was sympathetic to his plight, but firm. He recognized a limit to my sympathy, causing some resentment on his part, including a parting jab about how doctors made too much money.

His resentment toward doctors must have been superficial, because he went to his primary care doctor complaining of unhappiness. The doctor diagnosed depression and prescribed a psychotropic drug. The drug didn't completely refurbish Kevin's spirit—I still detected a feeling of emptiness in him and a touch of self-contempt—but he seemed less afraid. The drug worked just enough to turn off the alarms inside his mind. Rather than plan seriously for his future, Kevin submitted to circumstances, feeling no sense of urgency. He kept putting things off. Kevin had turned into one of those men who become aware of their failure only belatedly and who don't suspect trouble, while everyone else knows that things are spiraling down.

Kevin remained on the drug for several years. When he went off the medication, his fear and anxiety returned with full force, only this time he was past forty, with less career flexibility. Although it is possible that Kevin would not have changed his life even if he had not taken the drug, circumstantial evidence suggests otherwise. During his midthirties, at one of his low points, Kevin phoned me and cried, "I'm afraid! I'm afraid!" He had neither a job nor a plan for the future. I suggested that he go into nursing because there was a shortage of nurses, which meant a high likelihood of getting a job and enjoying a steady income. He seemed lukewarm to the idea but felt enough fear to send away for the college applications (in nursing and other fields), which he filled out and then sent to me so I could help with the essays. It was only after he took psychotropic medication that I noticed a slackening in his pace, to the point that he never mailed in the applications. Medication had robbed Kevin of his unhappiness at the moment he needed it most as an incentive to make a life change. He never recovered; in fact, things got worse. In the end, he died young, angry, and afraid.

Jane Allen is another person whom Artificial Happiness harmed. Hoping to marry her boyfriend and waiting anxiously for him to propose, she tried everything to make him come around, including housekeeping, sex-on-demand, and cooking, yet he refused to commit and basically strung her along. In the back of her mind, she had suspicions about his intentions, suspicions that flamed up, then sank down again. Still, she persevered in the relationship, keeping her doubts to herself, knowing that to appear needy would scare him off completely.

As time went on, the alternating contradictions in her state of mind grew more extreme. There were moments when she felt confident in her boyfriend's affection and that all the sweets of marriage would soon be hers; then there were times when she felt desperate and chided herself for being a fool. During the latter moments, she thought seriously about leaving him. Troubled by her feeling of unhappiness, she saw her primary care doctor, who prescribed Prozac. Because Prozac gave her Artificial Happiness, Jane stayed in her dysfunctional relationship for another year—a wasted year, it turns out, since her boyfriend never changed. When she went off Prozac, she became unhappy again, although this time her unhappiness reached critical mass and compelled her to leave him. When asked if she would have left her boyfriend the year before had she not been on Prozac, she said yes. She reluctantly admitted to wasting a year of her life in a dead-end relationship because of Prozac. By making her content, the drug had arrested her impulse to move on.

Love and work, Freud once said, are the two most important

things in people's lives. Not surprisingly, in the interviews I conducted for this book, much of the harm caused by Artificial Happiness occurred in one of these two areas. Like Kevin and Jane, the people I talked to found themselves in unhappy situations, each with unique circumstances but with a common theme. Something at work or at home was bothering them, making them unhappy; at the bottom of their consciousness, they knew something was wrong and even knew what they had to do; but instead they decided to treat their unhappiness as if it were a separate problem before tackling the bigger task of fixing their life. Little did they know that by treating their unhappiness they robbed themselves of both the energy and the reason to change their life. In essence, they paralyzed themselves with Artificial Happiness.

Fear can be good; unhappiness can be good; both sensations can be as vital to healthy living as physical pain. When touching a hot plate, we feel pain and instinctively pull back; were it not for the pain, we would keep touching the plate, thereby causing ourselves more harm. Fear and unhappiness can be equally protective. They signal to us that something is wrong in life that requires action. Rather than feel alarmed by their unhappiness, Kevin and Jane should have been thankful for it.

Grasping for Artificial Happiness brings to mind a child's approach to pain. In the operating room, children run away from me when they see the tiny needle that I must stick them with to start their anesthetic. The pain from the needle is slight and sometimes not nearly as painful as the disease for which they're getting operated on. Unlike adults, children can't weigh their pain in the present against some future benefit; they can't see the pain coming from the needle as necessary for some lifesaving operation. All they can think about is the pain *now*. Similarly, Kevin and Jane demanded Artificial Happiness because they felt unhappy *now*. They couldn't imagine any future benefit to their unhappiness, that their unhappiness might be an alarm telling them to change their lives so they could find new happiness. With the shortsightedness of children, they uncoupled their feeling of unhappiness from the narrative of their lives and focused solely on getting rid of the pain in the present.

Defenders of Artificial Happiness often accuse their critics of being spartan, ascetic, and opposed to all forms of happiness on principle. They jokingly refer to these critics as "psychopharmacological Calvinists," playing on the stereotypical Calvinist who keeps a stiff upper lip in the face of adversity and rejects all pleasure. The charge of psychopharmacological Calvinism wafted in my direction once during a television news piece. After I spoke gravely about the problems of overmedication, the camera cut to a woman on welfare pleading with a reporter that her only happiness in life came from Prozac. Although the official story line involved the consequences of Prozac going off patent, the story's subtext had me in the role of the cold, unfeeling professional denying a helpless woman her scrap of joy.

My criticism of Artificial Happiness is not in any way related to psychopharmacological Calvinism. I want people like Kevin Grimm, Jane Allen, and the woman on welfare to be deliriously happy. My concern is not that Artificial Happiness robs people of some character-building unhappiness but that it locks people in purgatory, lifting them only halfway out of misery while preventing them from making the changes they need to make to enjoy real happiness. My criticism of Artificial Happiness is tactical, not strategic.

I agree with the psychopharmacological Calvinists on one point: antidepressants stupefy people, just like alcohol does. Alcohol dampens certain aspects of brain function, creating an altered mental state, so much so that true reality becomes concealed from a person's consciousness. Drinking alcohol is a reliable method of dealing with unhappiness because it hides from view what people don't want to see with their minds. Antidepressants work similarly. Although people on antidepressants drive safely and don't vomit in the streets, they use antidepressants the way others use alcohol, to dampen brain functions, causing their minds to see life in a different light.

But once acknowledging the stupefying nature of antidepressants, my criticism of Artificial Happiness veers off in a different direction. Take, for example, the case of John Green, a man described in this book's introduction. Unhappily married but with a child, John had an important decision to make: whether he should stay married or leave his wife. Most people sift through contradictory thoughts and feelings when pondering a big decision; instead, John bleached out his negative feelings with Prozac. But without those feelings John couldn't make his decision as a whole man. True, he eventually decided to stay married, but who decided: John or John on Prozac? The two men are different. The real John would lie awake at night, stare at the ceiling, and think awful thoughts about his wife; John on Prozac lives contentedly and sleeps soundly. It was not John who decided to stay with his wife—it was John on Prozac, a man who felt differently, thought differently, and lived differently from the real John.

By stupefying John at a pivotal moment, Prozac deflected the course of his life. Even John admits that without the drug he'd probably have gotten a divorce, which makes Prozac the key factor in his decision. Perhaps worse, John's decision to stay married, made under Prozac's influence, condemns John to a future on Prozac. Since divorce grows financially more difficult with each passing year, Prozac kept John from divorcing his wife at an opportune moment. The possibility of having to spend a lifetime married to his wife grows more likely as the years roll by, causing John to cling more desperately to Prozac. Time compounds the effects of John's decision to stay married; because Prozac was the basis for that decision, Prozac begets more Prozac.

Unlike drunks, people on antidepressants retain the strength and ingenuity to make small life changes for the better. Kevin, for example, learned how to sail during his four years on Prozac. Jane cleaned out her closets. John Green orchestrated a wonderful birthday party for his son. Yet, all during their treatment, the heart of their respective situations remained untouched. By allowing themselves to be stupefied at a critical moment, Kevin, Jane, and John made many small decisions but dodged the most important life decisions.

Doug Sandler, like John Green, also calls into question the identity of people who make important decisions under the influence of Artificial Happiness. Living in the suburbs with his wife and two children, Doug had always dreamed of becoming a musician but played it safe and became an engineer. On weekends he kept his dream alive by busying himself in his basement with music. Over time, however, Doug began wrestling in his mind with whether he had done the right thing. Strumming on his guitar, he saw himself as an artist, a real artist, and regretted his career choice. Then at other times he imagined himself an impoverished musician grubbing for concert bookings and unable to support his family, which made him thankful that he became an engineer.

Gradually Doug's failed enthusiasm for his job grew into dissatisfaction with life, which he blamed on his career choice. He was gloomy when he went to the office in the morning; he was gloomy when he returned home. He began voicing aloud a serious plan to leave his job and try his hand at music professionally, although inwardly he knew that he lacked the gumption to act on it. His wife became alarmed, then angry, refusing to support him if he made the move and even threatening divorce. His mother was equally shocked. Reminding him that he had such a beautiful office at work, she asked him, "What else could a man possibly want?" Friends told him not to try, that he would ruin his life. Yet the phantom of regret haunted Doug, who felt he was taking part in some awful trade-off: security in exchange for pursuing his dream. Eventually his nagging unease grew into a merciless, all-consuming anxiety with no hope of being resolved since, deep down, Doug knew he lacked both the courage and the self-confidence to bolt his job and pursue music full-time. Feeling depressed and suffering from insomnia, he went to his primary care doctor, who prescribed him Zoloft.

Within two months Zoloft had refashioned Doug's cast of mind. "The cloud lifted," said Doug. In eight months, Doug felt sufficiently confident to leave his job and try his hand at music full-time. Before Zoloft, Doug lacked the strength of will to fight his family, his friends, and his own conscience. Zoloft gave him that strength. Doug now lives in a pathetic old apartment with shabby furniture and is separated from his wife. He's been pursuing his dream for only a few months, which means he still has time to succeed.

If Doug fails, Zoloft deserves the blame. Before taking Zoloft, Doug showed every intention of remaining an engineer—an unhappy engineer but still an engineer, with material security and a family. If Doug flops as a musician and spirals downward, Zoloft will be the cause. True, if Doug fails people may say he is unfortunate, unrecognized, and poor but at least he's honest—he's a man who gave his life to art. This is what Doug thinks, too. But this is not how the real Doug—the Doug before Zoloft—thought. The real Doug obsessed about material security and worried about what his friends said. Even if Doug fails as a musician and celebrates poverty he won't be honest while doing so, since the real Doug would not have done so.

However, even if Doug succeeds it won't be Doug's success but Zoloft's success. The natural Doug was not destined to become an American success story, for he lacked the requisite risk-taking personality. Even Doug admits that without Zoloft he would not have risked his material security for a career in music. Zoloft, and not any inherent qualities in Doug, will be responsible if Doug succeeds. No pat on the back is warranted if he does.

We have lost the guiding thread of Doug's life. Whether he succeeds or fails, Doug is no longer living his own life. He has lost traits that he formerly possessed—traits that can be useful to a person, such as caution, prudence, and a careful weighing of all the consequences of a decision before choosing. Obviously, his break with his past is not complete; there is still much continuity. But Doug is sufficiently changed so as to be on a path of life that he wasn't destined for.

When asked if he were the real Doug or an imposter, Doug replied:

> What is the camel? It's all loaded up, part of the caravan. Do you separate the camel from its load or are they one? Isn't the camel only itself when it's unburdened? And what does it say about the camel if its load is too cumbersome to carry? If you lighten its load and continue, is the camel different?
>
> I became overburdened and it showed. I felt it. Others could see it. My response: lighten the load. If I don't at some point accept the load as before, am I lesser for it?

Using the camel-load analogy, Doug divides himself into two

parts. One part is the person Doug wants to be—the camel. The other part is the psychology that kept him from becoming that person—the load. However, Doug's analogy is wrong. The camel's load is a foreign entity and not part of the camel, while Doug's personality traits, the product of countless experiences and interactions, are an essential part of him. Doug didn't remove an artificial load that had no business being there, he silenced certain modes of thinking that were basic to his identity. Doug concealed these modes of thinking from himself so that he could do what he would otherwise not do: leave work and pursue music full time. Basically, he lied to himself. Rather than become an unencumbered self, he became a stupefied self.

Falsehood can be useful sometimes. A woman goes to a party to meet men but is too shy to talk to anyone. So she drinks two glasses of wine and transforms herself from a wallflower into an accomplished flirt. In the end, she finds someone and has a good time. This is fine, since the stakes aren't that high, the alcohol effect is transitory, and the woman herself acknowledges what she's done. What Doug experiences is falsehood on an entirely different scale. His whole life has been affected. Moreover, Zoloft has so skillfully weaved itself into Doug's personality that he imagines he's the same person even though his behavior is that of someone totally different.

Alternative medicine-induced Artificial Happiness causes a paralysis of mind no less intense than psychotropic drugs, illustrated by the case of Beth Fallon.

Overworked and divorced, Beth spends long hours as a lawyer while also raising two teenage children on her own. Her life is hard. A year ago, feeling unhappy, she went to an alternative medicine doctor, who diagnosed her unhappiness as a "congested energy field," then prescribed her an herbal cocktail. Afterward, Beth felt Artificially Happy, noting:

> Before taking the herbs, I felt overwhelmed by life. I've got so much on my plate right now—kids, my career, a mortgage. Just yesterday my daughter dyed her hair a ridiculous color, and on top of that she had an allergic reaction to the dye, so I had to take her to the emergency room. It's too much. Herbal therapy is my "Band-Aid" for life.

She paused for a moment, then added, "I want to live my life, but not feel it so much. And why should I feel it? If I can't change my life, why shouldn't I change how I feel?"

At first glance, Beth's experience with Artificial Happiness differs from that of Kevin Grimm and Jane Allen, for Beth had no major life decision pending. The circumstances in Beth's life were so fixed that there was nothing for Artificial Happiness to influence, decide, or block. Artificial Happiness simply made her life bearable. However, on closer inspection, some big life changes were possible. Beth could have changed her priorities in life. She sent her children to the most expensive private school in town. She refused to sell her big house, despite the drain on her income, because she wanted to stay connected to a happier time in her life, when she was married. She worked sixty hours a week in a high powered law firm, in part for the money but also because the prestige associated with a busy practice fed her self-esteem. It was not life, but Beth's wants in life—and the enormous pressure those wants put her under—that lay at the root of her unhappiness.

I made this point to Beth. I told her that wants are like

balloons in a closed space. If reasonably inflated, the balloons have enough room for one another, but if extravagantly inflated, each balloon occupies too much space and crowds out the other balloons as well as itself, creating enormous pressure and causing the whole system to suffer. I told her that she suffered from extravagant wants, not a congested energy field; then I recommended that instead of taking herbs to feel Artificially Happy she change her priorities, starting with her house, her job, and her children's school.

She responded with excuses. "OK, if my life were slower and more spacious, then I wouldn't need this medicine. But I'm just not living that life right now." Then she got angry:

> What the hell do you expect me to do! Huh? You want my kids to lose out in life? You want me to live in some cheap apartment? You want me to become some third-rate lawyer on the mommy track, when I went to Harvard? Harvard! I'm not changing my life. OK, I take herbs, but at least I'm moving the boat forward.

At this point, I thought it best to end the interview. But Beth raises an important question that needs to be addressed. If a person is saddled with a stressful and depressing situation that is inescapable, then finds a safe modality that relieves the stress and depression, what's the harm? Beth's case is especially relevant, since at some point her children will be grown, the pressures will taper off, and she can relax. In the interim, why not let her use a safe modality to feel better?

The assumption here is that if Beth changed the conditions of her life now it would only make her unhappier. That assumption implies that her current conditions, which are making her unhappy, are acceptable, even logical. If Beth were locked in an abusive relationship amidst poverty, few people would encourage her to paralyze herself with Artificial Happiness, since no one in his right mind would find a semblance of happiness in an abusive relationship amidst poverty. But many people can find a semblance of happiness working for a big law firm, living in a mansion, and sending their children to the best schools, even when that happiness is poisoned by fear and anxiety. This is why Beth's use of alternative medicine is considered acceptable: Beth's life, unlike the life of a poverty-stricken person enduring an abusive relationship, is respected.

Beth's problem begins here. Beth is unhappy but, rather than rethink her approach to life, she submits to the guidance of the larger world. Since her days as a teenager, she has observed people desire Harvard, a fancy law firm, the best furniture, the best neighborhoods, and the best-dressed and best-educated children. These things filled the whole of life. She didn't understand why they were so important, but she heard people say they were. Her friends, who were equally in the dark, heard the same thing and ascribed to them the same significance. Today these friends endure similar stress, reassuring themselves with the idea that working in great law firms and living in huge mansions constitute the real business of life and are worth striving for because they are so highly prized. Beth and her friends assume that a life committed to getting these things has a rational explanation that someone in the world knows, even if they themselves don't.

Rather than cast doubt on the importance of these things, Beth's unhappiness simply heightens her desire to keep them, since they form the only definition of happiness she has ever known. This explains why she became angry with me: I threatened to take away the things that were making her so miserable. Is this life? All Beth's complicated, seething activity—her desperate juggling of wants to maintain a certain image of herself, her painful existence that she presumes is compulsory, although she's really a free person—is a source of misery for her.

Beth has never looked inside herself because she is unaccustomed to independent thinking. Her approach to life is strongly supported by her environment and influenced by the crowd. This is why she is unhappy. However, at the very moment when her unhappiness reached critical mass, pressing her to think about life for the first time, she used herbs to shut down the conversation she might otherwise have held within herself about the direction of her life. The herbs silenced her questions and doubts. They preserved in her the mind-set of a dumb animal, one that works efficiently but without understanding why or what for. They let her continue living a life purely external, where she sees nothing in the world beyond achievement.

Won't this be for just ten years, until Beth's children are grown? Even if it is, that is still a long time to thickly veil the mind, especially when herbs, unlike antidepressants, erect an incomplete barrier between the mind and real life. Beth admits that from time to time unhappiness peeps through. She knows living is necessary; she wants to live; her desires bid her to live; and yet she finds it impossible to live. This feeling of being in the middle of some irreconcilable contradiction saddens her. The Artificial Happiness she gets from alternative medicine is incomplete, just enough to stifle a conversation within herself but not enough to make her content.

I doubt Beth will change after her children are grown. As a teenager, Beth learned to prize the best retirement homes, the best vacations, and the best-dressed and best-educated grandchildren. Ten years from now, when her children are grown, she will likely develop new wants. Once recognized by her mind, these wants will grow to unlimited dimensions and she will find herself in the same situation she's in now—for the same reasons.

I don't expect Beth to move into a cheap apartment, stick her children in the worst schools, and confine her law practice to writing wills. She accused me of doing so because she wanted to eliminate the middle ground and prove to me that her situation was inescapable. But I think that Beth could modify her circumstances slightly, enough to satisfy personal pride, while also making her life less stressful. To do so, she must have clarity of mind with which to think anew about life, reexamine her wants, and decide what is important. She must awaken, look inside herself, and question the source and motivation for why she lives as she does. Artificial Happiness, however, keeps her asleep.

Exercise-induced Artificial Happiness causes a similar paralysis of mind. Anna Smith works in human resources for a boss nicknamed "the ogre." After work, she swims in my masters' swim class to "get her endorphins going." Several years ago, unhappy at work, she toyed with the idea of applying for a new job. Around the same time, she discovered exercise, which became a vent for her frustrations, siphoning off her drive to find another job. Anna credits exercise with helping her endure a hostile work environment. She exercises two hours a day, every day; the endorphin effect, she claims, lasts through most of the evening. She calls it a fair compromise: eight hours of unhappiness at work in exchange for eight hours of happiness at home.

Some of the Artificial Happiness Anna feels through exercise comes from more than the endorphin effect. Anna admits that being in good shape boosts her self-esteem. On days when she feels especially "beat up" at work, she trains extra hard and "beats herself up," as if by being her own taskmaster she balances some universal scale of justice. During fights with her boss she sometimes detaches herself from the conflict and gloats inwardly, *Yes, but I can swim a hundred yards in sixty seconds.* She repeats the phrase over and over again, like a mantra.

I don't expect every American with a difficult boss to uproot and find a new job. What troubles me is when exercise-induced unhappiness tips the balance in the decision. It's one thing for Anna to have balanced real happiness—perhaps from a steady partner, a family, or friends—against work; it's quite another for Anna to balance fake happiness against work. A woman without a family or a partner, and with few friends, Anna factored Artificial Happiness into her calculations when making her decision. Given the time she commits to Artificial Happiness (two hours of exercise every day by herself and another hour driving to and from the gym—again, by herself) Anna is not only miserable at work but also less likely to form friendships or meet a potential mate during her off-hours. The chance for real happiness becomes almost physically impossible.

People know life as a series of choices. Sometimes a choice has no clear outcome; in such cases, people make their best guess. Yet, even when guessing, people make the choice themselves. By robbing people of the desire to think or act differently, or robbing them of the ability to see the consequences of their actions, Artificial Happiness makes the choice *for* them. Whether it pushes them toward inaction, freezing them in their present circumstances no matter how noxious those circumstances might be, or conceals from them the outcome of different choices, Artificial Happiness disrupts the natural decision-making process by which people navigate life. Doctors abet this paralysis of mind by pushing drugs, alternative medicine, and obsessive exercise. They also contribute to the phenomenon by getting people to see unhappiness as something separate from life. This mind-set prepares people to seek or receive Artificial Happiness.

A case told to me by a prison psychiatrist illustrates how far people have taken this attitude. In jail for robbery and second-degree murder, one of the psychiatrist's patients complained of low self-esteem. The psychiatrist responded, "You have low self-esteem? Of course you have low self-esteem. You're a murderer and a thief!" The psychiatrist complained that too many of his patients these days saw self-esteem as something disconnected from life and to be given out in the form of a pill. To the extent that people today uncouple happiness from life, they are merely following the doctors' lead, while the doctors themselves fell into the clutches of this logic after several decades of faulty reasoning.

Doctors once saw unhappiness as something embedded in life. In the late 1960s, during the medical profession's first crisis, doctors began to reflect on the mechanics of unhappiness. During the course of their reflections, their attention shifted, first from life to the brain, then from the brain to neurons, then from neurons to synapses, and finally from synapses to neurotransmitters. They concluded that the whole unhappiness problem lay in neurotransmitters, which caused their entire understanding of life and happiness to be thrown out of gear. In a twisted way, they were right; their error was to reason without order and to put neurotransmitters ahead of life. This error led them to detach unhappiness from life and treat it separately. The public took the doctors' message to heart; eventually the whole country's deliberations on unhappiness lost their way. Because of this train of errors, Artificial Happiness is now the country's favored solution to unhappiness, concealing from people a proper understanding of the relationship between happiness and life.

TAMPERING WITH THE LIFE CYCLE

Brian Dunnigan is a forty-year-old man who likes twenty-year-old women. But twenty-year-old women rarely reciprocate his attentions. Most Friday nights he goes to his favorite bar wearing jeans and a black T-shirt, looking quite smart, yet the women treat him politely, even kindly—a sure sign of pity. Despite sitting alone on his stool, the oldest guy in the room, Brian still feels upbeat, thanks to Zoloft. Several months before, he told his primary care doctor that he felt blue because of his lousy social life. With the typical fast tempo of managed care, his doctor prescribed medication. Everything was short and to the point. Now when Brian sits alone at the bar he's content. Even after being rejected by a woman for the tenth time he feels good, thanks to the drug.

Compelled by circumstances, Brian had reached a point in life when he needed to rethink his approach to relationships. His unhappiness was natural, to be expected, and just the right catalyst to move things along. When Zoloft eliminated his unhappiness, the process stopped: Brian no longer felt the urge to change. To this day, he remains hooked on younger women—and he remains alone. Artificial Happiness fills up all the room in Brian's mind, crowding out any incentive he might have for another life. On reflection, we can see that Artificial Happiness did more than just arrest Brian's impulse to seek happiness in a new kind of life; it also blocked his progression from one life stage to another. This makes Artificial Happiness a sociological concern as well as a personal tragedy.

The traditional life cycle is divided up into stages based on age: childhood, adolescence, young adulthood, middle age, and old age. Each stage has its own special goal—such as dating, marriage, raising children, and retirement. Americans increasingly reject this traditional path through life. Compared to fifty years ago, their lives are less divided into stages based on age. In the 1950s, if you were thirty, chances are you were married; if you were forty, chances are you were raising children; if you were seventy, chances are you were retired. This is less true now.

By blocking people's progression from one life stage to another, Artificial Happiness further weakens the traditional life cycle. I'm not referring to the phenomenon where adults suddenly shirk all responsibility, sell their homes, and ride motorcycles across the country. In that pattern, adults regress to the same youthful stage; the traditional life cycle collapses because everyone tries to act young. In Artificial Happiness, the pattern is more textured and subtle. Happy Americans don't regress to teenage-hood; they simply remain in the stage of life where they found Artificial Happiness. People who become Artificially Happy at forty behave like forty-year-olds when they're sixty; people who become Artificially Happy at sixty behave like sixty-year-olds when they're eighty. Sometimes the behavior that's locked in is stereotypical—a forty-year-old man, for example, obsessing about younger women the way Brian did, which most men eventually grow out of, more or less. At other times, the behavior is person-specific; it is the particular outlook a person has when he or she induces Artificial Happiness. Such behavior may or may not define any recognizable life stage.

Not quite fifty, Vera Smith stares longingly at a picture of her ex-husband, who left her for another woman two years ago. I ask her why she gives the picture such a prominent place in her living room. Because he might come back, she says. In the most delicate fashion I can think of, I tell her that he's not coming back, that he's remarried. She winces. I ask her how things are going. She says meditation is a big part of her life now, an activity she gravitated toward during her divorce. She says she plays

New Age music and dims the lights while she meditates. Just yesterday, she imagined walking down a beautiful path and, later, someone pouring a mysterious orange liquid into her, cleansing her of bad memories. In her semiconscious state, Vera forgets her ex-husband and experiences Artificial Happiness.

Artificial Happiness keeps Vera from passing into the next stage of her life, that of a divorced woman. Although Vera escapes her own consciousness through meditation and keeps her unhappiness at bay, she also postpones any serious analysis of her situation. Her old ways of thinking carry on without end, her innermost nature fails to change, and she fails to progress to a new stage of life.

A person's relation to the world changes naturally, gradually, and imperceptibly—this is what passing through the stages of a life cycle means. Although their bond with the past may remain visible, people evolve and become different people. This explains why a forty-year-old laughs at the clothes he wore as a twenty-year-old or why a sixty-year-old laughs at the clothes he wore as a forty-year-old. Moving through life is like that. Unhappiness drives this progression in consciousness; although painful, it is an essential part of the life cycle. People grow unhappy as one life stage begins to wane. The possibility of a new kind of happiness beckons and they move from one stage to the next, often without being aware of it. By blocking this unhappiness, Artificial Happiness blocks this progression through life.

Life is a series of entrances and exits. People don't know how they arrive at a new state of consciousness or how they leave the old one. Change just happens. Sometimes people resist. They want things to stay the same; they fear stirring from their spot because they can't see what lies ahead; the thought of losing their present relationship to the world revolts them. At times, even their unhappiness is precious to them because it links them in some way to the world they want to hold on to. This was true of Vera. Still, in most cases, change inevitably occurs. People's minds detect the falseness of what they're trying to preserve and then reject it. Artificial Happiness keeps this from happening. It drowns out the feeling of revulsion toward the falseness and makes that particular dying stage of life seem viable a little while longer. This is what happened to both Brian and Vera. Artificial Happiness kept both of them from seeing the reality of their respective situations—from accepting that an old life stage was dying and a new one was dawning—thereby preventing them from moving forward in life.

A NEW KIND OF LIFE CYCLE

Artificial Happiness tampers with the traditional life cycle and also creates a new kind of life cycle. This new life cycle, when it dominates an entire society, creates new kinds of people: Happy Children, Happy Adults, and Happy Seniors. To understand this trend in American life and how these people differ from conventional children, adults, and seniors, it helps to understand how the life cycle has changed over the centuries.

The idea of a life cycle is relatively new in Western culture. In the preindustrial era, the concepts of neither adulthood nor childhood existed. The difference between adults and children turned merely on size and physical capacity. Boys became men when they were big enough to work; girls became women when they became fertile. Children were viewed as little adults; once they reached full size, their development ended.

The term *adult* first appeared in the Oxford English Dictionary in 1656. The term *adulthood* first appeared even later, in 1870, with several reasons accounting for the change. First, people began living longer, with less of life tied to raising children. Age groupings within adult life arose, with each group taking on distinct social roles and responsibilities. Life began to have stages. Second, adults functioning at the level of overgrown children sufficed in the premodern world, where people needed little knowledge to survive, but modernity brought autonomy and freedom. People had to be responsible; they had to participate in politics and government; they had to know more than before. In Western culture, the idea of the wise, informed adult began to take shape.

Increased longevity, industrialization, and the spread of democracy fed the emerging social concept of adulthood, which most Americans lived by well into the 1960s—an adult man is paid for his labor in the industrial economy and advances socially within the public sphere; an adult woman performs labor in the household economy (without pay) and advances socially within the private sphere. The concept reached its zenith in the 1950s, during the era of the Organization Man when adults passed through different life phases based on clear social markers. The Organization Man went to school; went to work for the Organization; dated; got married; moved to the suburbs; raised children; had barbeques; joined the Rotary Club; became a pillar of the community; and then retired. The Organization Woman went to school; became a nurse, a teacher, or a secretary; found a man; got married; quit her job; moved to the suburbs; had babies; joined the PTA; joined the garden club; became president of the PTA; became president of the garden club; and then retired with her husband. Those people who didn't follow this social track to adulthood were seen as childish, even abnormal. The track became known as the traditional life cycle.

During the 1950s, psychologists working within the structure of social adulthood created their own psychological interpretation of adulthood, matching each social accomplishment with a psychological one. Psychologist Erik Erikson published *Childhood and Society* in 1950, in which he described eight stages of life, with three of the stages occurring in adulthood and correlating with the Organization Man's rhythm of life. The first adult stage, called "intimacy versus isolation," represented marriage. The second adult stage, called "generativity versus stagnation," represented parenthood. The third and final adult stage, called "integrity versus despair," represented retirement. Erikson's model practically endorsed the Organization Man's rhythm of life. Getting off the track, he argued, led to all sorts of psychological trouble, including despair, confusion, and midlife crisis.

In her 1976 best seller *Passages*, author Gail Sheehy embellished Erikson's model, organizing the phases of life by decade. "Intimacy versus isolation" became the "trying twenties" and "generativity versus stagnation" became the "Catch-30s." In another book, titled *New Passages*, she extended her model to include midlife and old age—the "flourishing forties" gave way to the "flaming fifties," followed by the "serene sixties." In both books, Sheehy showed life progressing like clockwork, with each stage of life tied to a specific age.

The search for happiness drives the life cycle, so once the social model of adulthood stopped making people content they rejected it. In an idealized version of life in the 1950s, people lived happily in the suburbs, raised children, and had barbeques, with the journey through life almost preplanned. By the 1960s, many Americans saw this plan for life as stifling. The sexual revolution, feminism, and the decline in the Organization as omnipotent protector brought new freedoms, new ways of living, and new paths to happiness.

Cheryl Merser captured the collapse of the traditional life cycle in her 1987 book *Grown-ups*. Unable to find herself in

Sheehy's passages, Merser showed how the old life cycle was no longer relevant to people's lives and that Americans weren't necessarily marrying in their twenties and parenting in their thirties. New opportunities in education, careers, and living arrangements meant that being a twentysomething or thirtysomething was no longer a reliable predictor of anything.

Merser and her cohorts found happiness in these new opportunities. At the same time, they found living without a life cycle confusing and depressing, for they no longer understood what it meant to be an adult. Their confusion played into the hands of psychologists, who conceived a different path to adulthood, one disconnected from either social markers or age. In the psychological model of adulthood, instead of advancing socially toward adulthood, a person advances mentally. Psychologist Abraham Maslow spoke of a development that proceeds from within rather than from without, toward individuality, and ending when the person behaves "purely expressively." In the new order, children were self-aware and adults were self-actualized. Becoming an adult no longer depended on age or social position. A repressed middle-aged businessman with a house and a family could be less of an adult than a thoughtful twentysomething who lived alone and slept on a futon. The key to adulthood was achieving a certain psychological state. But people found even less happiness in the psychological model than in the social model. Moving to the suburbs and hosting barbeques brought at least some joy; achieving a higher consciousness brought none. Nothing pleasant existed in the psychological model to draw people forward in life. In the end, the psychological model became a set of values more than a path through life.

Artificial Happiness rushed onto the scene during this crisis, offering a second alternative to the declining social model of adulthood. Because people feel Artificial Happiness independent of life or age, the life cycle generated by Artificial Happiness has nothing to do with moving forward in life. In the traditional life cycle, a new kind of happiness beckons at each stage, but in Artificial Happiness people have no reason to advance through stages, since they enjoy happiness independent of life's progression. Although Happy Children become Happy Adults, who in turn become Happy Seniors, the whole process lacks a sense of movement with direction.

All life cycles begin with childhood, and the attention now being paid to the problem of teenage depression is an ominous sign of what is to come. The U.S. Department of Health and Human Services published in 2005 a National Survey on Drug Use and Health (NSDUH) report stating that 14 percent of American teenagers, or 3.5 million youths, had experienced major depression in their lifetime. Accompanying the report's release were calls for doctors to get more aggressive in treating the problem. Dr. David Fassler, a psychiatry professor at the University of Vermont, said, "The real tragedy, as the report notes, is that there are still so many young people who aren't receiving the appropriate and effective treatment they need and deserve." The tone of both the report and the response recalls the medical profession's thinking during the first stage of the medical practice revolution, when the Nielson-Williams article, published in 1980 and discussed in this book's second chapter, declared the prevalence of minor depression in the general population to be 12 percent, and charged primary care doctors with underdiagnosing and undertreating the problem. The Nielson-Williams article set the stage for an explosion in antidepressant use among adults. The NSDUH report plays the same role among teenagers, with doctors eager to prescribe medication in these patients and using the report to justify their aggressive approach.

The NSDUH report may lead to an even greater percentage

of teenagers being treated for depression than the percentage of adults recommended for treatment in the Nielson-Williams article since the NSDUH estimate for the prevalence of *major* depression among teenagers approximates the Nielson-Williams estimate for the prevalence of *minor* depression among adults. Because the incidence of minor depression in any given population is roughly four times that of major depression, approximately half of American teenagers can be expected to have some kind of depression, major or minor, with all of them candidates for Artificial Happiness.

The new emphasis on teenage depression pushes Artificial Happiness into unchartered territory. Artificial Happiness harms millions of people now, but only individually; the overall social impact has yet to be felt. This is because most users of Artificial Happiness are adults, who may ruin their own lives with Artificial Happiness but who have little effect on the lives of others while doing so. Inducing Artificial Happiness in children, and on a mass scale, has far greater social repercussions. A whole species of humanity stands ready to emerge in which Artificial Happiness has blunted psychological development during a crucial period in life—childhood. As children, these people are given Artificial Happiness to drive off feelings of sadness. Avoiding sadness becomes a habit for them. When the next downturn in life occurs, the Artificial Happiness experience is repeated. These Happy Children go on for months, even years, standing before the same life dilemmas and not moving a step toward their solution, stifling the growth of their consciences through repeated bouts of stupefaction. They become Happy Adults and then Happy Seniors, using the same method throughout their lives to deal with unhappiness. What emerges is an entire life cycle based on Artificial Happiness.

Before describing these character types of the future, I need to make one last point. These characters are just that—of the future. What I describe is a world that may emerge if Artificial Happiness solidifies its hold on American culture; its broad outlines are just barely visible now.

THE HAPPY CHILD

In the 1950s, children were told to wear certain clothes and brush their hair a certain way to win friends. They were advised, "Take a good look at those who are popular. Try to be like them." A child's mission during this era was to be normal, for being normal was the way to happiness. This mission also had a larger purpose: fitting in, belonging, and being well-rounded were vital behavioral patterns in a society organized around the traditional life cycle. For a child, happiness came from being liked on the playground; for a teenager, it came from being liked in the fraternity or sorority; for a young adult, it came from being liked in the Organization; for an older adult, it came from being liked by the neighbors. Happiness changed its spots over the course of the traditional life cycle, but at each stage the key to happiness was being liked and the key to being liked was being normal.

Even the psychological model of adulthood emphasized the importance of being normal. Although the psychological model put less emphasis on a child's school clothes or on whether a child had nice teeth, a child had to assimilate a set of core values to be liked, including tolerance, empathy, and understanding. The child felt pressure to adopt these values, which formed the new definition of normal. Failure to comply carried the risk of being disliked and unhappy.

Under an Artificial Happiness regime, the Happy Child is not normal; he is *functional*. The Happy Child is expected to perform certain rudimentary tasks that earlier models of child development considered mere baseline: showing up to class, obeying school rules, not fighting with the other kids, and not terrorizing the teacher. Little else is expected of the Happy Child (certainly not that he be popular or empathetic). All society asks of him is that he not be a nuisance to others. In past eras, children learned to be normal because normalcy determined likeability and therefore happiness. In Artificial Happiness, the Happy Child receives happiness from drugs, alternative medicine, or obsessive exercise—from a source independent of life. Happiness no longer turns on whether the Happy Child is liked. On the contrary, chances are the Happy Child will not be liked, since he sees no benefit to endearing himself to others.

The concept of the Happy Child comports with important cultural values. In a society that emphasizes individuality over the group nothing is more resented than the concept of normal. In the 1950s, children's minds were chipped and pruned in preparation for living in a society that demanded conformity. Children who failed to conform suffered miserably. The Happy Child, on the other hand, feels no such pressure to conform. He does his schoolwork, participates in school activities, and goes home, all without causing trouble. He feels no pressure to compare himself to others; in fact, all society expects of him (and wants from him) is that he behave and achieve.

The Happy Child is the third child character type to emerge in American cultural history. Writing in the 1950s, sociologist David Riesman described the first two types in his book, *The Lonely Crowd*. According to Riesman, the nineteenth century American child was "inner-directed." Religion gave the inner-directed child an internal gyroscope, forcing the child to behave in certain ways no matter what his surroundings were. Because the inner-directed child received his behavioral cues from a belief system rather than from a group of peers, being normal mattered less; guided from within rather than from without, the nineteenth-century American child could be quirky and idiosyncratic. Being liked was not the driving force behind his actions.

The child during the era of the Organization Man was other-directed. Eager to shave off quirks and idiosyncrasies to be liked, the other-directed child took his behavioral cues from his peers, not from some internal belief system. How others saw him loomed large in his mind, constraining how he behaved and deciding how much happiness he felt.

Hovering on America's cultural horizon is the Happy Child, a new character type. Like the inner-directed child, the Happy Child is guided from within, except that Artificial Happiness rather than religion guides him. He experiences happiness not because he fulfills some religious command (or because he's liked by others) but because of what medicine does to him. If anything, happiness is the cause of his behavior rather than the consequence. In the past, authority figures told inner-directed and other-directed children that if they behaved a certain way they would be happy. Happy Children, on the other hand, are made happy so that they will behave—or, at the very least, so that they will function.

Already this dictum is being translated into medical reality. With the rate of violent crime among teenagers more than doubling since 1985 and the number of violent deaths among children threefold higher since the 1950s, doctors are exploring the brain chemistry behind juvenile violence in preparation for treating it. Dr. Markus Kruesi, head of the division of the Institute for Juvenile Research at the University of Illinois, argues that low serotonin levels predict aggression in children with multiple disruptive behavioral disorders. Dr. Emil Coccaro, head of the division of clinical neuroscience research at the Medical College of Pennsylvania, claims that serotonin modulates the brain response to external stimuli; he has already used Prozac to decrease aggressive behavior in forty adults. Psychologist Oliver James ventures to say that a chemical hierarchy exists in society, that some people are predisposed to immoral behavior because of their brain chemistry, and that medication might correct the imbalance. Low serotonin levels, he claims, have already been discovered in children who torture animals and treat their mothers badly. He suggests that treating these children with antidepressants, thereby making them happier, will also make them orderly.

Although the treatment goal of all these doctors is to make dysfunctional children functional, normal children in Happy America will aspire to the same goal. This is because the gap between dysfunctional children and normal children will narrow. In the past, there were three levels of adolescent behavior: dysfunctional, functional, and normal. In Happy America, there will be only two: dysfunctional and functional, with normal defined down to functional.

Fear is palpable among the authorities who deal with Happy Children. They appease children with Artificial Happiness, turning happiness into a kind of bribe. All the authorities want is a clean school, without vandalism or bullies, and an orderly playground with functional children. Normalcy, once so vital to a child's development, is viewed as a luxury. The authorities settle for peace and quiet.

The Happy Child is well-behaved on the playground because Artificial Happiness erases feelings that would otherwise cause him to lash out—not because his mind calculates how God or his peers might judge him. Having lost the habit of making such calculations, the Happy Child's inner experience shrinks from lack of use. Without the need to be liked by his peers, the

Happy Child doesn't learn empathy or understanding. Nothing in his life pushes him to reflect on how other people feel, let alone how they feel about him, reflections that would trim his behavior accordingly. Without a need for a belief system, the Happy Child doesn't learn respect or humility because nothing in his life forces him to settle a conflict between personal happiness and duty, since his happiness comes automatically from medicine. The Happy Child is a very simple organism: he functions, which is all that society really asks of him.

The abuse of stimulants among teenagers today offers an example of this shrunken inner experience. Emulating classmates with ADHD who improve their grades on Ritalin, many healthy teenagers secretly take the drug as a "study pill" to improve their own scores. Although the authorities condemn Ritalin abuse, they police the problem less aggressively than other forms of drug abuse, seeming almost warmed by the teenagers' desire to function at such a high level. Teenagers learn from the authorities' tepid response that any action is permissible in the quest to be high functioning. Instead of sensing a gap between their real-life capabilities and what they aspire to, and feeling unhappy as a result, they close that gap artificially through stimulants and grow accustomed to using medicine whenever they feel a divergence between how they live and how they want to live.

The Happy Child is honest when he can afford to be, not because his conscience tells him to be. He silences his conscience with Artificial Happiness whenever it threatens him with criticism. Sometimes, as in the case of stimulants, he changes how he functions to comport with what his conscience expects of him. He fastens his constancy not to a belief system or to the watchful eye of his peers but to a sensation. That sensation conceals any discord he may feel between how he lives and how he wants to live.

The aspiration to be functional complements the psychological effect of Artificial Happiness. *Normal* involves a much higher standard, which incites unhappiness in those unable to attain it. *Functional* signifies the lack of any such standard, since practically anyone can be functional. Without the more rigorous standard, which feeds into a person's conscience and creates the critic within, a person is less likely to feel tension between how he lives and how he wants to live. The part of the mind that appraises and judges is kept from developing, since the bar in life is kept so low.

The Happy Child doesn't develop toward adulthood, for nothing in his mind that pertains to adulthood really develops. The whole purpose of a Happy Childhood is to prevent a person's conscience from growing, which might bite back in the form of criticism, thereby making the child unhappy. Instead, the Happy Child simply carries certain characteristics forward inside an increasingly bigger body.

THE HAPPY ADULT

Posted at my gym are before and after pictures of a fifty-year-old man. In the before picture, the man is fat and unhappy; in the after picture, he is slim and happy. In fitness culture, he is the epitome of the successful fifty-year-old, although his success is concocted. In real life, fifty-year-olds succeed in fifty-year-old ways; only at the gym do fifty-year-olds succeed in this other way. Posted next to his pictures are pictures of children, young adults, and seniors, all going from fat to thin. With well-defined muscles far more than what good health requires, these people are also fitness successes. The same success story is told in all the before and after pictures at the gym, with people of different ages supplying the only variation. The whole picture series recalls old Hollywood B movies that portrayed the same boring love story against different backgrounds (e.g., a medieval castle, a Spanish galleon, a tropical island). In fitness culture, there is only one criterion for success—fitness—and the same success story is told against the background of a ten-year-old, a fifty-year-old, or an eighty-year-old.

There is something poignant about these people having turned their backs on real life as a source of good feeling and obsessively exercising to experience Artificial Happiness. And there is something unpleasant about their happiness, something lacking in warmth. There is nothing sunny in the sun; it's more like a hot moon. Their happiness radiates unwholesomeness because it emanates from an unnatural source, not from real life.

Fitness culture symbolizes the unreality of Happy Adulthood; it also illustrates Happy Adulthood's lack of stages. The traditional life cycle separated life into stages according to age, with each stage associated with a particular social condition. In Happy Adulthood, both age and social condition are meaningless, as the same Artificial Happiness spreads out over the entire age continuum. The only difference between Happy Children, Happy Adults, and Happy Seniors lies in the amount of drug they consume, or, in the case of exercise, the amount of weight they lift. Like the Happy Child, the Happy Adult feels happiness independent of life. Because the Happy Child and the Happy Adult share in this vital sensation, the two figures grow alike, recalling the premodern era when the life cycle didn't exist. In a regime governed by Artificial Happiness, Happy Children truly are little Happy Adults.

In *Brave New World*, Aldous Huxley describes a world similar to the one governed by Artificial Happiness, where adults find joy outside of a life, although with an important difference. In his society of the future, people take the drug Soma to feel euphoric, as if they're on holiday, which makes them less troublesome to the authorities. In *Brave New World*, Soma controls people, relieving the police of having to use harsher means. Artificial Happiness, on the other hand, does not make people less troublesome; rather it gives people a durable feeling of happiness—happiness beyond risk, beyond attack—while keeping their ambition and pride intact. And there is nothing more dangerous to authority than a man drunk with pleasure but who retains an interest in public affairs, who has the capacity to feel passionately and reason unscrupulously, and who does so without fear that his happiness is at risk. A man who cares little if he's liked, or who lacks religious conviction to keep him true, and whose happiness comes from a source unrelated to life is a dangerous man. Unlike the docile people on Soma, Happy Adults are potential revolutionaries.

In *Democracy in America*, Tocqueville roots the stability of the American political system in a principle he calls "self-interest rightly understood." People act moderately when their personal happiness is at stake; they participate in civic life out of conviction, but also because they fear a threat to their own happiness if the work of the community goes undone. Tocqueville also noted the heightened empathic qualities in democratic citizens. Citizens feel for each other because each of them senses that his or her happiness is equally vulnerable. A common fear makes people law-abiding, moderate, charitable toward others, and merciful in punishment.

A century later, anthropologist Daniel Lerner made a similar observation about modern society in *The Passing of Traditional Society*. He notes that what separates a modern, stable society from a less advanced one is the heightened sense of empathy among its citizens, more specifically, the ability of citizens to get into each other's minds and, once feeling for one another, to understand and tolerate one another.

The Happy Adult doesn't adhere to the principle of self-interest rightly understood because his happiness doesn't depend on community life. Lacking a vested interest in the community's fate, he tends to withdraw into private life. Yet the Happy Adult also contains within him a countervailing tendency, which is where the danger arises. Because he retains ambition and drive, unlike the person on Soma, the Happy Adult sometimes gets involved in public life, only without the Tocquevillian American's prudence, since his happiness isn't contingent on any outcome. In such cases, rather than being motivated by self-interest, the Happy Adult is motivated by more mysterious impulses. Rather than behave matter-of-factly, he is romantic; rather than worry about the practical side of things, he sees visions. Without fearing the loss of his happiness, the Happy Adult may leave the realm of moderation and compromise altogether and cleave to radical, reckless, and revolutionary ideas. In purest form, the Happy Adult is a man of energy, a lover of danger, and a passionate creature, overflowing with the self-confidence that comes from knowing that, whatever happens to society, his happiness is secure.

The Happy Adult is mere conjecture at this point, but research performed today suggests his plausibility. Psychological studies show that happy people, like angry people, are more likely to racially stereotype because they are less prone to calm, analytical thought. Strong emotion clouds judgment. The happy people studied were able to modify their antisocial behavior when given more information, but not always. These studies involved people who were happy at a particular moment and who, during the course of their lives, cycled through unhappiness and neutrality the way most people do. When happiness is fixed through medication—and has been for years—the effect on judgment will in all likelihood last longer, to the point that it becomes wired into the personality.

In another example, I interviewed a woman who had been on Prozac for a year while going through a divorce and caring for her two children. When she came off Prozac she confessed that her method of raising children had been different while on medication. On Prozac, whenever her children got out of hand, she rarely disciplined them (in her words, "cracked down"). Artificial Happiness made her feel so content and at peace with herself that she wanted to feel "peace everywhere," so she let her children's reckless behavior pass. Such a relaxed, carefree attitude, bordering on irresponsibility, is characteristic of the Happy Adult. Once off Prozac, her approach grew more balanced. She saw the consequences of letting her children's bad behavior get out of hand and, although she still loved them dearly, she saw that firmness was necessary at times, even if it meant shattering the peace. No longer under the influence of Artificial Happiness, her romantic, dreamy approach to raising children had given way to something more moderate and sensible.

The Happy Adult's potential radicalism takes a more ominous turn when combined with his lack of empathy. The Happy Adult doesn't need other people to feel happy. As a Happy Child, he learned nothing about kindness, since any reciprocal kindness shown to him was superfluous from the perspective of his own happiness. The Happy Adult is not cruel, but he is cold and brutal; little touches him; he has learned the habit in life of ignoring other people. Without the principle of self-interest rightly understood to ground him, he is eccentric and contemptuous of the ordinary course. Lack of empathy causes him to disregard the troubles of others. From a political perspective, the Happy

Adult is best left alone and asleep. He is morally immovable; if aroused, he is almost ungovernable.

To date, the literature linking a person's shrunken capacity to feel unhappiness to more aggressive behavior is small. In one study, Michaela Hau, an animal physiologist and behavioral scientist at Princeton University, showed how testosterone implants in male birds decrease their responsiveness to pain, possibly by boosting their endorphins. Extrapolating to humans, he concluded, "If men are less sensitive to pain, there is more willingness to fight and participate in further fights." By extrapolating further, one can imagine Happy Adults enjoying a constant source of happiness, unable to feel unhappiness, and for this reason acting more brutally.

Trouble lurks in the Artificial Happiness creed. The happiness one normally gets from life has little charm for the Happy Adult, since he gets happiness through another outlet. Unused to searching his conscience, he is prone to inspiration and intoxication at the expense of others. The Happy Adult has a kind of Dr. Jekyll and Mr. Hyde quality about him. He might retreat into his private sphere, savor his Artificial Happiness, and leave others alone; or he might mix politics with mystery and glamour, throw caution and wisdom to the wind, and join antidemocratic causes. Simply put, the Happy Adult is trouble.

THE HAPPY SENIOR

Doctors instinctively resist dividing life into stages, since most human beings reach their final form by age fifteen or twenty. Children differ from adults, but mostly in size, which is why doctors see children the way people saw children in the Middle Ages, as little adults. It's no surprise that pediatrics emerged as a medical specialty quite late, toward the end of the nineteenth century, and even then only because public opinion decreed adults and children to be different. Nor should it surprise anyone that geriatrics emerged as a medical specialty even later, in 1909, since elderly adults and young adults differ even less than adults and children. Again, doctors acted in response to public opinion. The idea of creating an entire specialty around older adults seemed fishy to doctors; to this day, there is still debate within medicine over whether geriatrics should be a subdivision of internal medicine or a specialty in its own right. Even as late as the 1980s, medical professors taught students to see diseases of the elderly as generic organ problems rather than as a special disease subset.

Although doctors view adulthood as a single biological phase, they do recognize subtle changes. They recognize *aging*. Out of a total of ten billion nerve cells, the brain loses roughly 50,000 a day. Neuropathologists detect senescent changes in brain matter starting in the fourth decade in life. As a general rule, people lose 1 percent of their function every year after age thirty. Adulthood and aging become synonymous under an Artificial Happiness regime. Interpreted biologically rather than sociologically, adulthood becomes one continuous phase starting at age thirty, marked by slow and steady decline. Already, college libraries shelve books on aging next to works on the sociology of adulthood.

Blending adulthood with aging creates a bias in favor of Artificial Happiness. When doctors see decline, whether physical or psychological, their instinct is to arrest it. As the chance of unhappiness increases with age, doctors tend to see unhappiness as one more example of decline, especially when research shows a decrease in neurotransmitters with age. Most doctors recognize that change with age is not necessarily pathological— menopause, for example—but when psychotropic drug ideology governs doctors' thinking, the temptation to equate unhappiness with decline is too great and doctors tend to treat unhappiness to arrest this decline.

Such logic touched my own family. When my father grew depressed a year after he retired, his doctor questioned whether retirement was really the cause. Although retirement is a normal life cycle stage, and the unhappiness associated with it a normal transitional feeling, medical research also shows that asymmetric changes in brain activity can predispose elderly people to depression. If my father's unhappiness were sociological, he wouldn't need treatment; if it were biological, he would. My father showed some cerebral atrophy on his CT scan; his doctor associated this finding with his unhappiness and recommended drug therapy. I protested, explaining to him that my father had a Russian heritage and that Russians are always a little depressed; perhaps my father was slightly more depressed than usual, but that didn't necessitate medication, especially when the shock of retirement still lingered and gave him every good reason to feel unhappy. My argument failed to persuade; the doctor still wanted to start treatment. In the end, we compromised, agreeing to start my father on a low dose of antidepressant to raise his spirits just a little—to the level of Russian, I joked darkly, but not beyond.

The Happy Adult lives with a pleasant sensation, one that makes life monotonous but safe. Disconnected from the vicissitudes of life, the Happy Adult lives a lie; he feels happy without any good reason. Because Artificial Happiness is so durable, reality stays a safe distance away and the whole charade continues for decades. Inevitably, however, the Happy Adult ages and falls ill, making it impossible for him to keep reality at bay. At that point, the Happy Adult becomes a Happy Senior.

During the transitional period, the Happy Senior is unhappy, since life breaks through his defenses. At no point, whether as a Happy Child or a Happy Adult, has the Happy Senior learned how to cope with life. With Artificial Happiness having shielded him all these years, the Happy Senior's heart is wholly unacquainted with life's tribulations, leaving him unprepared for the crisis now upon him. With nothing in his inner experience to comfort him, he falls back on more medication. Doctors dutifully help him rebuild his defenses with stronger stuff.

This works for a time, but eventually the Happy Senior's health worsens and the end looms. The Happy Senior struggles psychologically in a way that he never has before. Panicking, he thinks to himself: *I will cease to be; I will die; all that I value in life will die; my happiness will die; I should not die; yet I am dying.* He tries to hide death's approach with more medication, but no amount of Artificial Happiness works; he knows his annihilation is imminent. He seeks consolation in religion's idea of a happy afterlife, but medical science has governed his whole outlook in life and this lie is too hard for him to swallow. In the end, unable to uphold any delusion and now quite afraid, the Happy Senior reaches for death the way some people, fearing for their lives, commit suicide to escape torture.

The broad outlines of this mentality can already be discerned in the physician-assisted suicide movement. Although one branch of the movement argues that people should have a right to end their lives when they suffer from intractable pain, another, equally important branch argues that suffering should not be an essential prerequisite to assisted suicide. If a person doesn't have a good "quality of life," then, for all practical purposes, that person's life is already at an end and dying is a mere formality. Without the possibility of happiness, which Happy Seniors view as life's purpose—an idea sown in their minds as Happy Children—Happy Seniors want to die.

And die they will. In the not-so-distant future, the doctor will stand at the Happy Senior's bedside, poised to act on the Happy American's behalf one more time, like the faithful servant of yesteryear who accompanied his master on life's journey—washed his master at birth, dressed him as a child, cooked for him as an adult, tended to his pains as an old man, and, when his master died, shut his eyelids for good. Like that faithful servant, the doctor has always been there for the Happy American, comforting the Happy American with drugs, alternative medicine, or exercise ever since the Happy American was a Happy Child, fortifying him against life and preserving for him a happy spot no matter how terrifying or menacing life seemed. Now, with the end in sight, the doctor prepares the Happy Senior for an all-absorbing, invincible sleep, knowing that fear and anguish have struck root in the Happy Senior's mind—for good—and that no medical instrument can obscure life's stark reality. The doctor will perform his last act. With a smile on his face—perhaps a residue of Artificial Happiness—the Happy Senior will drop off.

CONCLUSION

FRIENDS SOMETIMES ASK me why I specialized in anesthesiology, given my intellectual interests outside of medicine. For a doctor who likes philosophy and literature, psychiatry would have been a better fit than a branch of medicine organized around gases and tubes.

I decided to become an anesthesiologist when I was twenty-four years old, an age when few decisions receive the serious attention they deserve. At the time, I liked wearing scrubs, which saved on the clothing bill; besides that, rushing to and from the emergency room seemed kind of macho. Yet even at that young age I had a sense of what being a doctor in the modern era would be like. Holed up in the laboratory, the world of ideas far away, I found myself sinking into forgetfulness through the monotony of hard science. My mind growing indolent amidst cadavers and specimens, I saw that doctoring meant the end of all intellectual adventure for me and that I was destined in life to become a physician-engineer. Rather than resist, and being competitive by nature, I decided to become the best physician-engineer I could be, which meant mastering the most "engineering" of all medical fields, the field recognized by all doctors as being closest to chemistry and physics—anesthesiology. Once I made this decision, psychiatry seemed too soft and unserious, too reminiscent of the watered-down science classes that humanities students take in college to satisfy their course requirements. Going into anesthesiology was my way of making peace with myself and with medicine.

On reflection, I was right in my estimation of modern medical practice, but wrong to think that physician-engineering could never intersect with the world of ideas, for the entire medical practice revolution and the subsequent fight between medicine and religion arose from a system of ideas conceived by physician-engineers. At each stage in the Artificial Happiness movement, a crisis pushed doctors out of their narrow scientific world into the more hazardous and unknowable realm of belief. In an act of creative synthesis totally out of character for these professionals, doctors enacted a new vision of life, in part to save their own skins but also to solve humanity's greatest riddle: the problem of unhappiness. These doctors were revolutionaries, visionaries, and populists—all names that apply to agitators who upset the status quo.

So determined were doctors to change things that when they spoke about life and happiness, supposition slipped into fact; ideology blended into certainty, which, in fact, was baseless. The American people, eager to satisfy their own aspirations for a happy life, enthusiastically went along, compounding the doctors' error. The result was folly on a nationwide scale: Artificial Happiness. But even if the doctors created a false vision their philosophizing still amazes me. I discovered during the writing of this book that practicing medicine didn't mean leaving the world of ideas, after all. Ideas were in my own backyard the whole time.

Nevertheless, the product of those ideas—Artificial Happiness—is a threat. Artificial Happiness arrests the individual's impulse to change life when life needs changing. This passivity can have even more consequences than action can. By settling for Artificial Happiness a person makes a conscious decision to live a lie. The only challenge left to him is to convince himself that the lie is not really a lie and that his happiness is real, which, of course, it's not. Sometimes Artificial Happiness blinds an individual to the consequences of his decision, biasing the decision-making process. With his caution erased by a good feeling, he chooses a path in life without clarity of mind. His entire identity grows murky as he follows a path he wasn't destined for.

The number of Happy Children, Happy Adults, and Happy Seniors in America today is large enough to define distinct character types, but not so large as to change vital social statistics. Still, the Artificial Happiness movement is only forty years old. If Artificial Happiness solidifies its hold on America, these three populations will continue to grow and so will their impact. The question remains of how to curtail the phenomenon or, better yet, how to reverse it. I have never believed that the solution to a knotty problem is the opposite of what common sense dictates. If the aggressive use of psychotropic drugs is wrong, then so is their miserly use. Many Americans suffering from clinical depression and ADHD need these medications and they shouldn't be denied them as part of a larger scheme to rid society of Artificial Happiness. It would be better to heighten awareness of Artificial Happiness, especially among the primary care doctors who prescribe these drugs, and use common sense.

If after reading this book doctors see unhappy patients in their offices and think twice about writing a drug prescription, knowing that the drug may do more harm than good, then this book will have served its purpose.

Curtailing Artificial Happiness arising from alternative medicine and obsessive exercise is trickier, since Artificial Happiness in those cases is often self-inflicted, especially in the case of exercise. Doctors who prescribe alternative medicine for unhappiness deceive people, making it hard for them to moderate their behavior: they can't just deceive people a little less. However, if these doctors confined their alternative medicine prescriptions to physical disease and avoided treating everyday unhappiness with alternative medicine, then, again, progress will have been made.

One reason I wrote this book was to put a mirror to people's faces. In the case of drug-induced Artificial Happiness, both doctors and patients have a vested interest in perpetuating certain myths. For doctors, if unhappiness is a disease then the search for happiness begins and ends in science. There is nothing more to decide; everything has been decided already—medication is the answer. Psychotropic drug ideology makes medical practice quick, easy, and clean. On the other side, no one can live a lie if they truly believe it to be a lie. To enjoy Artificial Happiness, patients must be convinced that their unhappiness is a disease, that taking medication is natural and proper, and that the happiness they feel on medication is the real thing. Both doctors and patients want the deceit and need the deceit perpetuated by psychotropic drug ideology. In such an environment, Artificial Happiness flourishes without criticism. Hopefully, this book will upset this tight relationship.

Phasing out managed care would barely influence the Artificial Happiness trend. Even if managed care disappeared overnight and doctors spent more time with their patients, the Artificial Happiness movement would continue, since primary care doctors, not managed care executives, form the movement's major impetus. Nor would emphasizing psychiatry at the expense of primary care necessarily change things for the better. Unhappy patients need neither expensive specialists nor medication nor specialized counseling; they simply need sensible people to talk to. Wise generalists are always preferable to psychiatrists when dealing with everyday unhappiness—if only primary care doctors could be wise generalists! Pushing unhappy patients toward psychiatrists would simply raise costs while perverting in a different way the care of unhappiness.

The transformation of doctors into physician-engineers stands at the origin of the Artificial Happiness movement and here lies the best hope for corrective action. That transformation launched a chain reaction of events: the public's dissatisfaction with health care, the rise of psychotropic drug ideology, the rise of alternative medicine ideology and exercise ideology in reaction to the psychotropic drug phenomenon, the rise of managed care, and the fight between the medical profession and organized religion. Since medical schools create the physician-engineers that feed the Artificial Happiness movement, the answer is for medical schools to turn out a different product. I argue for a second major reform in medical education to counter the Flexner Report published at the beginning of the twentieth century, which practically institutionalized the physician-engineering creed.

In 1910, after leading a team of researchers from the Carnegie Foundation through the nation's medical schools, Abraham Flexner, a former secondary school teacher from Lexington, Kentucky, published a report that revolutionized medical education. At the time, medical education in the United States was grossly uneven, with serious university-based medical schools on one end of the spectrum and private institutions with no educational standards whatsoever on the other. To correct what he termed the abysmal nature of medical training in this country, Flexner advised several reforms, including more biochemistry and physics in premedical education, a greater role for basic science in medical school, and a requirement that medical school faculty pursue research. Quickly acted on, his reforms continue to inspire American medical education to this day; every American medical school churns out competent physician-engineers because of his recommendations.

By reforming medical education, Flexner elevated medical practice in this country, making it more likely that a sick patient would see a competent physician-engineer than a quack. Yet, as in all reforms, there was a trade-off. Artificial Happiness arose in the late 1960s when physician-engineers proved incapable of dealing with people's everyday unhappiness. Flexner opened the door to physician-engineering, but also to its inevitable crisis and the medical practice revolution that followed.

The trouble posed by Artificial Happiness demands a new set of educational reforms—not in specialty medicine but in primary care. Since the Flexner Report's publication, specialty medicine has fulfilled its promise. Specialists are scientific, precise, and skilled; they represent the best of physician-engineering. Primary care, on the other hand, lost its way during the twentieth century. Even as medical student, I sensed primary care's outlier status. When I asked professors why a patient with anemia would go to a primary care doctor rather than to a hematologist, or why a patient with asthma would go to a primary care doctor rather than to a pulmonologist, they temporized. Although acknowledging the specialists' greater skill, they said primary care doctors compensated for their deficit by being better coordinators of patient care. For example, if a patient had anemia and asthma, primary care doctors would guard against conflicting treatments. Yet, once made aware of potential conflicts, internists with subspecialties are equally capable of coordinating care. Even a nurse practitioner can coordinate care as well as any doctor. Again, I asked, why would a patient go to a primary care doctor? My professors fell back on the argument that primary care doctors make excellent gatekeepers under managed care. But gatekeeping is an administrative task assigned by the insurance companies, not a medical skill inherent in primary care. Any doctor can be a gatekeeper. The reason managed care makes primary care doctors gatekeepers is because they cost less—again, because they lack any specific skill.

With mental health now taking up such a large portion of primary care, primary care doctors need a specific skill. They need to become wise generalists, and more than just physician-engineers. The time has come to divide medical training into two different tracks: for specialists, the current system that trains physician-engineers, and for primary care doctors, a new system altogether. A few medical schools have already substituted clinical clerkships for basic science classes, teaching students medicine through direct patient care in an effort to give them greater exposure to life. Although this strategy may humanize primary care doctors, it also makes for dumber physician-engineers. Those medical students destined to become specialists need these basic science classes.

Students planning careers in primary care need a separate curriculum altogether, starting from day one. To treat everyday unhappiness, primary care doctors must become fundamentally different creatures from specialists. They must be able to counsel and advise unhappy patients and not just write a psychotropic drug prescription. They must become thoughtful, subtle, and urbane, like doctors who existed before the Flexner Report, and they must be part doctor, part social worker, part minister, and part educated layman, and not just physician-engineers. This means exposing these doctors to more nonscience, both in college and medical school, perhaps even making nonscience a third of the medical school curriculum for them.

Primary care doctors trained as physician-engineers drive Artificial Happiness in this country. Shutting down their production would starve Artificial Happiness at the roots.

RELIGION, TOO

Artificial Happiness has another source: the change in organized religion's mission over the last half century. I speak of change, not of decline. On the contrary, America is now undergoing a religious revival, with over 90 per cent of Americans believing in God and organized religion more popular than ever. But this religious revival smells funny amid a simultaneous explosion in the use of psychotropic drugs, alternative medicine, and obsessive exercise. The parallel movement suggests that many Americans are only superficially religious, outwardly professing belief in God while crossing over to medicine for help when life really grows difficult. If people truly believe in God, they should have no need of artificial ways toward a better mood, a sense of purpose, or improved self-esteem.

The change in organized religion's mission also accounts for the paradox that religious people treat their unhappiness with medicine. Starting in the 1950s, well-being became religion's mission. This point once reached, the next step inevitably followed. Religious leaders pursued various paths to well-being. Progressives focused on wealth redistribution and social services; traditionalists championed morality and family values; a third group sought well-being for the solitary individual, independent of the family or the economy. In all three cases, religious leaders drummed into people's minds the notion that happiness in this life was achievable. When Artificial Happiness came along and worked better than religion at providing the sensation of well-being, secular people naturally gravitated toward it. Given organized religion's own emphasis on well-being, religious people followed along, oblivious to any contradiction. This explains the paradox of a religious revival concurrent with the rise of Artificial Happiness. To dam up this second source of Artificial Happiness, the nation's religious leaders need to awaken a new sense in themselves and others.

Although I oppose Artificial Happiness because it keeps people from finding real happiness in life, on deeper reflection, one must admit, there is something preposterous about life and happiness. The universal goal in life is lasting happiness, yet it is impossible to find lasting happiness. Such happiness might be attainable if everyone cooperated, but everyone is too busy looking for their own happiness to do so. Even if everyone did cooperate, more enduring reasons for unhappiness would inevitably surface, including change, boredom, sickness, and death. Lasting happiness is a pipe dream.

This is a terrible contradiction, which all organized religions today address in one of two ways. The first way is to replace the desire for conventional happiness with the desire for a more peculiar kind of happiness, one that is easily satisfied and almost indestructible, the happiness that comes from denial and humility—the happiness of the monk, the ascetic, and the philosopher. Most people, however, want to feel happy in the conventional way. They want life to be merry and agreeable; they want to pass the time pleasurably; they don't want to sacrifice enjoyment now for the sake of some rosy palace of unreality, like heaven or nirvana, lying in the distant future. They would rather feel Artificial Happiness.

The second way is to hold forth examples of happy families and happy communities, proclaim conventional happiness in this life possible, and then veil the fact that it isn't. People inevitably discover the truth—in private—then simply go through the motions of religion, extracting a little happiness from knowing that they have followed the rules of propriety and custom and done their sacred duty. Still, in moments of deep despair, this rarely suffices. People ask, "Why do I bother?" In the end, they, too, reach for Artificial Happiness.

Both roads lead to Artificial Happiness. Before Artificial Happiness existed, it mattered less in what spirit people practiced religion. Even if religion couldn't supply happiness, people had nowhere else to turn. They just endured the best they could. Now, with Artificial Happiness available, it does matter. So long as people practice religion to enjoy happiness, even in the form of consolation, Artificial Happiness remains irresistible, like some heaven-sent opportunity. Religious people will want it just like everyone else does. Already their embrace of Artificial Happiness is one of those indisputable but ambiguous situations that are at once recognized and ignored by polite society, like sex out of wedlock. Religious leaders, in particular, prefer to brush the whole Artificial Happiness problem under the carpet.

Religious leaders need to think anew about people's spirit of belief, since embracing religion to get happiness leads sooner or later to Artificial Happiness. They need to guide people toward seeing the desire for happiness as a boundary in life. On one side of the boundary is conventional life—the futile striving for permanent happiness, the search for enjoyments that give only a semblance of happiness, and the real happiness that is subject to annihilation from a thousand different quarters. On the other side of the boundary is the religious life, which recognizes the search for personal happiness as a kind of defect in human nature. Religious leaders need to encourage people to look inward and ask themselves why they worship. If their goal is personal happiness, in whatever form, they need to rethink, and religious leaders need to hound them until they do. True, very few people can live an authentically religious life—the pull of personal happiness being too strong—yet simply understanding the contradiction that exists between the personal desire for happiness and the life of the world can go a long way toward steeling people against Artificial Happiness when life turns sour. The most terrifying thing about unhappiness is not the sensation itself but the failure to understand it. Religious leaders shirk their duty when they conceal from people the dark truth about lasting happiness and in the end they just drive people toward Artificial Happiness.

Reforming religion's mission might not only reverse the Artificial Happiness trend but also create a milder atmosphere along a continuing battlefront—the fight over abortion, stem cell research, and other beginning-of-life issues.

When organized religion properly understands its mission, it rarely conflicts with science. Organized religion puts the outer life and inner life of human beings in perspective, knowing that nothing scientists discover in their labs will ever change the eternal condition of the human soul. Thus, most people live in fear or boredom no matter how technically advanced a society is. Even a genetically engineered baby is likely destined for a dull childhood, a painful adolescence, and a restless adulthood spent staring out an office window. This is religion's promise, which is why people need religion to change their outlook. Under such conditions, organized religion focuses on the problems of the inner life and offers only general guidelines for scientific research. Scientists cannot murder or forcibly experiment on people;

otherwise, organized religion is content to let science do its thing.

But there are times when organized religion grows confused about its mission. At that point it panics and cracks down hard on science. An erroneous mission brings religion into matters of the outer life, putting organized religion in direct competition with science, with religious leaders imagining themselves fighting science for the same turf. In the seventeenth century a mission change thrust the Christian church into competition with astronomers. Connecting the inner life of human beings with the relative positions of the earth and sun, church leaders feared that Galileo's discoveries might undermine the doctrine of the soul, so they punished him. In the second half of the twentieth century, a similar event happened. Organized religion changed its mission to well-being, again putting the church into competition with science. The inner life ceased to be the invisible human soul and instead became small things that affected well-being, like neurotransmitters, cell nuclei, and DNA.

When religious leaders made this leap they wrongly concluded that religion and science were fighting for the same turf, and because science has a better understanding of small things than religion does, some religious leaders developed an inordinate fear of science, imagining that scientists were closing in on the secret of life—that all the scientists needed was a bigger microscope—which threatened religion. As a consequence, some religious leaders warned that genetic research and the manipulation of stem cells would initiate a long chain of human degradation and that God himself—divine and unshakeable—was threatened by what the doctors did.

The tension between religion and science is an old problem. In the fourth century, Christians and scientists were deadlocked over the matter of the earth's shape. Saint Augustine, a wise man who knew the difference between the outer life and the inner life, wrote:

> What concern is it of mine whether heaven is like a sphere and the earth is enclosed by it and suspended in the middle of the universe, or whether heaven like a disk above the earth covers it over on one side? These facts would be of no avail for my salvation.

Augustine attached little importance to science and left it alone. If a reading of the Bible conflicted with a scientific view that was certain truth, he humbly admitted that he had interpreted the Bible erroneously. He could afford to be humble, for in his inmost convictions he looked upon science the way a master looks upon his pet, as a creature with intelligence but lacking in higher understanding, and something irrelevant to the search for meaning in life. Putting organized religion's mission back on track—meaning a focus on the true inner life of human beings rather than on the small things connected with science—might allow today's religious leaders to rediscover the same relaxed indifference toward medical science.

The word "happiness" is very simple and very clear. Everyone knows what it means as the definition was decided on long ago. In addition, the central fact in most people's lives is the desire for the feeling. Yet the word's simplicity and clarity has misled doctors into a banal interpretation of the phenomenon. Having invented Artificial Happiness, doctors think they have solved the unhappiness problem, that everything has been arranged, all eventualities have been foreseen, and that only a few soft touches remain to be applied. In supreme confidence they push on, impervious and self-satisfied, convinced that they have brought humanity from a lower phase of life based on religion into a new and higher phase of life based on science, in which doctors satisfy people's deepest psychological needs.

Yet the inexplicable human spirit has eluded them; doctors have utterly misjudged human beings. And nothing is more telling than the fact that doctors, despite all their accomplishments, remain unable to answer the most basic question about life, the question that gives life its coherence and when answered makes happiness and contentment possible. That question is: How should one live?

During the first half of the twentieth century, before the rise of Artificial Happiness, some scientists thought they could answer this question, believing that it was ultimately a question of social science but that real science needed to be done in preparation. Emboldened by discoveries that made life kindlier and happier, scientists advised people to be patient, that an answer to this question was forthcoming but that a few more questions of chemistry and physics needed to be solved first. However, by midcentury, after science had produced great wealth but also great weapons, which were used in two world wars to kill millions, people began to lose faith in science's ability to answer this question, let alone to make life better.

In the second half of the twentieth century, doctors picked up where the scientists left off, but rather than try to answer this question they dismissed it. The underlying theme in Artificial Happiness is the irrelevance of life to happiness, since people can feel Artificial Happiness independent of life. Doctors dodged the question of how to live, instead inventing an elegant rationale for going through life stupefied. But answering this question is not only essential to all real happiness but also incredibly easy. People can find answers to this question by just going to a local bookstore, and for fifty dollars buying books on all the world's great faiths and philosophies, reading them in a month, and discovering all the answers about how to live that humanity has ever known. People can then apply this knowledge to their lives, change their behavior, and live in accord with the demands of their consciences—no neurotransmitters involved, no drugs involved, no alternative medicine involved, no obsessive exercise involved, no doctors involved. This glaring truth sheds light on what is probably Artificial Happiness's greatest defect: the whole thing is so . . . unnecessary.

BIBLIOGRAPHY

Ader, Robert, and Nicholas Cohen. "Behaviorally Conditioned
Immunosuppression." *Psychosomatic Medicine* 37, no. 4 (July–
August 1975): 333–39.

Aftanas, L. I., and S. A. Golocheikine. "Human Anterior and
Frontal Midline Theta and Alpha Reflect Emotionally Positive State and Internalised Attention." *Neuroscience Letters* 310,
no. 1 (2001): 57–60.

Albernaz, Ami. "Why It's Good to Feel Good." *Science and Spirit*
(November–December 2004).

Annas, G. J. "Why We Should Ban Human Cloning." *NEJM*
332, no. 2 (July 9, 1998): 122–25.

"Anzio Beachhead: The Breakthrough" at www.army.mil/cmh-
pg/books/wwii/anziobeach/anzio-break.html.

Aries, Phillipe. *Centuries of Childhood*. Translated by Robert
Baldick. New York: Vintage Books, 1962.

Artal, Michael. "Exercise Against Depression." *The Physician and Sportsmedicine* 26, no. 10 (October 1998).

Augustine. "The Literal Meaning of Genesis." Translated by John Taylor. New York: Newman Press, 1982. Quoted in Richard Blackwell. *Science, Religion, and Authority*. Milwaukee: Marquette University Press, 1998.

Azari, N. P. "Neurocorrelates of Religious Experience." *European Journal of Neuroscience* 13 , no. 8 (2001): 1649–52.

Babyak, Michael, "Exercise Treatment for Major Depression: Maintenance of Therapeutic Benefit at 10 Months." *Psychosomatic Medicine* 62 (2000): 633–38.

Batson, C. D., and W. L. Ventis. *The Religious Experience*. New York: Oxford University Press, 1982.

Beard, George. *American Nervousness*. New York: Arno Press, 1972 (c1881).

Beaton, Lindsay. "A Doctor Prescribes for His Profession." *Harper's*, October 1960, 151–52.

Beck, Stanley. "Science and Christian Understanding." *Dialog*, Autumn 1963.

Beecher, Henry. "Pain in Men Wounded in Battle." *Annals of Surgery* 123, no. 1 (January 1946): 96–105.

———."The Powerful Placebo." *JAMA* 159, no. 17 (December 24, 1955): 1602–6.

———. "Resuscitation and Sedation of Patients with Burns Which Include the Airway." *Annals of Surgery* 117, no. 1 (June 1943): 825–33.

Benson, Herbert. "Relaxation Response: Bridge Between Psychiatry and Medicine." *Medical Clinics of North America* 61 (1977): 929–38.

———. *Timeless Healing*. New York: Simon and Schuster, 1997.

Bentz, W. K. "Consensus Between Role Expectations and Role

Behavior among Ministers." *Community Mental Health Journal* 4 (1968): 301–68.

Bergin, A. E. "Religiosity and Mental Health." *Professional Psychology: Research and Practice* 14, no. 2 (1983): 170–84.

Berkel, J., and F. de Waard. "Mortality Pattern and Life Expectancy of Seventh Day Adventists in the Netherlands." *International Journal of Epidemiology* 12, no. 4 (1983): 455–9.

Berryman, Jack. *Out of Many, One: A History of the American College of Sports Medicine.* Champaign, Illinois: Human Kinetics, 1995.

Bloch, Sidney, and Peter Reddaway. *Soviet Psychiatric Abuse: The Shadow over World Psychiatry.* Boulder, Colorado: Eastview Press, 1985.

Blumenthal, James. "Effects of Exercise Training on Older Patients with Major Depression." *Archives of Internal Medicine* 159, no. 19 (October 25, 1999): 2349–56.

Brock, L. G., J. C. Coombs, and J. C. Eccles. "The Recording of Potentials from Motorneurones with an Intracellular Electrode." *Journal of Physiology* 17 (1952): 431–60.

Brosse, Alisha. "Exercise and the Treatment of Clinical Depression in Adults." *Sports Medicine* 32, no. 12 (2002): 741–60.

Brown, Frank. "ADHD: A Neurodevelopmental Perspective." *Contemporary Pediatrics* 13, no. 6 (June 1996): 25–44.

Brown, Warren, Nancey Murphy, and H. Newton Malony, eds. *Whatever Happened to the Soul?* Minneapolis: Fortress Press, 1998.

Bryce, James. *The American Commonwealth.* 2 vols. New York: Macmillan Company, 1911.

Buechi, Patrick J. "Review of Kathleen Riley's *Fulton J. Sheen.*" *Western New York Catholic* (September 2004; online version).

Bunge, Mario. *The Mind-Body Problem*. Oxford: Pergamon Press, 1980.

Carlson, Rick. *The End of Medicine*. New York: John Wiley and Sons, 1975.

Carney, Patricia. "How Physician Communication Influences Recognition of Depression in Primary Care." *Journal of Family Practice* 48, no. 12 (December 1999): 958–64.

———. "Recognizing and Managing Depression in Primary Care." *Journal of Family Practice* 48, no. 12 (December, 1999): 965–72.

———. "Variations in Approaching the Diagnosis of Depression." *Journal of Family Practice* 46, no. 1 (January 1998): 73–82.

Carroll, Linda. "Violence as a Biomedical Problem: Natural Born Killers." www.columbia.edu.

Chase, Edward. "The Politics of Medicine." *Harper's*, October 1960, 125–31.

Colt, Edward. "The Effect of Running on Plasma Beta-Endorphin." *Life Science* 28, no. 14 (1981): 1637–40.

Comstock, G. W., and K. B. Partridge, "Church Attendance and Health." *Journal of Chronic Diseases* 25, no. 12 (1972): 665–72.

Cousins, Norman, ed. *Nobel Prize Conversations*. New York: Norton, 1985.

Cowan, W. Maxwell. "The Emergence of Modern Neuroscience." *Annual Review of Neuroscience* 23 (2000): 343–91.

———. "Prospects for Neurology and Psychiatry." *JAMA* 285, no. 5 (February 7, 2001): 594–600.

Crick, Francis. *The Astonishing Hypothesis*. New York: Charles Scribner's Sons, 1994.

Cronan, Thomas and Edward Howley. "The Effect of Training on Epinephrine and Norepinephrine Excretion." *Medicine and Science in Sports* 6, no. 2 (1974): 122–25.

Dain, Norman. *Concepts of Insanity in the U.S.—1789–1865.* New Brunswick, New Jersey: Rutgers University Press, 1964.

Damasio, Antonio. *Descartes' Error.* New York: G. P. Putnam, 1994.

D'Aquili, Eugene. "Human Ceremonial Ritual and the Modulation of Aggression." *Zygon* 20, no. 1 (1985): 21–30.

Delude, Cathryn. "Crisis of Confidence." *Harvard Public Health Review*, Fall 2004.

Dennett, Daniel. *Consciousness Explained.* Boston: Little, Brown, and Co., 1991.

———. *Content and Consciousness.* New York: Humanities Press, 1969.

Destono, David. "Prejudice From Thin Air: The Effect of Emotion on Automatic Intergroup Attitudes." *Psychological Science* 15, no. 5 (May 2004): 319–24.

Diagnostic and Statistical Manual of Mental Disorders: DSM-IV. Washington, D.C.: American Psychiatric Association, 1994.

Dodds, T. Andrew. "Richard Cabot: Medical Reformer during the Progressive Era." *Annals of Internal Medicine* 119, no. 5 (September 1, 1993): 417–22.

Donahue, M. J. "Intrinsic and Extrinsic Religiousness: A Review and Meta-Analysis." *Journal of Personality and Social Psychology* 48, no. 2 (1985): 400–19.

Dwyer, J. W. "The Effect of Religious Concentration and Affiliation on County Cancer Mortality Rates." *Journal of Health and Social Behavior* 31, no. 2 (1990): 185–202.

Eccles, Helena, and Hans Biersack, eds. *Sir John Eccles: In Memoriam—A Tireless Warrior for Dualism.* Germany: Ecomed, 2000.

Eccles, J. C. "The Effect of Silent Thinking." In *The Brain-Mind Problem*, edited by John Eccles. Leuven: Leuven University Press, 1987.

————. "Evolution and the Conscious Self." In *The Human Mind*, edited by John Roslansky. Amsterdam: North Holland Publishing Co., 1969.

————. *Evolution of the Brain*. London: Routledge, 1989.

————. *How the Self Controls Its Brain*. Heidelberg: Springer Verlag, 1994.

————. *Neurophysiological Basis of Mind*. Oxford: The Clarendon Press, 1952.

————. *The Understanding of the Brain*. New York: McGraw-Hill, 1973.

Edelman, Gerald. *Bright Air, Brilliant Fire*. New York: Basic Books, 1992.

Edelman, Gerald, and Giulio Tononi. *Consciousness: How Matter Becomes Imagination*. London: Penguin Books, 2000.

Eisenberg, D. M. "Trends in Alternative Medicine Use in the U.S., 1990–1997." *JAMA* 280, no 18 (1998): 1569–75.

————. "Unconventional Medicine in the U.S." *NEJM* 328, no. 4 (January 28, 1993): 246–52.

Elrick, Harold. "A New Definition of Health." *Journal of the National Medical Association* 72, no. 7 (1980): 695–99.

Erikson, Erik. *Childhood and Society*. New York: Norton, 1950.

Esfeld, Michael. "Is Quantum Indeterminism Relevant to Free Will?" *Philosophia Naturalis* 37 (2000): 177–87.

Favazza, A. "Modern Christian Healing of Mental Illness." *American Journal of Psychiatry* 139, no. 6 (June 1982): 728.

Faxon, N. W., and E. D. Churchill. "The Cocoanut Grove Disaster in Boston." *JAMA* 120, no. 17 (December 26, 1942): 1385–88.

Fenwick, Peter. "The Neuroscience of Spirituality." Spirituality and Psychiatry Special Interest Group, Newsletter No. 13, October 2003, The Royal College of Psychiatrists, www.rcpsych.ac.uk.

Foote, Sandra, and Lynn Etheredge. "Increasing Use of New Prescription Drugs: A Case Study." *Health Affairs*, July–August 2000, 165–70.

Foucault, Michel. *Madness and Civilization*. Translated by Richard Howard. London: Tavistock, 1977.

Frankel, B. G. "Religion and Well-Being among Canadian University Students: The Role of Faith Groups on Campus." *Journal for the Scientific Study of Religion* 33, no. 1 (1994): 62–73.

Fugh-Berman, Adriane, and Jerry Cott. "Dietary Supplements and Natural Products as Psychotherapeutic Agents." *Psychosomatic Medicine* 61 (1999): 712–28.

Gallo, Joseph. "Attitudes, Knowledge, and Behavior of Family Physicians Regarding Depression in Later Life." *Archives of Family Medicine* 8 (1999): 249–56.

Gambert, Steven. "Running Elevates Plasma Beta-Endorphin Immunoreactivity and ACTH in Untrained Human Subjects." *Proceedings of the Society for Experimental Biology and Medicine* 168 (1981): 1–4.

Gartner, J., D. B. Larson, and G. D. Allen. "Religious Commitment and Mental Health: A Review of the Empirical Literature." *Journal of Psychology and Theology* 19, no. 1 (1991): 6–25.

Gerrity, Martha. "Improving the Recognition and Management of Depression." *Journal of Family Practice* 48, no. 12 (December 1999): 949–57.

Goffman, Erving. *Asylums: Essays on the Social Situation of Mental Patients and Other Inmates*. Chicago: Aldine Publishing Co., 1962.

———. *The Presentation of Self in Everyday Life*. New York: Doubleday Anchor, 1959.

Goldman, Larry. "Diagnosis and Treatment of ADHD in Children and Adolescents." *JAMA* 279, no. 14 (April 8, 1998): 1100–07.

Goldstein, Avram. "Opioid Peptides (Endorphins) in Pituitary and Brain." *Science* 193, no. 4258 (September 17, 1976): 1081–86.

Greenberg, Selig. "The Decline of the Healing Art." *Harper's*, October 1960, 132–37.

Greenwald, A. G., and Banaji, M. R. "Implicit Social Cognition: Attitudes, Self-esteem, and Stereotypes." *Psychological Review* 102 (1995): 4–27.

Greist, John. "Running as a Treatment for Depression." *Comprehensive Psychiatry* 20, no. 1 (January–February 1979): 41–54.

Grembowski, David. "Managed Care, Access to Mental Health Specialists, and Outcomes Among Primary Care Patients with Depressive Symptoms." *Journal of General Internal Medicine* 17 (April 2002): 258–69.

Grobstein, Clifford. *From Chance to Purpose: An Appraisal of External Human Fertilization*. Reading, MA: Addison-Wesley, 1981.

Gross, Mortimer. "Origin of Stimulant Use for Treatment of Attention Deficit Disorder." *American Journal of Psychiatry* 152, no. 2 (February 1995): 298–99.

Grossman, Ashley. "Endorphins: 'Opiates for the Masses.'" *Medicine and Science in Sports and Exercise* 17, no. 1 (1985): 101–05.

Grossman, Ashley, and John Sutton. "Endorphins: What Are They?" *Medicine and Science in Sports and Exercise* 17, no. 1 (1985): 74–80.

Guenin, Louis. "Morals and Primordials." *Science* 292, no 5522 (June 1, 2001): 1659.

Hankin, Janet. "Use of General Medical Care Services by Persons with Mental Disorders." *Archives of General Psychiatry* 39 (February 1982): 225–31.

Harrington, Anne, ed. *The Placebo Effect*. Cambridge, MA: Harvard University Press, 1997.

Harris, Corra. *A Circuit Rider's Wife.* Philadelphia: Henry Altemus, 1910.

Harris, R. C. "The Role of Religion in Heart-Transplant Recipients' Long-Term Health and Well-Being." *Journal of Religion and Health* 34, no. 1 (1995): 17–31.

Hau, M. *Hormones and Behavior* (2004). Published online, doi:10.1016/j.yhbeh.2004.02.007.

Healy, David. *The Antidepressant Era.* Cambridge, MA: Harvard University Press, 1997.

———. *The Creation of Psychopharmacology.* Cambridge, MA: Harvard University Press, 2002.

———. *The Psychopharmacologists II: Interviews.* London: Altman, 1998.

———. *The Psychopharmacologists III: Interviews.* London: Arnold, 2000.

Heavey, Susan. "About 1 in 10 U.S. Teens Face Major Depression," Reuters, Dec. 29, 2005.

Houpt, J. "The Role of Psychiatric and Behavioral Factors in the Practice of Medicine." *American Journal of Psychiatry* 137 (1980): 37–47.

Howley, Edward. "The Effect of Different Intensities of Exercise on the Excretion of Epinephrine and Norepinephrine." *Medicine and Science in Sports* 8, no. 4 (1976): 219–22.

Hrobjartsson, Asbjorn, and Peter Gotzsche. "Is the Placebo Powerless?" *NEJM* 344, no. 21 (May 24, 2001): 1594–99.

Huba, Stephen. "Many Empty Church Pews." *Cincinnati Post,* April 19, 1998.

Hughes, John. "Isolation of an Endogenous Compound from the Brain with Pharmacological Properties Similar to Morphine." *Brain Research* 88 (1975): 295–308.

Hunter, James Davison. *The Death of Character.* New York: Basic Books, 2000.

Huxley, Aldous. *Brave New World*. New York: Harper, 1932.

Illich, Ivan. *Medical Nemesis*. London: Calder and Boyars, 1975.

Jackson, Stanley. *Melancholia and Depression*. New Haven: Yale University Press, 1986.

James, Oliver. "Up on a Higher Level." Sunday Review, *Independent* (U.K.), August 18, 1996.

Joranson, David. "Trends in Medical Use and Abuse of Opioid Analgesics." *JAMA* 283, no. 13 (April 5, 2000): 1710–14.

Kabat-Zinn, J. "Four-Year Follow-Up of a Meditation-Based Program for the Self-Regulation of Chronic Pain." *Journal of Behavioral Medicine* 8 (1986): 163–90.

Katz, S. J. "Appropriate Medication Management of Depression in the United States and Ontario." *Journal of General Internal Medicine* 13 (1998): 77–85.

Kiegolt-Glaser, J. K. "Marital Quality, Marital Disruption, and Immune Function." *Psychosomatic Medicine* 49 (1987): 13–18.

Kienle, Gunver, and Helmut Kiene. "A Critical Re-Analysis of the Concept, Magnitude, and Existence of Placebo Effects." In *Understanding the Placebo Effect in Complementary Medicine*, edited by David Peters. Edinburgh: Churchill Livingstone, 2001.

Knapp, P. M. "Short-term Immunological Effects of Induced Emotion." *Psychosomatic Medicine* 54 (1992): 133–48.

Koenig, Harold, and Harvey Jay Cohen, eds. *The Link between Religion and Health: Psychoneuroimmunology and the Faith Factor*. New York: Oxford University Press, 2002.

Kramer, Peter. *Listening to Prozac*. New York: Penguin, 1993.

Krejci-Papa, Marianna. "Better in the Long Run." *Science and Spirit*, March–April 2005.

Kritzman, Lawrence, ed. *Michel Foucault*. New York: Routledge, 1988.

Lambert, Craig. "Risk Factors and Life Style: A Statewide Health Interview Survey." *NEJM* 306, no. 17 (April 29, 1982): 1048–51.

Langdon, Christine. "Tired? Pop Your Pal's Ritalin." *New York Post*, May 28, 2000, p. 8.

Larson, David, James Swyers, and Michael McCullough (eds.). *Scientific Research on Spirituality and Health: A Consensus Report*, 1998.

Lasch, Christopher. *The Culture of Narcissism*. New York: W. W. Norton, 1979.

Lawlor, Debbie, and Stephen Hopker. "The Effectiveness of Exercise as an Intervention in the Management of Depression." *BMJ* 322 (March 31, 2001).

Lazarus, Jeremy, and Steve Sharfstein, eds. *New Roles for Psychiatrists in Organized Systems of Care*. Washington D.C.: American Psychiatric Press, 1998.

Lerner, Daniel. *The Passing of Traditional Society*. Glencoe, Illinois: Free Press, 1958.

Leutwyler, Kristin. "The Price of Prevention." *Scientific American*, April 1995, 124–29.

Levin, J. S., and H. Y. Vanderpool. "Is Religion Therapeutically Significant for Hypertension?" *Social Science and Medicine* 29, no. 1 (1989): 69–78.

Lobstein, Dennis, and A. H. Ismail. "Decreases in Resting Plasma Beta-Endorphin/Lipotropin after Endurance Training." *Medicine and Science in Sports and Exercise* 21, no. 2 (1989): 161–5.

Maclean, C. R. K. "Altered Cortisol Response to Stress after Four Months' Practice of the Transcendental Meditation Program." Presented at the Eighteenth Annual meeting of the Society for Neuroscience, Anaheim, California, October 30, 1992.

Mandell, A. J. "The Second Second Wind." *Psychiatric Annals* 9

(1979): 57–68. In "Affective Beneficence of Vigorous Physical Activity." William Morgan. *Medicine and Science in Sports and Exercise* 17, no. 1 (1985): 94.

Markoff, Richard. "Endorphins and Mood Changes in Long-Distance Running." *Medicine and Science in Sports and Exercise* 14, no. 1 (1982): 11–15.

Martin, Joseph. "The Integration of Neurology, Psychiatry, and Neuroscience in the 21st Century." *American Journal of Psychiatry* 159 (May 2002): 695–704.

Maslow, Abraham. *Motivation and Personality* (3rd ed.). New York: Harper & Row, 1970.

McHugh, Paul. "The Death of Freud and the Rebirth of Psychiatry." *Weekly Standard*, July 17, 2000.

McKnight-Trontz, Jennifer. *How to Be Popular*. San Francisco: Chronicle Books, 2003.

Meldrum, Marcia. "A Capsule History of Pain Management." *JAMA* 290, no. 18 (November 12, 2003): 2470–80.

Mercugliano, Marianne. "What Is Attention-Deficit/Hyperactivity Disorder?" *Pediatric Clinics of North America* 46, no. 5 (October 1999) 831–43.

Merser, Cheryl. *Grown-ups: A Generation in Search of Adulthood*. New York: New American Library, 1988.

Micozzi, Marc, ed. *Fundamentals of Complementary and Alternative Medicine*. New York: Churchill Livingstone, 2001.

Miller, Douglas, and Marion Nowak. *The Fifties: The Way We Really Were*. New York: Doubleday, 1977.

Miller, Geoffrey. *The Mating Mind*. New York: Doubleday, 2001.

Millman, Marcia. *The Unkindest Cut: Life in the Backrooms of Medicine*. New York: William Morrow, 1976.

Mills, C. Wright. "A Pagan Sermon to the Christian Clergy." *Nation*, March 8, 1958.

Mirkin, Gabe. "Placebos," *NEJM* 344, no. 21 (May 24, 2001).

Mollica, Richard. "A Community Study of Formal Pastoral Counseling Activities of the Clergy." *American Journal of Psychiatry* 143, no. 3 (March 1986): 323–28.

Moreland, J. P. "Restoring the Soul to Christianity." *Christian Research Journal* 23, no. 1.

Morgan, William. "Affective Beneficence of Vigorous Physical Activity." *Medicine and Science in Sports and Medicine* 17, no. 1 (1985): 94–100.

Munoz, Ricardo. "On the AHCPR Depression in Primary Care Guidelines: Further Considerations for Practitioners." *American Psychologist* 49, no. 1 (January 1994): 42–61.

Nelson, Laura. "Why It Hurts Less to Be a Man." www.bioedonline.com, June 15, 2004.

Newberg, A. "The Measurement of Regional Cerebral Blood Flow During the Complex Task of Meditation." *Psychiatry Research* 106, no. 2 (2001): 113–22.

Nielsen, Arthur, and Thomas Williams. "Depression in Ambulatory Medical Patients." *Archives of General Psychiatry* 37 (September 1980): 999–1004.

Olfson, M., and G. L. Klerman. "The Treatment of Depression: Prescribing Practices of Primary Care Physicians and Psychiatrists." *Journal of Family Practice* 35, no. 6 (1992) 627–35.

———. "Trends in the Prescription of Psychotropic Medications: The Role of Physician Specialty." *Medical Care* 31, (1993): 559–64.

O'Malley, Patrick. "Antidepressant Therapy for Unexplained Symptoms and Symptom Syndromes." *The Journal of Family Practice* 48, no. 12 (December 1999): 980–89.

Orleans, C. T. "How Primary Care Physicians Treat Psychiatric Disorders: A National Survey of Family Practitioners." *American Journal of Psychiatry* 142 (1985): 52–57.

Oxman, Thomas, and Anjana Sengupta. "Treatment of Minor Depression." *American Journal of Geriatric Psychiatry* 10 (June 2002): 256–64.

Paul, Joan. "The Health Reformers: George Barker Windship and the Boston's Strength Seekers." *Journal of Sport History* 10, no. 3 (Winter 1983): 41–57.

Pelletier, Kenneth. "Current Trends in the Integration and Reimbursement of Complementary and Alternative Medicine by Managed Care, Insurance Carriers, and Hospital Providers." *American Journal of Health Promotion* 12, no. 2 (November–December 1997): 112–23.

———. "Current Trends in the Integration and Reimbursement of Complementary and Alternative Medicine by Managed Care Organizations and Insurance Providers: 1998 Update." *American Journal of Health Promotion* 14, no. 2 (November–December 1999): 125–33.

Pelletier, Kenneth, and John Astin. "Integration and Reimbursement of Complementary and Alternative Medicine by Managed Care and Insurance Providers: 2000 Update." *Alternative Therapies* 8, no. 1 (January–February 2002): 38–48.

Perneger, Thomas. "Mental Health and Choice Between Managed Care and Indemnity Health Insurance." *American Journal of Psychiatry* 152, no. 7 (July 1995): 1020–25.

Pert, C. B., and D. L. Bowie. "Behavioral Manipulation of Rats Causes Alterations in Opiate Receptor Occupancy." In *Endorphins and Mental Health*, edited by E. Usdin, W. E. Bunney, and N. S. Kline, 93–104. New York: Oxford University Press, 1979.

Pert, C., and S. Snyder. "Opiate Receptor: Demonstration in Nervous Tissue." *Science* 179 (March 9, 1973): 1011–14.

Peters, David, ed. *Understanding the Placebo Effect in Complementary Medicine*. Edinburgh: Churchill Livingstone, 2001.

Pignone, Michael. "Screening for Depression." *Annals of Internal Medicine* 136, no 10 (May 21, 2002): 760–64

Pincus, Harold. "Prescribing Trends in Psychotropic Medications." *JAMA* 279, no. 7 (February 18, 1998): 526–31.

Pinker, Steven. *How the Mind Works.* New York: Norton, 1997.

Plyushch, Leonid. *History's Carnival.* New York: Harcourt Brace Jovanovich, 1979.

Popper, Karl, and John Eccles. *The Self and Its Brain.* New York: Springer International, 1977.

Potts, Michael. *Beyond Brain Death.* Dordrecht: Kluwer Academic Publishers, 2000.

Pragman, D., and M. Baker. "Running High: Enkephalin Indicted." *Journal of Drug Issues* 10, no. 3 (1980): 341–49.

Price, Bruce. "Neurology and Psychiatry: Closing the Great Divide." *Neurology* 54 (2000): 8–29.

Prioleau, L. "An Analysis of Psychotherapy versus Placebo Studies." *Behavioral and Brain Sciences* 6 (1983): 275–310.

Puri, B. K. "SPECT Neuroimaging in Schizophrenia with Religious Delusions." *International Journal of Psychophysiology* 40, no. 2 (2001): 143–8.

Reed, Barbara. "Physicians and Exercise Promotion." *American Journal of Preventive Medicine* 7, no. 6 (1991): 410–15.

Regier, Daniel. "The De Facto U.S. Mental Health Services System." *Archives of General Psychiatry* 35 (June 1978): 685–93.

Reich, Charles. *The Greening of America.* New York: Random House, 1970.

Reid, M. C. "Use of Opioid Medications for Chronic Noncancer Pain Syndromes in Primary Care." *Journal of General Internal Medicine* 17, no. 3 (2002): 173–9.

Riesman, David. *The Lonely Crowd.* New Haven: Yale University Press, 1950.

Robertson, J. A. "Human Cloning and the Challenge of Regulation" *NEJM* 332, no. 2 (July 9, 1998): 119–21.

Rose, Nikolas. "Becoming Neurochemical Selves." In *Biotechnology, Commerce, and Civil Society.* Edited by Nico Stehr. New Jersey: Transaction Press, 2004.

Rotenberg, Vadim. "Psychoneuroimminology: Searching for the Main Deteriorating Factor." *Genetic, Social, and General Psychology Monographs* 122 (1996): 329–46.

———. "Search Activity in the Context of Psychosomatic Disturbances, of Brain Monoamines and REM Sleep Function." *Pavlovian Journal of Biological Science*, 1984.

Rutstein, David. "Do You Really Want a Family Doctor?" *Harper's*, October 1960, s144–50.

Ryle, Gilbert. *The Concept of Mind.* New York: Barnes and Noble, 1949.

Sabom, Michael. *Light and Death.* Grand Rapids, Michigan: Zondervan, 1998.

Safer, Daniel. "Increased Methylphenidate Usage for ADD in the 1990s." *Pediatrics* 98 (1996): 1084–88.

———. "A Survey of Medication Treatment for Hyperactive/ Inattentive Students." *JAMA* 260, no. 15 (October 21, 1988): 2256–58.

Salkind, M. R. "Beck Depression Inventory in General Practice." *Journal of the Royal College of General Practitioners* 18 (1969): 267–73.

Schildkraut, Joseph. "The Catecholamine Hypothesis of Affective Disorders: A Review of Supporting Evidence." *American Journal of Psychiatry* 122 (1965): 509–22.

Schlesinger, Mark. "A Loss of Faith: the Sources of Reduced Political Legitimacy for the American Medical Profession." *The Milbank Quarterly* 80, no. 2 (June 2002): 185.

Schneider, R. H. "In Search of an Optimal Behavioral Treatment for Hypertension: A Review and Focus on Transcendental Meditation." In *Hypertension*, edited by E. H. Johnson, Washington, D.C.: Hemisphere, 1992.

Schrodinger, Edwin. *What is Life?* New York: Macmillan, 1945.

Schulberg, H. C. "Assessing Depression in Primary Medical and Psychiatric Practice." *Archives of General Psychiatry* 42 (December 1985): 1164–70.

Schurman, Rachel. "The Hidden Mental Health Network." *Archives of General Psychiatry* 42 (January 1985): 89–94.

Schurmann, Franz. *Ideology and Organization in Communist China*. Berkeley: University of California Press, 1968.

———. *The Logic of World Power*. New York: Pantheon Books, 1974.

Shao, Wei-Ann. "Knowledge and Attitudes About Depression Among Non-Generalists and Generalists." *Journal of Family Practice* 44, no. 2 (February 1997): 161–68.

Shapiro, Arthur, and Elaine Shapiro. *The Powerful Placebo*. Baltimore: Johns Hopkins University Press, 1997.

Sharfstein, Steven. "Psychiatric Care and Health Insurance Reform." *American Journal of Psychiatry* 150, no. 1 (January 1993): 7–18.

Sheehy, Gail. *New Passages*. New York: Random House, 1995.

———. *Passages*. New York: Dutton, 1976.

Shore, James. "Psychiatry at a Crossroad: Our Role in Primary Care." *American Journal of Psychiatry* 153, no. 11 (November 1996): 1398–1403.

Shorter, Edward. *A History of Psychiatry*. New York: John Wiley and Sons, 1997.

Shuman, Joel, and Keith Meador. *Heal Thyself*. New York: Oxford University Press, 2003.

Simon, Eric. "History." In *Endorphins*. Edited by Jeffrey Malick and Robert Bell. New York: M. Dekker, 1982.

Smith, Richard Dean. *The Rise and Fall of Managed Care*. New York: Nova Science Publishers, 2002.

Solberg, Leig. "The Need for a System in the Care of Depression." *Journal of Family Practice* 48, no.12 (December 1999): 973–79.

Solomon, George, and Rudolf Moos. "Emotions, Immunity, and Disease." *Archives of General Psychiatry* 11 (December 1964): 657–74.

Sommers, Christina Hoff, and Sally Satel. *One Nation Under Therapy*. New York: St. Martin's Press, 2005.

Spitzer, R. L. "Utility of a New Procedure for Diagnosing Mental Disorders in Primary Care." *JAMA* 272 (1994): 1749–56.

Starr, Paul. *The Social Transformation of American Medicine*. New York: Basic Books, 1982.

Stein, Marvin. "The Establishment of the Department of Psychiatry in the Mount Sinai Hospital: A Conflict Between Neurology and Psychiatry." *Journal of the History of Behavioral Sciences* 40, no. 3 (Summer 2004): 285–309.

Stephens, Thomas. "Physical Activity and Mental Health in the U.S. and Canada: Evidence from Four Population Surveys." *Preventive Medicine* 17 (1988): 35–47.

Stevens, Robert, and Rosemary Stevens. *Welfare Medicine in America*. New York: Macmillan, 1974.

Stevenson, Richard, and Mark Wolraich. "Stimulant Medication Therapy in the Treatment of Children with ADHD." *Pediatric Clinics of North America* 36, no. 5 (October 1989): 1183–97.

Stoll, Oliver. "Endogenous Opiates, 'Runner's High,' and 'Exercise Addiction,'—The Rise and Decline of a Myth." *Leipziger Sportwissenschaftliche Beitrage* 8, no. 1 (1977).

Stoll, Oliver, and P. Wagner. "Beta-Endorphin Immunoreactive Material in the Blood-Plasma and Mood-Changes in Ultra-Long Distance Running." In *Motivation, Emotion, Stress*.

Edited by J. R. Nitsch and R. Seiler, 169–73. Sank-Augustin: Academia, 1994.

Sudsuang, R. "Effect of Buddhist Meditation on Serum Cortisol and Total Protein Levels." *Physiology and Behavior* 50 (1991): 543–48.

"Suicidal Thoughts among Youths Aged 12 to 17 with Major Depressive Episode." In National Survey on Drug Use and Health Report. Office of Applied Studies, Substance Abuse and Mental Health Services Administration, Sept. 9, 2005.

Taggart, M. "The Professionalization of the Parish Pastoral Counselor." *Journal of Pastoral Care* 27 (1973): 180–88.

Tiedens, L. Z., and S. Linton. "Judgment Under Emotional Certainty and Uncertainty: The Effects of Specific Emotions on Information Processing." *Journal of Personality and Social Psychology* 81 (2001): 973–88.

Tocqueville, Alexis de. *Democracy in America.* 2 vols. Translated by Henry Reeve. New York: Vintage Books, 1990.

Turk, D. C. "Physicians' Attitudes and Practices Regarding the Long-Term Prescribing of Opioids for Non-Cancer Pain." *Pain* 59, no. 2 (November 1994): 201–8.

Waldrop, Ron. "Selection of Patients for Management of ADHD in a Private Practice Setting." *Clinical Pediatrics* (February 1994): 84–7.

Weber, Max. *The Protestant Ethic and the Spirit of Capitalism.* Translated by Talcott Parsons. New York: Charles Scribner's Sons, 1958.

———. "The Protestant Sects and the Spirit of Capitalism." In *From Max Weber.* Translated by H. H. Gerth and C. Wright Mills. New York: Oxford University Press, 1949.

Wechsler, Henry. "The Physician's Role in Health Promotion—A Survey of Primary-Care Practitioners." *NEJM* 308, no. 2 (January 13, 1983): 97–100.

Weiss, Margaret, and Candice Murray. "Assessment and Management of Attention-Deficit Hyperactivity Disorder in Adults." *CMAJ* 168, no. 6 (March 18, 2003): 715–31.

Wells, Kenneth. "Do Physicians Preach What They Practice." *JAMA* 252, no. 20 (November 23/30, 1984): 2846–48.

———. "The Practices of General and Subspecialty Internists in Counseling about Smoking and Exercise." *American Journal of Public Health* 76, no. 8 (1986): 1109–13.

Whorton, James. *Nature Cures: The History of Alternative Medicine in America.* New York: Oxford University Press, 2002.

Whyte, William, Jr. *The Organization Man.* New York: Doubleday, 1956.

Williams, John. "Primary Care Physicians' Approach to Depressive Disorders." *Archives of Family Medicine* 8, no. 1 (1999): 58–67.

———. "Treatment of Dysthymia and Minor Depression in Primary Care." *JAMA* 284, no. 12 (September 27, 2000): 1519–26.

Williford, Henry. "A Survey of Physicians' Attitudes and Practices Related to Exercise Promotion." *Preventive Medicine* 21 (1992): 637–53.

Wilson, James Q. *Moral Judgment.* New York: Basic Books, 1997.

Windship, George. "Autobiographical Sketches of a Strength-Seeker." *Atlantic Monthly* 9 (January 1862): 102–15.

Wolraich, Mark. "Stimulant Medication Use by Primary Care Physicians in the Treatment of ADHD." *Pediatrics* 86, no. 1 (July 1990): 95–101.

Wootton, Jacqueline, and Andrew Sparber. "Surveys of Complementary and Alternative Medicine Usage." *Seminars in Integrative Medicine* 1, no. 1 (March 2003): 10–24.

Worthington, Everett. "Empirical Research on Religion and

Psychotherapeutic Processes and Outcomes." *Psychological Bulletin* 119, no. 3 (May 1996): 448–87.

Wurtzel, Elizabeth. *Prozac Nation.* New York: Penguin, 1994.

www.brainyquotes.com

www.publicagenda.org

Wysowski, Diane, and Carlene Baum. "Outpatient Use of Prescription Sedative-Hypnotic Drugs in the U.S., 1970 through 1989." *Archives of Internal Medicine* 151 (September 1991): 1779–83.

Yin, Sandra. "Grandpa Gets Fit." *American Demographics,* November 2001. (Original source: "Fitness American Style: 2001." Report by Roper Starch. Worldwide for IHRSA.)

Zarin, Deborah. "Treatment of Attention-Deficit Hyperactivity Disorder by Different Physician Specialties." *Psychiatric Services* 49, no. 2 (February 1998): 171.

Zung, William. "Recognition and Treatment of Depression in a Family Medicine Practice." *Journal of Clinical Psychiatry* 4 (January 1983): 3–6.

I would also like to thank the following media for permission to reprint sections of articles written first for their pages:

Parts of Chapter 2 first appeared in Ronald Dworkin, "Why doctors are down," *Commentary,* May 2001.

Parts of Chapter 2 first appeared in Ronald Dworkin, "The medicalization of unhappiness," *Public Interest,* no. 144, Summer 2001.

Parts of Chapter 4 first appeared in Ronald Dworkin, "Science, faith, and alternative medicine," *Policy Review,* August–September 2001.

Parts of Chapter 9 first appeared in Ronald Dworkin, "The

wellness gospel and the future of faith," *Policy Review*, April–May 2002.

Parts of the conclusion first appeared in Ronald Dworkin, "Confident faith doesn't fear science," *Baltimore Sun*, op-ed page, August 19, 2002.

NOTES

ONE: TOO MUCH HAPPINESS

p. 16 The explanation lies . . . a "realm of ideology": Schurmann, ("Logic"), p. 13.

TWO: UNHAPPINESS BECOMES AN ENGINEERING PROBLEM

p. 23 Even Dr. Richard Cabot . . . "passing into oblivion": Dodds.

p. 25 Already in the 1960s . . . "our professional men": Rutstein; Chase; Greenberg; Beaton; for quote, see Chase, p. 129.

p. 25 Books like Ivan . . . with machines: Carlson, p. 34.

pp. 25–26 From 1968 to 1975 . . . most of the decline: Schlesinger; Delude.

p. 29 By 1970 an . . . of these prescriptions: Rose.

pp. 33–34 The prescription . . . started to plummet: Wysowski and Baum.

p. 34 From 1967 to 1975 . . . to over hundred million: Smith ("Small Comfort"), p. 31–32.

p. 34 Compared with the psychiatrists . . . much of the increase: Olfson and Klerman ("The Treatment of Depression").

p. 34 The number of antidepressants . . . to over thirty million: Smith ("Small Comfort"), p. 31–32.

p. 34 Since Prozac's creation . . . most of the increase: Foote and Etheredge, p. 166.

p. 34 Contrast this with . . . relatively stable: Pincus, p. 526.

p. 34 Psychiatrists correctly blamed . . . 60 million: Foote and Etheredge, pp. 167–68.

pp. 34–35 In one study . . . the same treatment: Williams ("Primary Care").

p. 35 Given the high ratio . . . many more patients: Oxman and Sengupta.

p. 37 Not surprisingly . . . with counseling: Williams ("Primary Care").

p. 38 Wondering how . . . rural areas elsewhere: Schurman, p. 93.

p. 41 To the extent . . . legitimize their prescriptions: Regier, p. 692; Schurman, p. 91.

p. 42 Psychiatrists envisioned . . . as was then the case: Schurman, p. 91.

p. 43 For example, in one study . . . was raised to 17: Salkind.

p. 44 These articles . . . this number: For example, Zung; Schulberg.

p. 44 The articles' goals . . . in primary care: Houpt; Hankin, p. 231.

p. 47 Program graduates . . . than older doctors: Gallo.

THREE: FROM IDEOLOGY TO INTERESTS TO SCANDAL

pp. 49–50 A psychiatrist warned . . . "in the evening": Bloch and Reddaway, p. 88.

p. 50 In one 1985 . . . barrier to care: Orleans.

p. 50 Patient resistance . . . *Listening to Prozac*: Williams ("Primary Care"); Katz.

pp. 50–51 Primary care doctors . . . not just psychiatrists: Foote and Etheredge, p. 167.

p. 52 In one study . . . were depressed: Carney ("Variations"), p. 78.

p. 52 "Some people . . . dig for it": Carney ("Variations"), p. 78.

p. 52 "You have to . . . any better": Carney ("Variations"), p. 79.

p. 53 In another MacArthur-funded . . . a headache: Carney ("Recognizing").

p. 54 In one . . . patient's reactions: Carney ("Variations"), p. 80.

p. 55 To apply . . . eight minutes: Williams ("Primary Care"); Spitzer.

p. 55 Even when . . . often unnecessary: Williams ("Treatment"); Healy ("Antidepressant Era"), p. 103.

p. 55 One study . . . kicks in: Williams ("Treatment"); Oxman.

p. 56 Dr. Charles Bradley . . . loss of spinal fluid: Gross.

p. 56 He attributed . . . neurological deficit: Mercugliano, p. 833.

p. 58 Ritalin's mass prescription . . . for antidepressants: Zarin; Wolraich.

p. 58 Between 1985 . . . *sevenfold*: Pincus, p. 529.

p. 58 By 1995 . . . took Ritalin: Safer ("Increased"); Goldman.

p. 58 As a condition . . . have the condition: Weiss and Murray.

p. 59 During the 1980s . . . rambunctious children: Safer ("A Survey"), p. 2258.

p. 59 Adults with ADHD . . . holding up banks: Weiss and Murray, p. 718.

p. 59 They cited . . . social skills: Waldrop; Brown; Wolraich.

p. 59 They diagnosed ADHD . . . and home: Wolraich, p. 99–100; Brown.

p. 59 And they succeeded . . . visits for ADHD: Zarin ("Treatment of") p. 171.

p. 61 U.S. consumption of . . . until 1985: International Narcotics Control Board, courtesy of Pain and Policy Studies Group, University of Wisconsin.

p. 61 Narcotic prescriptions . . . 1150 percent, respectively: Center for Substance Abuse Treatment, Substance Abuse and Mental Health Services Administration.

p. 61 Primary care doctors . . . noncancer pain: Turk; Reid; Author's conversation with representative from Purdue Pharma.

FOUR: THE REVOLT OF THE ENGINEERS

p. 65 Caught between . . . moles at work: See "Anzio Beach-head" (Web site).

p. 66 Beecher tended . . . their hysteria: Beecher ("Resuscitation").

p. 66 Three-quarters of the . . . asked for the drug: Beecher ("Pain in Men").

p. 66 One nineteen-year . . . "lying on his rifle": Beecher ("Pain in Men").

p. 66 One day . . . it was morphine: Mirkin.

p. 67 To explain . . . morphine needs: Beecher ("Pain in Men").

p. 69 From 1990 to 1997 . . . 45 percent: Eisenberg ("Trends in").

p. 69 By 2000 . . . cover them: Wootton and Sparber.

p. 69 Although alternative medicine . . . or depression: Eisenberg ("Unconventional").

p. 76 Another article . . . against Beecher: Hrobjartsson and Gotzsche.

p. 79 Although statistics . . . primary care doctors: Author's conversation with spokesmen for the two organizations.

p. 81 First, in public . . . "nincompoopery." Whorton, p. 282.

p. 81 One editor . . . smelled marijuana: Whorton, p. 268.

p. 83 As sociologist . . . through the state: Schurmann ("Logic"), p. 138.

p. 83 Allopathic physicians . . . even resigned: Whorton, p. 294.

pp. 83–84 By 1994 . . . own practices: Whorton, p. 299.

p. 84 According to a report . . . medical modalities: Private correspondence from Marc Micozzi.

p. 86 As the editor . . . "down the rules": Whorton, p. 269.

p. 89 Some studies showed . . . strengthened it: Rotenberg ("Psychoneuroimmunology").

p. 89 In one study . . . lymphocyte activity: Kiegolt-Glaser; Rotenberg ("Psychoneuroimmunology").

p. 89 However, other . . . accompanying behavior: Knapp.

p. 89 Happiness and unhappiness . . . system suppression: Rotenberg ("Search"); Rotenberg ("Psychoneuroimmunology").

p. 96 In 1977 . . . quality of life: Benson ("Relaxation Response").

p. 96 In 1986 . . . blood pressure reduction: Kabat-Zinn; Schneider; Maclean.

p. 96 In the 1980s . . . home and work: Denise Rodgers, "Mind-body Interventions," p. 225, in *Fundamentals of Complementary and Alternative Medicine.*

FIVE: ENGINEERING FOR THE MASSES

p. 103 "There goes the" . . . college green: Windship, p. 102.

p. 103 Sick of the abuse . . . "rest of his life": Windship, p. 104.

p. 106 "Thirty minutes out" . . . "found it so everywhere": Mandell.

pp. 107–8 Avram Goldstein . . . terminal "e": Simon, p. 6.

p. 109 In a second study . . . during exercise: Discussed in Stoll.

pp. 109–10 In 1982 . . . with running: Markoff.

p. 110 In another study . . . sedentary people: Lobstein.

p. 110 A third study . . . marathon runners: Stoll and Wagner.

p. 111 If endorphin theory . . . everyday gym people: Stoll.

p. 112 "As long" . . . about lifestyle: Wells ("Do Physicians"), p. 2848.

p. 113 Even as late as 1984 . . . to exercise: Wells ("The Practices").

p. 113 "They believed . . . shortened lifespan: Berryman, p. 13.

p. 113 Unheard since . . . "Mending Heart!": Berryman, p. 64.

p. 114 A few large-scale . . . was unclear: See Brosse.

p. 119 While the medical . . . twice weekly: Lambert.

p. 121 Exercise ideology's . . . times a week: Stephens, p. 45.

p. 121 By 1991 . . . physical illness: Reed, Williford.

p. 122 According to one study . . . the "hard look": Yin.

p. 127 Sociologist Franz . . . of prediction: Schurmann ("Logic"), p. 15.

SIX: HAPPINESS HITS THE ASSEMBLY LINE

p. 138 Some psychiatrists . . . gatekeepers themselves: Shore.

p. 141 The pamphlet . . . "line of treatment": Munoz.

p. 143 A peculiar aspect . . . "perfectibility of man": Tocqueville (vol. 2), p. 33.

p. 143 Moreover, drugs . . . "little neurotic": McHugh.

p. 146 In his critical . . . "programs whatsoever": Smith, p. 31.

p. 146 In his study . . . "quite limited": Pelletier (1997), p. 119.

p. 147 Pelletier writes . . . "specific diagnosis": Pelletier (1997), p. 119.

p. 148 Only three preventive . . . childhood immunizations: Leutwyler; Smith, p. 33, 35.

SEVEN: MORE REVOLUTION

p. 156 Rather than duck . . . organized religion: Robertson; Annas.

p. 156 *Science* magazine also . . . "at conception": Guenin.

p. 161 "They [mountain people]" . . . "wither soon": Harris, p. 185.

p. 162 Alexis de Tocqueville . . . "foot of the altar": Tocqueville (vol. 2), p. 126.

p. 162 James Bryce . . . "without bigotry": Bryce (Vol. 2), p. 290.

p. 162 Max Weber . . . "had to offer": Weber ("Protestant Ethic"), p. 166.

p. 163 "The savage" . . . "kills himself": Beard, p. 121.

p. 164 The discovery of . . . from the soul: Healy ("Antidepressant Era"), p. 31.

p. 164 Some clergymen . . . only salvation: Dain, p. 184–85.

p. 165 In their weakened state . . . science with clergymen: Dain, p. 186.

p. 165 As Edwin Hubbell . . . "with the infinite": *www.brainy quotes.com*.

p. 167 Writing in 1958 . . . "it reacts": Mills, p. 200.

p. 167 Rather than to fulfill . . . Communist threat: For a discussion of the new emphasis on well-being, see Miller and Nowak, p. 92–93.

p. 167 Norman Vincent . . . "a continual feast": *www. brainyquotes.com*.

p. 167 Billy Graham . . . "all right": *www.brainyquotes.com*.

p. 167 Bishop Fulton . . . "the modern world": Buechi.

p. 168 As one bulletin . . . "for you": Miller and Nowak, p. 93.

p. 168 In the country . . . end of affluence: Johnson, p. 497.

p. 169 In the early 1900s . . . separate ways: For discussion of this, see Healy ("Antidepressant Era"), pp. 37–8.

p. 170 Peale's message . . . in Manhattan: Miller and Nowak, p. 95.

p. 170 What Peale did . . . American Catholics: Miller and Nowak, p. 85.

p. 172 Weekly church . . . mid-thirties: Huba.

p. 173 By the 1970s . . . calls "psychologizing": Shorter, pp. 288–89.

p. 173 In the 1960s . . . and rabbis: Favazza.

p. 170 Many clergymen . . . practices and convictions: Bentz; Taggart.

p. 170 But psychology . . . to be the case: Prioleau.

pp. 182–83 Attitudes toward . . . 67 percent: Gallup Organization, June 1947 and March 1999, in Public Agenda (*www.publicagenda.org*).

EIGHT: THE PLIGHT OF SIR JOHN ECCLES

p. 190 When Eccles spoke . . . pact with the Devil: *Sir John Eccles*, p. 35.

p. 191 In a critical . . . neurotransmitters: Brock, Coombs, and Eccles.

pp. 191–92 One theory repudiated . . . "liver secretes bile": Quoted in Crick, p. 3.

p. 193 He argued . . . during thinking: Eccles ("Neurophysiological").

p. 193 In the 1960s . . . theory of evolution: Eccles ("Evolution and the Conscious").

p. 195 "A psychoanalyst" . . . neurology department: Stein, p. 291.

p. 200 Eccles theorized . . . own energy: Eccles ("Effect of").

pp. 200–1 All this happened . . . two universes: Eccles ("Effect of"), p. 53.

p. 201 Let's say the mind . . . *regular* way: Esfeld.

p. 202 Their philosophy lives . . . "associated molecules": Crick, p. 3.

p. 202 They called . . . individual has alone: Bunge, p. 6.

p. 203 Atoms lack . . . with science: Bunge, p. 187.

p. 203 A brain needs . . . evolutionary development: Edelman, p. 14.

p. 204 Like the emergent . . . gave rise to them: *Nobel Prize Conversations*, p. 67.

p. 206 In "Restoring the soul" . . . "Christian theology": Moreland.

pp. 206–7 Some of them hoped . . . soul still existed: For an example of this, see *Whatever Happened*, chapter 6 ("Nonreductive Physicalism: Philosophical Issues").

p. 207 Giving tacit support . . . renegade doctors: For an example of this, see Sabom; Stevenson.

p. 208 His new year's . . . "other way to go": *Sir John Eccles*, p. 35.

p. 208 Five days before . . . "I will get it": *Sir John Eccles*, p. 185.

NINE: THE LAST BATTLE

p. 212 Dr. Gerald Edelman . . . *"your environment"*: Author's conversation with Dr. Edelman.

p. 216 An article in a 1972 . . . heralded change: Comstock and Partridge.

p. 216 One study . . . visits to the dentist: Levin and Vanderpool; Harris ("The Role of Religion"); Dwyer; Frankel and Hewitt.

p. 217 In the mid-1980s . . . self-control, and responsibility: Bergin; for a literature review see Gartner, Larson, and Allen; see also Worthington.

p. 218 According to one . . . years to life: Interview with Duke sociologist Linda George in Krejci-Papa. Also see Berkel and de Waard.

p. 220 Psychologist Barbara . . . hard times: Interview with psychologist Barbara Fredrickson in Albernaz.

p. 221 Evolutionary biologist Geoffrey . . . ornate nests: Miller ("Mating Mind").

p. 221 In 1985 . . . sensory stimuli: D'Aquili.

p. 222 Stanley Beck . . . "believe in evolution": Beck, pp. 316–17.

pp. 225–26 Studies showed . . . truly believed: Donahue; Batson and Ventis.

p. 226 Dr. Benson's . . . attitude and health: Benson ("Timeless Healing").

p. 227 During the 1990s . . . three different paths: For a review of the literature, see Fenwick.

pp. 227–28 They discovered . . . stress hormone: Sudsuang.

p. 228 Second, doctors performed . . . to baseline: Puri; Newberg; Aftanas and Golocheikine.

p. 228 In one study . . . telephone directory: Azari.

p. 228 Third, doctors . . . the cerebral cortex: Discussed in Fenwick.

p. 228 In a 1998 conference . . . "search for the sacred": "Scientific Research on Spirituality and Health," p. 21.

pp. 228–29 Two glaring examples . . . spirituality research: "Scientific Research on Spirituality and Health," p. 90.

TEN: THE HAPPY AMERICAN

p. 257 The term adult . . . in 1656: For a discussion of adulthood's origin, see Merser.

p. 260 Psychologist Abraham . . . "purely expressively": Maslow, p. 66.

p. 261 Dr. David Fassler . . . "need and deserve": Quoted in Heavey.

p. 263 They were advised . . . "be like them": McCrady, quoted in McKnight-Trontz, p. 19.

p. 265 With the rate . . . for treating it: For statistics, see Carroll.

p. 266 Psychologist Oliver James . . . the imbalance: James.

p. 267 Emulating classmates . . . their own scores: Langdon.

p. 270 In *Democracy in America* . . . "self-interest rightly understood": Tocqueville (vol. 2), p. 121.

p. 271 Psychological studies . . . analytical thought: DeSteno; Tiedens and Linton; Greenwald and Banaji.

p. 273 In one study . . . their endorphins: Hau.

p. 273 Extrapolating to humans . . . "further fights": Hau, quoted in Nelson.

CONCLUSION

p. 291 "What concern" . . . "my salvation": Augustine.

ACKNOWLEDGMENTS

THIS BOOK BEGAN as a series of magazine essays on some of the topics discussed in these pages, which in no way were connected. To find the connection I had to go back twenty-five years, to a political science class at Swarthmore College taught by my friend and mentor, Professor James Kurth, who has greatly influenced the course of my intellectual life. In that class, I was introduced to the works of sociologist Franz Schurmann, which I enthusiastically devoured. Although Professor Schurmann wrote about American foreign policy, I found his understanding of the relationship between interests and ideology, and the origins of popular movements to be relevant to the practice of medicine. Two years ago, while surveying the essays I had already published, and with a sixth sense that an important change had occurred in American society—a change that tied all the essays together, it was my memory of Professor Schurmann's work that guided me toward an understanding of what that change was, enabling me to build this book's unifying theme.

Still, a theme and a few ideas do not necessarily make a book. To have been able to go from the former to the latter I owe enormous thanks to my agent, John Wright, who helped organize my thinking into a readable product, emphasizing clarity above all else. Along the way, he threw several pearls of wisdom in my direction, including the dictum that when a reader finds something confusing, "Remember, it's always the writer's fault." John is excellent at doing the things that agents do, but he also knows well the world of ideas and the art of communicating those ideas to others. His sound advice will last me a lifetime.

I want to thank Philip Turner, my editor at Carroll and Graf. In his case, I benefited from working with a man who loves what he does and who loves books, which is an immeasurable benefit to someone who tries to write one.

Walter Bode offered invaluable advice during the editing process, which I greatly appreciate. Along with John and Philip, he sits in the first tier of those in the publishing world who made this book possible.

I also want to thank the fellows and staff at the Hudson Institute, especially Dr. Ken Weinstein, Hudson's CEO. Hudson not only gave me an office in which to write but also access to a great number of smart and thoughtful people with whom I could share ideas. That interesting environment, where people routinely think "outside the box," stretched the limits of my own imagination, thereby making this book possible.

I want to thank the doctors, nurse anesthetists, and administrative staff at Greater Baltimore Medical Center, who form my little platoon of life. They also helped make this book possible—in some ways, more than anyone else—for it is by working day-to-day at the hospital and listening to other people's observations about medicine that I began to understand the deep structure of the revolutions I describe in this book. My own contact with these revolutions, which occurred at the hospital, made these events come alive.

Many other people helped me during the research for this book, whether by consenting to be interviewed or by directing me to important research material. They include Peter Berkowitz, Marc Micozzi, Adriane Fugh-Berman, Vernon Mountcastle, Jack Berryman, Gerald Edelman, Solomon Snyder, Masao Ito, Piergiorgio Strata, and Lorraine McCoy.

Closer to home, I thank my mother, Alyse, and my brother John. At home itself, I thank my wife, Sandy, who is a very smart and talented person and who has a way with words; she actually thought up the title for this book. Finally, thank you to my baby daughter Grace, who kept me company lying in her cradle next to my desk while I insanely scribbled.

INDEX

Index

Index

ABOUT THE AUTHOR

RONALD W. DWORKIN received his BA from Swarthmore College in 1981, his MD from the University of California at San Diego in 1985, and his PhD in political philosophy from Johns Hopkins University in 1995. He practices anesthesiology in Baltimore while also working as Senior Fellow at the Hudson Institute in Washington, D.C. His has written on culture, politics, and medicine for the *Baltimore Sun*, the *Weekly Standard*, *Commentary, Policy Review,* and other publications. He lives in Baltimore with his wife and daughter.